To Do This...	Select...	Then Select...	Then Do This...	Icon	Keyboard Shortcut
Select rectangular or elliptical area	Marquee	Rectangle or ellipse	Drag selection		M
Crop an image	Marquee	Crop	Drag selection		C
Move selection border	Any selection tool		Drag border		M/L/W
Move contents of selection	Move		Drag selection		V
Select hand-drawn area	Lasso/Freeform	Lasso	Draw selection		L
Select polygonal area	Lasso/Freeform	Freeform	Draw selection		L
Select pixels by tone	Magic Wand		Click in selected area		W
Paint with brushes	Brush		Draw strokes		B
Paint with airbrush	Airbrush		Draw strokes		A
Draw with pencil	Pencil		Draw strokes		Y
Erase pixels	Erase		Erase pixels		E
Clone an area	Rubber Stamp		ALT/OPTION-click at source point; then draw		S
Smudge pixels	Smudge		Smudge pixels		U
Sharpen pixels	Sharpen/Blur	Sharpen	Sharpen pixels		R
Blur pixels	Sharpen/Blur	Blur	Blur pixels		R
Darken an area	Dodge/Burn/Sponge	Burn	Darken pixels		O
Lighten an area	Dodge/Burn/Sponge	Dodge	Lighten pixels		O
Remove color from area	Dodge/Burn/Sponge	Sponge	Reduce color		O
Draw curves and lines	Pen		Draw		P
Add points to line or curve	Pen	Pen+	Click point to add		P
Remove anchor points	Pen	Pen–	Click point to remove		P

W9-CYE-214

To Do This...	Select...	Then Select...	Then Do This...	Icon	Keyboard Shortcut
Change corner point to curve point	Pen	Convert Anchor Point	Click point to change		P
Create text	Text	Font/Size, etc.	Type Text		T
Draw straight line	Line		Drag mouse cursor to draw line		N
Color with a gradient	Gradient	Colors and style	Drag gradient		G
Fill selection with color	Paint Bucket		Click within area to be colored		K
Change background to an image color	Eyedropper		OPTION/ALT-click on desired color		I
Change foreground to an image color	Eyedropper		Click on desired color		I
Move document image	Hand		Drag document image		H
Zoom larger	Zoom		COMMAND/ CTRL-click		Z, COMMAND/ CTRL-click
Zoom smaller	Zoom		OPTION-ALT-click to choose –		Z, ALT/ OPTION-click
Choose specific foreground color	Foreground Color Control Box	Desired color from Color Picker	Foreground		
Choose specific background color	Background Color Control Box	Desired color from Color Picker		Background	
Exchange foreground and background colors	Exchange Colors		Exchange		X
Restore default colors	Default Colors		Restore defaults		
Change to Quick Mask	Quick Mask				Q
Turn off Quick Mask	Normal Mode				Q
Switch to standard screen display	Standard Display				F
Display screen with menus only	Menu Only				F
Display full screen with no menus	Full Screen				F
Hide palettes	TAB key				TAB
Access Adobe Web site	About Photoshop				

Photoshop 4

Answers!
Certified Tech Support

David Busch

Osborne **McGraw-Hill**
Berkeley • New York • St. Louis • San Francisco
Auckland • Bogotá • Hamburg • London
Madrid • Mexico City • Milan • Montreal
New Delhi • Panama City • Paris • São Paulo
Singapore • Sydney • Tokyo • Toronto

Osborne/**McGraw-Hill**
2600 Tenth Street
Berkeley, California 94710
U.S.A.

For information on translations or book distributors outside the U.S.A., or to arrange bulk purchase discounts for sales promotions, premiums, or fund-raisers, please contact Osborne/**McGraw-Hill** at the above address.

Photoshop 4 Answers!
Certified Tech Support

1234567890 AGM AGM 901987654321098

ISBN 0-07-882456-7

Publisher	**Copy Editor**
Brandon A. Nordin	Dennis Weaver
Editor-in-Chief	**Proofreader**
Scott Rogers	Stefany Otis
Acquisitions Editor	**Indexer**
Joanne Cuthbertson	Rebecca Plunkett
Project Editor	**Computer Designer**
Nancy McLaughlin	Roberta Steele
Editorial Assistant	**Series Design**
Stephane Thomas	Michelle Galicia
Technical Editor	**Cover Design**
Susan Glinert	Matthew Nielsen

For Anthony Godby-Johnson,
a young author who taught me
that the very best writing comes
from the heart, and not from the mind.

Contents

Acknowledgments

Many thanks to the technical experts whose scrutiny helped ensure the accuracy of the solutions I collected for this book. They include Susan Glinert, Ph.D., and Stream International. Other instigators who helped move this project forward are Osborne/McGraw-Hill's Joanne Cuthbertson, who selected me from among the other 11,293 Photoshop book authors to write this one; Nancy McLaughlin, who worked extra hours to keep things moving smoothly; Stephane Thomas, who managed to keep track of the hundreds of individual pieces of text, art, and commentary that make up this book; and Dennis Weaver, whose editing and suggestions made my prose more concise and readable.

I'd also like to thank my wife and the country of Spain for giving me something beautiful to photograph for the examples.

Introduction

Computers are useless. They can only give you answers.
—Pablo Picasso

It is better to ask some of the questions than to know all of the answers.
—James Thurber

If you were to ask a graphics professional to name their most vexing problem, as well as the most ingenious solution to a tormenting quandary, it's even money that both answers would involve Adobe Photoshop.

Although it started modestly enough as an image editor for the Apple Macintosh, Photoshop has since engulfed both the Mac OS and Windows pixel-pushing worlds, and now serves as the standard tool for manipulating photos, compositing images, alleviating defects with retouching, and color balancing graphics destined for prepress.

Like any product with such far-reaching influence, Photoshop has become a minor industry of its own. Vast multitudes, ranging from photographers and picture editors to graphics professionals, make their livings using Photoshop. Successful companies, such as MetaCreations, have built their enterprises on a foundation of Photoshop add-ons like Kai's PowerTools. And, judging from the crowded shelves at the bookstores, there's a thriving demand for books that painstakingly explain how to use Adobe's flagship product.

However, as in the television show *Jeopardy*, having the answers to everything won't help unless you also know the questions—the *right* questions. That's especially true now that Adobe has layered on feature after new feature in bringing the latest edition of Photoshop to market.

The most recent release makes it easy to automate tasks involving a single file, or a batch of files, with macro-like Actions. Creating, moving, and copying selections are done in new ways. Roughly 100 filters are bundled right in the Photoshop box. Prepress professionals will find new methods for creating color separation tables based on printer profiles. Photographers can protect their work with invisible digital watermarks. Adjustment layers make it simple to apply effects only to selected layers, and can undo the transformation instantly. In short, there is a towering number of new and complex capabilities, and the latest edition of Photoshop has prompted more questions than any previous release.

That's why I'm pleased to bring you this collection of answers to the most common queries that any Photoshop user is likely to encounter. *Photoshop Answers!* addresses more than 400 issues that you're likely to encounter as you explore this program more deeply. It bristles with common-sense questions, straightforward solutions, and *answers*. You'll find it the next best thing to having a Photoshop customer support technician at your side. This book is even better in some ways—you won't have to wait on hold, for example, to find out what you need to know!

Note   *Photoshop operates almost exactly the same way on both Macintosh and Windows platforms. The key exception is that the Mac's* OPTION *key corresponds to the* ALT *key on a Windows machine's keyboard, and the Mac's* COMMAND *key is the equivalent (at least within Photoshop) of the PC's* CONTROL *key. In this book, I'll indicate most shortcut keystrokes using the conventions* COMMAND/CTRL *and* OPTION/ALT. *Whenever you see an instruction like this one,*

Press COMMAND/CTRL-G, followed by OPTION/ALT-F1...

you should use the correct keys for your platform.

Top Ten FAQs

Answer Topics!

? **I need to position objects very precisely, but Photoshop's rulers measure in fractions of an inch. How can I gain more control over where I place the cursor and individual objects?**

Using inches as your unit of measurement won't give you fine enough increments for precise positioning. Try switching to pixels as your basic ruler unit, then learn how to use grids and guides to help you place things exactly where you want them. Just follow these steps:

1. From the File menu, select Preferences | Units & Rulers. You'll see the dialog box shown in Figure 1-1.

2. From the drop-down list in the Rulers box, choose pixels.

3. Another drop-down list of each of the Photoshop preference options appears at the top of the dialog box.

4. Choose Guides & Grid, and make sure the "Gridline every" field shows "1 pixels."

5. Click OK to return to Photoshop's main screen.

6. Make sure you have rulers, grids, and guides visible. You can toggle them by pressing COMMAND/CTRL-R to turn rulers on and off, COMMAND/CTRL-; (semicolon) to turn guides on and off, or COMMAND/CTRL-" (quotation mark) to turn grids on and off.

7. If you'd like to have selections and objects snap to the guides you create, press SHIFT-COMMAND/CTRL-; (semicolon).

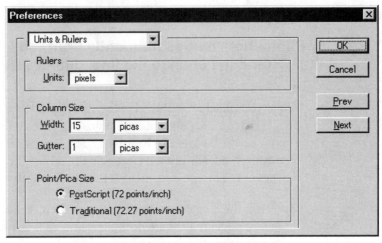

Figure 1-1. Photoshop's Preferences dialog box is used to set units.

You can now drag a guide onto your screen by placing the cursor on the left or top rulers, holding down the mouse button, and releasing it when the guide is positioned properly. You'll find more information on setting up preferences in Chapter 2, "Setup and Preferences," and additional tips on positioning selections and objects in Chapter 5, " Selections and Paths."

❓ How much memory do I need to run Photoshop?

Photoshop uses a lot more RAM than you might think, and eats it up in different ways, depending on whether you're using a Windows machine or a Macintosh. However, a safe rule of thumb is to have four to five times as much memory as the largest file you plan to edit, plus an additional 8MB or more of RAM for Photoshop itself and your operating system. That is, if you frequently work with 3MB files, you should have a minimum of 12 to 15MB available for Photoshop, plus 8 to 16MB or more for your OS and the application. In practical terms, that means you'll need 24 to 32MB of memory to avoid making Photoshop swap out part of your image to your hard disk (which is thousands of times slower than memory). I run Photoshop on a Power Macintosh with 64MB of RAM, and a pair of Windows NT and Windows 95 machines that each have 192MB of memory.

The reason that Photoshop is such a memory hog is that, in essence, it duplicates a file in memory each time you do things like create a layer, take a snapshot, or apply a filter that the program may have to later undo. For more tips on memory optimization, see Chapter 2.

❓ My Photoshop images frequently print too large, or too small. How can I change the final output size on my printer?

While you can change the relative size of your document with most printer drivers' Scaling option, Photoshop gives you an easier way. There's no need to resize the image and perhaps sacrifice some quality. Instead, simply tell Photoshop to adjust the final size whenever the image document is printed. Just follow these steps:

1. Select the area you want to print, or, if you'd like to print the entire page, make sure nothing is selected, using Select | None, or by pressing COMMAND/CTRL-D.

2. Access the Image | Image Size dialog box, shown in Figure 1-2. You can press OPTION/ALT-I twice if you'd like to practice the keyboard shortcut.

3. In the Print Size area, type in either the width or height that you want for your final image or selection. If the Constrain Proportions box is checked, a chain icon linking the width and height fields will show. When you type a value into either field, the other one changes to reflect the other size using the same proportions.

4. Click OK.

The new size you've indicated will be used automatically whenever the image is printed from within Photoshop.

It's bothersome to have to locate the Options palette every time I want to change the attributes for the current tool. Is there a faster way?

To change attributes for a given tool, just double-click the button on the Tools palette for the given tool and the Options tab will pop to the front. You can then change any attributes related to that tool.

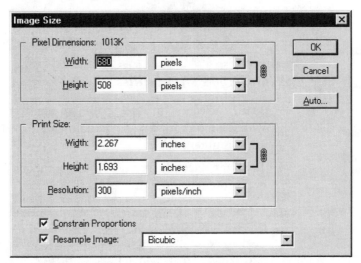

Figure 1-2.   The Image Size dialog box is used to adjust the print size of an image.

? How do I duplicate a selection?

To duplicate a selection on a layer, just point at the selected object with the Move tool while holding down the OPTION/ALT key. Then drag away from the selection and a duplicate will now be selected. To place a duplicate of a selection on its own new layer, press COMMAND/CTRL-C, followed by COMMAND/CTRL-V (the Copy and Paste commands). The duplicate will be placed on a new layer, and will remain selected.

? How can I quickly fill a selection with the foreground or background color?

You'll need to learn several techniques, because Photoshop handles fills on transparent layers differently than on layers that already contain a background color, and you'll need to access the Fill dialog box, shown here, if you want to use less than a 100 percent fill in your selection.

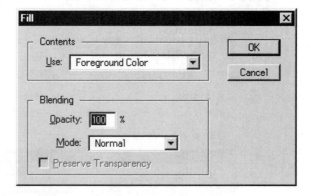

Adding 100 Percent Fills

⇨ To fill a selection on a transparent or non-transparent layer with the foreground color, hold down the OPTION/ALT and DEL keys simultaneously.

⇨ To fill the selection on a non-transparent layer with the background color, simply press the DEL key.

⇨ Photoshop won't fill a selection on a transparent layer with the background color when you press the DEL key. Instead, you'll need to swap the foreground and background colors (by pressing X to exhange them), then press OPTION/ALT-DEL to fill the selection

with the "new" foreground color. Press X again to return the
foreground and background colors to their former status.

⇨ To apply the foreground color only to the areas in a transparent
layer that contain image pixels without needing to make a
selection first, press OPTION/ALT-SHIFT-DEL.

⇨ To fill with the background color only to areas in a transparent
layer that contain pixels, press COMMAND/CTRL-DEL.

Filling Using a Percentage

To fill using a percentage of the foreground or background colors,
you'll need to access the Fill dialog box. Just follow these steps:

1. Press SHIFT-BACKSPACE (in Windows) or SHIFT-DEL (on the
   Macintosh) to display the Fill dialog box.

2. In the Use field, you can select Foreground or Background from
   the drop-down list. You can also choose Black, White, 50 percent
   gray, or fill from a snapshot, saved version, or pattern. More
   information about filling from a snapshot, saved version, or
   pattern can be found in Chapter 6, "Retouching and Compositing."

3. In the Blending area, type in the amount of opacity you want,
   from 0 percent (transparent) to 100 percent (completely filled).

4. If you want to fill only the areas of a transparent layer that contain
   pixels, check the Preserve Transparency box.

5. To merge the fill with the rest of the image in the selection, choose
   a blending mode from the drop-down Mode list. I'll answer some
   questions about these modes in Chapter 6.

❓ How do I select an image found on one layer?

Many veteran users of Photoshop have had problems making the
transition to the significant changes Adobe made in how layers are
handled in Photoshop 4.x. In the previous version, you could select
the layer you want to work on from the Layers palette, then select the
whole layer by using the COMMAND/CTRL-A keys or by using
Select I All. You then needed to use the Move tool and move the layer
slightly, which commanded Photoshop to select only the parts of the
layer with an image on it.

The procedure has been simplified in Photoshop 4.x. Just hold
down the CTRL key while clicking on the layer you want to use in the

Layers palette. Photoshop automatically selects whatever pixels are in use on that layer.

❓ How can I make my Photoshop 4.0 files compatible with other versions, programs, and platforms?

First, find out what file format can be handled by the platform your Photoshop file is destined for. Then, use File I Save A Copy and select that format. Photoshop will only save files in image formats. Here are some tips:

⇨ Most file formats saved by Photoshop can be read easily by another copy of Photoshop, regardless of the platform. Macs and PCs can each read TIF, PCX, PICT, and PSD files created on the other system.

⇨ The exception to the first tip is when a user is working with Photoshop 2.5. When exchanging files with a Photoshop 2.5 owner, use the TIF format. You can also use the Files I Preferences I Saving Files dialog box, shown in Figure 1-3, to tell Photoshop to save in a Photoshop 2.5 format by default.

⇨ TIF and PSD formats both preserve saved selections, but only Photoshop's native PSD format preserves your layers.

⇨ If your file will be read by a non-Photoshop application, the TIF format is usually your best choice. Some older applications have difficulty reading compressed TIF files, so you may want to uncheck the LZW Compression box in the TIFF Options dialog box that pops up when you save a TIF file.

⇨ To transport a file between Windows machines and Macintoshes, use PC-compatible disks, if possible. Most recent Macintoshes can read PC media directly.

❓ How do I change the foreground and background colors?

The color swatches on the bottom of the toolbox determine the foreground and background colors. To change a color, use one of these techniques:

⇨ In the Swatches palette, click on any color patch in the library to change the foreground color to that hue. Note that the cursor changes to an eyedropper when it passes over the Swatches

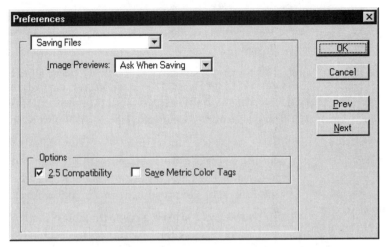

Figure 1-3.   Change Photoshop's Saving Files preferences to ensure
Photoshop 2.5 compatibility.

palette. You can create your own libraries of swatches and save
them for later reuse. Hold down the OPTION/ALT key to change
the Background color to that of the current patch.

⇨ To "dial in" colors, access the Color palette, shown here:

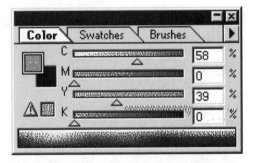

You can click on either the foreground or background color
swatches, then use the sliders to create a specific color using red,
green, and blue values.

⇨ The color ramp at the bottom of the Color palette can also be used
to select a foreground and background color quickly. The cursor
changes into an eyedropper when passed over the color ramp.
Just click to set the foreground color, or OPTION/ALT click to set the
background.

⇨ For more precise color selection, double-click the Foreground or Background swatches on the toolbox to produce the Color Picker, shown in Figure 1-4. You can type in values for red/green/blue, as well as for hue, saturation, and brightness; cyan, magenta, yellow, and black; or the L*a*b components L (lightness), a (green to red), and b (blue to yellow). More information about these color models can be found in Chapter 10, "Color Models and Balancing."

⇨ The Color Picker also has a large Color palette that can be used to choose a specific hue by clicking in the area containing the color you want. The color range of this palette can be changed with the rainbow slider in the middle of the dialog box.

⇨ To choose a color from a color-matching system, such as Pantone or Trumatch, click the Custom button on the Color Picker, and select the system and hue you want.

Even after changing dialog box settings, I find that a filter is too strong. Is there anything I can do?

Press COMMAND/CTRL-SHIFT-F to produce the Fade dialog box. You can move the slider to reduce the effect of the filter from 100 percent all

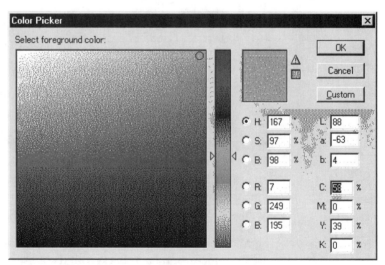

Figure 1-4.   The Color Picker has multiple color selection options.

the way down to zero. If the Preview checkbox is marked, you'll be able to see the effects of your changes on the original image as you make adjustments. The Fade dialog box can be moved to one side to give you a good look at the image workspace. You may also blend the filter effect and the underlying image it was applied to by choosing a mode from the drop-down list.

Setup and Preferences

Answer Topics!

Photoshop's Setup and Preferences @ a Glance

Photoshop can be customized to a certain extent so that it will operate the way you prefer each time you load it. These settings are stored in Photoshop's preference files, which may be located in your Photoshop folder's Prefs subdirectory (Windows) or in your System Folder's Preferences folder (Macintosh).

⇨ Photoshop "remembers" three kinds of information on your behalf: data on your preferred methods for using tools, saving files, or various management tasks; color management information that boosts color accuracy with the monitor, printing press, or color separation system; and Photoshop's state when you last exited, including the size and position of Photoshop's window, the names of the last four files you worked with (displayed in the File menu), and the settings of the filters as you last used them.

⇨ Your overall preferences can be changed using the File | Preferences menu item. A fast way to jump to Preferences is to press COMMAND/CTRL-K. This produces the General Preferences dialog box. At the top of this dialog is a drop-down list you can select from to access any of the other preferences.

⇨ The other seven Preference dialog boxes control Saving Files; Display & Cursors; Transparency & Gamut; Units & Rulers; Guides & Grid; Plug-ins & Scratch Disk; Memory & Image Cache.

⇨ Color calibration is set from the File | Color Settings menu, which includes four choices: Monitor Setup; Printing Inks Setup; Separation Setup; and Separation Tables. We'll cover calibration in Chapter 13, "Output: Printing and Preparing for the Press."

BASIC SETUP INFORMATION

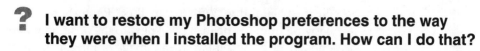 **I want to restore my Photoshop preferences to the way they were when I installed the program. How can I do that?**

On the Macintosh, open the Preferences folder in the System Folder and drag the Adobe Photoshop 4.0 Prefs file to the Trash. With Windows machines, delete the PHOTOS40.PSP file in the Prefs subdirectory inside the Photoshop directory. Photoshop will create a new Preferences file using its default values the next time you load the program. Some less critical information for Windows users, such as the name of the last directory you worked in and the names of the last four files you opened, are stored in PHOTOS40.INI. You can back up this file, too, if you wish, to be on the safe side. It does store the path to your Photoshop and plug-ins directories.

?   I just changed one preference, clicked OK, then remembered I needed to make another change in that dialog box. Is there a shortcut to return me to the same dialog?

Press COMMAND/CTRL-OPTION/ALT-K to return to the last Preferences dialog box you used.

?   Someone changed some of my preferences. Can I restore them without going through each dialog box?

You can restore your settings if you remembered to make a backup copy. Drag the Adobe Photoshop 4.0 Prefs file from the Macintosh System Folder, or the PHOTOS40.PSP file from the Prefs subdirectory inside your Windows 95 Photoshop directory, to a safe location, such as another hard disk, directory, or floppy disk. If your preferences are changed, copy the backup to its original location and your preferences will be restored.

?   How can I configure Photoshop to give me the best possible quality when resampling images?

You'll need to make sure that Bicubic is selected from the drop-down list in the File | Preferences | General dialog box. Each time you change the resolution of an image, even if the size remains the same, or make an image smaller, Photoshop must create new pixels, or throw some away, using a process called interpolation. Your three choices are

⇨ **Nearest Neighbor** With this method, Photoshop adds pixels by copying from the nearest pixel next to the position where the new one will go (when enlarging an image or increasing resolution), or to determine the value of a pixel that will replace others (when reducing an image or its resolution). On very slow computers (such as older 486 Windows systems or 680×0-based Macs), this faster system can speed up the process significantly. However, it works best with line art rather than continuous tone images, because the process doesn't take much account of the fine gradations that occur in tonal transitions.

⇨ **Bilinear** This method bases its calculations on the values of the pixels above, below, and to either side of the new or replacement pixel. While not as fast as Nearest Neighbor, it produces better quality.

⇨ **Bicubic** This interpolation method uses sophisticated algorithms to calculate a new pixel based on surrounding pixels. Unless you have a very slow computer, this choice should be your default, as it produces much finer gradations and significantly higher quality. Actually, even those who own slowpokes are better off using bicubic interpolation and just scheduling a coffee break during resampling.

Figure 2-1 shows an image resampled using each of these three methods.

? Can I customize my palettes so the ones I use the most are more accessible?

You can create your own collection of palettes, and direct Photoshop to place them in the position you prefer each time the program starts. Just follow these steps:

1. Make sure all four of Photoshop's default palette sets are visible on your screen. The quickest way to do this is to press COMMAND/CTRL-K, then press OPTION/ALT-E (or click the Reset Palette Locations to Default button.)

2. Click the Save Palette Locations box if it is unmarked, then click OK to return to Photoshop's main window. You should see four palettes arrayed at the right side of the screen. One contains the Navigator, Info, and Options palettes; the one below includes the Color, Swatches, and Brushes palettes; below that is the solitary

Figure 2-1.   Image resampled using Nearest Neighbor, Bilinear, and Bicubic algorithms

Actions palette; the bottom collection houses the Layers, Channels, and Paths palettes.

3. You can now drag the title tab for each palette to a location of your choice. If you drop it on the desktop, it will appear as a single palette. You might want to do this for a palette like Layers, which you access quite often. Palettes can also be dragged from one collection to another. If you rarely use the Paths, Color, and Info palettes, it might make sense to place them together, and then close their window by clicking on the Close box. Any of those palettes can be recalled to the screen with the Window menu choice. If you need to free up space on your display screen, four or five palettes can be dragged to a single collection, and the others minimized or closed altogether, as shown in Figure 2-2.

4. Each time you load Photoshop, the palette arrangement and positions you've specified will be restored.

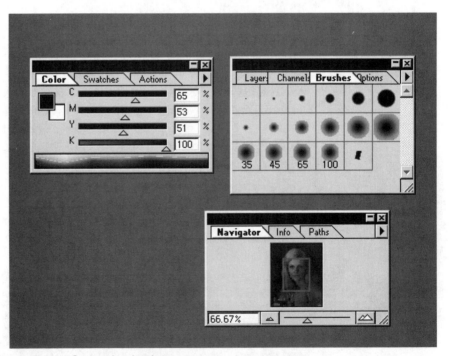

Figure 2-2.   Customized palettes are easy to set up.

? **Someone customized my palettes. I want them to look the way they did when I first installed Photoshop each time I load the program. How can I do that?**

Press COMMAND/CTRL-K, then press OPTION/ALT-E, or click the Reset Palette Locations to Default button. The palettes will be restored to their "factory" defaults. Next, uncheck the Save Palette Locations box if it is marked, then click OK to return to Photoshop's main window. The four Photoshop palette collections will be arrayed at the right side of your screen each time you load Photoshop, even if you or someone else has repositioned them or dragged individual palettes to new locations.

? **Sometimes Photoshop pauses or slows my system down when I exit the program or move to other applications. Can I configure the program to prevent this?**

To optimize its speed, Photoshop keeps a private clipboard with information about the most recent image data you cut or pasted. When you leave the program, it transfers that information to your operating system's shared Clipboard in a format compatible with that repository. If the image information is large, this can take some time, especially on slower machines or those without a great deal of RAM. If you find you rarely need to paste down information cut from Photoshop into other applications, press COMMAND/CTRL-K to view the General Preferences dialog box, and uncheck the Export Clipboard box.

? **My computer is rather slow, doesn't have a lot of RAM, and when I am applying a complex filter, loading a large file, or performing some other time-consuming task, I often turn to other work while I am waiting. Can I configure Photoshop to alert me when it has finished the current task?**

Press COMMAND/CTRL-K to load the General Preferences dialog box, and check the Beep When Done box. Photoshop will emit a sound when finished.

SAVING FILES

? **I'd like to be able to preview images before I load them into Photoshop. Can I configure Photoshop to let me do this?**

Photoshop doesn't have a preview capability built in for all files; however, you can save a thumbnail with each file you store in JPG or TIF format. Photoshop can display the thumbnail image when you select a file in the File | Open menu. Choose File | Preferences | Saving Files, and select Always Save from the Image Previews drop-down list. If you'd rather be asked (each thumbnail takes up only 2K of disk space), choose Ask When Saving instead. Select Never Save to turn off this capability entirely. Figure 2-3 shows the thumbnail previews you'll see when you open a file that's been saved with a thumbnail.

OPTIONS FOR DISPLAY AND CURSORS

? **How do I interpret the meaning of the differently-shaped cursors used in Photoshop? Can I change the way they appear?**

Most tools, except for the Type tool (which uses an I-shaped Insertion Bar), the Move tool, the Zoom tool, and the Pen tool use one of three common cursors, shown in Figure 2-4. These three cursors offer three different kinds of information about the tool:

⇨ **Standard** The standard cursor resembles the icon for the tool itself, such as a brush or eyedropper, usually with a "hot" spot at the tip. The chief value of this type of cursor is that it constantly reminds you what tool you're using. Beginners might like the standard cursor until they become used to the Photoshop interface. Glancing over to the toolbox to see which tool is selected is a faster way. A line of text in the status bar at the bottom of the screen also tells you the function of the currently selected tool, but not its name. The Standard cursor applies to all tools.

⇨ **Precise** The precise cursor looks like a crosshair. The center dot shows the hot spot where the tool will begin its work when the mouse button is clicked. This cursor can be applied to all tools

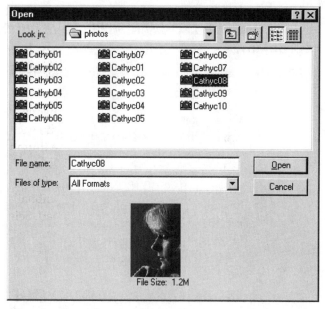

Figure 2-3.   Thumbnail previews make it easy to select the file you want.

except for the Hand, Type, Move, and Zoom tools. When you click with the precise cursor, a circle appears inside the crosshair to show that you are selecting a point on the image.

⇨ **Brush Size**   This cursor changes in size to reflect the coverage area of the currently selected brush when painting with the Airbrush, Paintbrush, Pencil, Rubber Stamp, the Paint Bucket, and the Gradient tools, or erasing with the Eraser. Normally, a brush-shaped cursor is round, but if you're working with an odd-shaped user-defined brush, it will assume that shape as well.

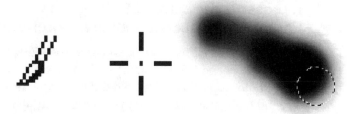

Figure 2-4.   Photoshop has three basic cursor shapes for its tools: a tool icon, a precise cursor, and a brush-shaped cursor.

? Why do the cursors change shape when I press the OPTION/ALT and COMMAND/CTRL keys? Is this a setup problem?

The change in cursor shape signals a modification in the action of the cursor, as follows:

⇨ When a standard cursor is active for any drawing tool except the Pen, holding down the OPTION/ALT key changes the cursor into an eyedropper, unless the eyedropper is already the current tool. Click on a color in that mode, and the color becomes the foreground color. If the eyedropper is already the current tool, pressing OPTION/ALT picks up the color you select as the *background* color. Keep this in mind to avoid becoming confused. If that isn't perplexing enough, the OPTION/ALT key has varying effects on nondrawing keys like the selection tools, Hand tools, and Zoom tools.

⇨ When a standard or precise cursor is active, holding down the COMMAND/CTRL key changes the cursor into the Move tool. Continue to hold the COMMAND/CTRL key while you drag to move the selected object.

⇨ When the precise cursor is active for any tool except the Hand, Type, Move, and Zoom tools, or the brush size cursor has been activated, holding down the OPTION/ALT key turns the cursor into the selection cursor (the one with the circle inside the crosshair). The cursor mode/key combinations are shown in Table 2-1.

 Warning: *If you click while pressing the OPTION/ALT key while using the precise cursor, the color under the cursor becomes the foreground color.*

? Sometimes I want to know the exact area a painting tool will affect; other times, I'd rather see which pixel represents the center of the brush stroke. Can I set Photoshop to accommodate my preferred way of working?

Just access File | Preferences | Display & Cursors and set the Painting Cursors and Other Cursors to the mode you want as a default. Photoshop actually has two different cursors it can use to represent all tools, and three for representing painting tools, which include Airbrush, Paintbrush, Pencil, Rubber Stamp, the Paint Bucket, the Eraser, and the Gradient tools.

Table 2-1.   Tool/Key Combinations

Tool	No Key	OPTION/ALT	COMMAND/CTRL
Airbrush	Standard/Brush	Precise Cursor	Move
Paintbrush	Standard/Brush	Precise Cursor	Move
Eraser	Standard/Brush	Precise Cursor	Move
Pencil	Standard/Brush	Precise Cursor	Move
Rubber Stamp	Standard/Brush	Precise Cursor	Move
Smudge	Standard/Brush	Precise Cursor	Move
Blur	Standard/Brush	Precise Cursor	Move
Dodge	Standard/Brush	Precise Cursor	Move
Pen	Crosshair	Precise Cursor	Move Point
Type	Insertion Bar	Precise Cursor	Move
Line	Crosshair	Precise Cursor	Move
Gradient	Crosshair	Precise Cursor	Move
Paint Bucket	Standard/Crosshair	Precise Cursor	Move
Eyedropper	Crosshair-FG Color	Crosshair/BG Color	Move
Hand	Hand	Zoom Out	Zoom In
Zoom	Zoom In	Zoom Out	Move

OPTIONS FOR TRANSPARENCY AND THE GAMUT

 I find the grid Photoshop uses to represent transparency distracting. Can I change it?

You can change the way this grid appears, or remove it entirely. Just follow these steps:

1. Choose File | Preferences | Transparency & Gamut to bring the Transparency & Gamut Preferences dialog box to the screen. The dialog box is shown in Figure 2-5.

2. Choose from Small, Medium, or Large grid sizes, or None, from the drop-down list. A preview of the grid size you select is shown in the panel to the right of the list box. If you choose None, layers will be filled with nothing, but will appear on your screen as if they are white (this is one good reason to use the transparency grid).

3. From the Grid Colors list box, choose Light, Medium, or Dark Gray, or Light Red, Orange, Green, Blue, or Purple. A color sometimes makes it easier to tell what portions of an image are transparent.

4. If you'd rather select a custom color, choose Custom from the list box. The Photoshop Color Picker appears. Choose a color using the Color Picker's options.

5. Click OK to save your preference and return to the main Photoshop window.

? How do I make the gamut warning more noticeable?

Unless you're extraordinarily fussy, the gamut warning won't tell you much. The color gamut is the range of colors that a particular color model or output device can reproduce, and the gamut warning alerts you to pixels that can't be represented in those colors using a target system. You may find that most of the off-color pixels aren't important to the image anyway, and so Photoshop's approximation when converting from one color system to another will be acceptable. If you rely on the gamut warning and want to make it more noticeable, access the Transparency & Gamut dialog box using File | Preferences | Transparency & Gamut, click on the color box,

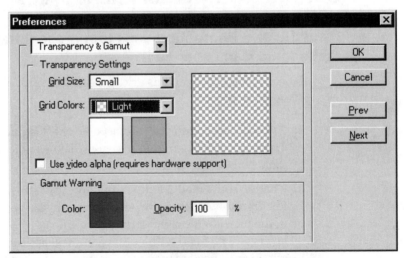

Figure 2-5.   Transparency and Gamut preferences are set here.

then choose a bright, easily recognizable color from the Color Picker. You may also type an opacity percentage. You'll find more about gamuts and color correction in Chapter 9, "Color Models and Color Balancing" and in Chapter 12.

OPTIONS FOR UNITS AND RULERS

When I use type in an image, it isn't exactly the same size as the same font in a printed document, even though I've scaled it to 100 percent. What's happening here?

If you're measuring type in points, a point isn't always a point. Traditional printers figure a point as 72.27 to the inch, while the Macintosh world adopted a slightly larger point of 72 to the inch, and this measurement spread to Windows. Usually, the difference doesn't matter, but if you must have an exact match, you can visit the File | Preferences | Units & Rulers dialog box, and click the appropriate radio button in the Point/Pica Size area. The default is PostScript (72 points per inch), but you can switch to traditional (72.27 points per inch) as shown in Figure 2-6.

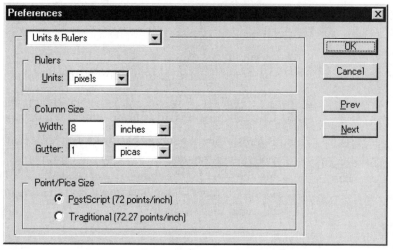

Figure 2-6.   The size of a point can be changed in the Units & Rulers Preferences dialog box.

? Can I set up Photoshop so its rulers display units in another format?

I showed you one method for changing the units used by rulers in Chapter 1. Here's another way:

1. Press F8 to make the Info palette visible, if it isn't already shown on your screen.

2. Select the Info palette's fly-out menu by clicking the right-pointing triangle at the right corner of the palette.

3. Choose Palette Options. The following dialog box will appear:

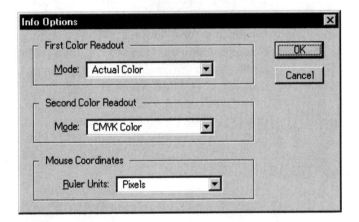

4. In the Mouse Coordinates area, choose the units you want from the Ruler Units drop-down box. You may select pixels, inches, centimeters, or points.

5. Click OK to return to your document window.

6. Photoshop will now use the units you have selected to show the position of the mouse cursor in the Info palette. Those units will also be used for the rulers. If you check the File | Preferences | Units & Rulers dialog box, you'll find that the units have been changed there as well.

OPTIONS FOR GUIDES AND GRIDS

? I want to customize my grids to better suit the kind of projects I do. For example, can I create a grid that represents feet and inches?

Unfortunately, Photoshop doesn't have a feet/inches option for its units, since most documents can be easily measured using only inches or some smaller increment. Drawing programs may be better suited for this kind of design, but if you need Photoshop's pixel-editing prowess, there's a workaround. Just follow these steps, then check the finished example grid in Figure 2-7.

1. Access the Guides & Grid dialog box by selecting File | Preferences | Guides & Grid.

2. For Guides Color, select a hue that will contrast with your grid, such as red, from the drop-down Color box. You can also select a Custom color and specify its values from the Color Picker.

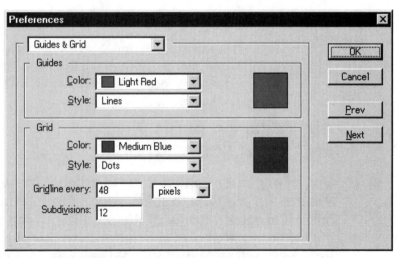

Figure 2-7.   A customized grid can include any increments you need.

3. Also in the Guides area of the dialog box, choose the Style you want for guides. The Lines choice makes the guides easier to see (you can always turn them off completely), while dashed lines are less obtrusive and may be kept visible at all times.

4. In the Grid area, select a color that contrasts with your guides, such as blue, from the drop-down Color box.

5. For a Style, choose between lines, dashed lines, and dots.

6. Select a distance between the gridlines—which will represent feet—appropriate to the scale of your image. You might want 48 pixels between gridlines if the object you are creating is less than about a dozen feet wide, or as few as 12 pixels for larger objects.

7. In the Subdivisions field, type in 12. This will divide each of the spaces in your grid into 12 increments, representing inches. With 48-pixel grid spacing, each "inch" will measure four pixels, while with a 12-pixel spacing, your "inch" markings will be one pixel apart.

8. Click OK, and the grid you've designed will be set as Photoshop's default.

This method is a workaround only. Your ruler's increments will no longer match your grid (since Photoshop has no feet/inches option) and the same grid will apply to every Photoshop image you work with, unless you change it. You'll find information on creating a customized grid on a separate Photoshop layer in Chapter 5, "Paths, Selections, and Layers."

OPTIONS FOR PLUG-INS AND YOUR SCRATCH DISK

One of my other applications is compatible with Photoshop plug-ins, but insists on storing them in its particular folder. Some of the plug-ins which come with my other applications are better than the plug-ins found in Photoshop. Can I configure Photoshop to share plug-ins with another program?

Photoshop allows you to use any folder on your hard disk to store your plug-ins. Just access the File | Preferences | Plug-ins & Scratch Disk dialog box, click Choose, and locate the folder you want to point to. All plug-ins must be in this folder or one nested within it, so if you want several applications to use a single collection, you may have to copy some of your plug-ins from their current location to the destination folder you want.

❓ How about sharing plug-ins over a network? Is that possible?

If your computer is installed over a network, you may even share a collection of Plug-ins among several users. If you're using Microsoft Windows 95 or Windows NT, you must map a network drive and assign it a drive letter on your computer, as Photoshop's Plug-ins & Scratch Disk Preferences folder chooser doesn't have a network option.

There are several other reasons to relocate your Plug-ins folder. You may wish to free up some hard disk space on the volume containing Photoshop, and moving plug-ins to another location—especially over a network—is one way to lighten the load.

❓ I have lots of memory, but Photoshop keeps telling me my scratch disk is full, and refuses to carry out a function. Can I stop this from happening?

You can easily make more room for the scratch files Photoshop creates on your hard disk to free up memory. Just follow these steps:

1. Access the File | Preferences | Plug-ins & Scratch Disk dialog box.

2. In the Scratch disk area, choose from the drop-down Primary list on your hard disk drive that has the most free space and is the fastest. If you have one drive that's fast and full, and another that's slower but nearly empty, choose the roomier drive. You must choose a physical hard disk on your system; selecting a network drive would defeat the purpose of the scratch disk anyway, which is to provide a decently fast substitute for RAM.

Tip: *Photoshop defaults to your startup disk (the one you boot from). This is often the worst disk to use for scratch files since you're likely to have another hard drive that's less busy and has more space than your boot disk. If you start up your computer from an IDE disk drive, but also have a fast SCSI drive in your system, the SCSI drive will almost always provide a better scratch disk.*

3. In the Secondary field, select your second most vacant, fast hard drive. Photoshop will use this if your primary scratch disk fills. If you have just one hard drive on your system, your primary and secondary scratch disks may be the same drive; if you have just two, you may get the best performance when your startup disk is your secondary scratch disk, and your other disk is set to be your primary.

4. Click OK to set these preferences.

Once you've used Photoshop for any length of time, you'll find that it's *never* possible to have enough memory. Once you've loaded a clutch of images, start working with large image files, or manage to create a bunch of layers and channels, you'll find the program has consumed all your memory (it happens even on our 192MB machines) and begins to substitute hard disk space for RAM.

Keep in mind that a scratch disk, also called virtual memory, is much slower than RAM, since hard disk accesses are measured in milliseconds, while memory operates on a nanosecond scale. The difference between the two measures is roughly the equivalent of saying, "I'll talk to you in a second" (RAM) but not replying for more than 32 years (hard disk).

❓ How much scratch disk space do I need?

You need at least as much scratch space as your RAM allocated to Photoshop. If scratch space is smaller, Photoshop uses only as much RAM as your available scratch space. That is, if you have 128MB of RAM allocated to Photoshop, but have only 64MB free on all your scratch disks, Photoshop will use no more than 64MB of the RAM.

That's because the program writes its entire RAM contents to the scratch disk during idle times, even if you haven't used all your available RAM. The upside of that process is that when you really do need to start using scratch space because your RAM is used up, Photoshop has already written some or all of the data that it needs to offload to your hard disk, during moments when no other work was being accomplished. This makes the scratch disk seem to operate faster. However, if you have less scratch space than you have RAM, Photoshop will use only as much RAM as it can offload to the hard disk. If your scratch disk is really crowded, Photoshop may be constantly swapping data back and forth between your disk and RAM, making it seem like your computer has much less memory than it really has.

While you can't control how much of your hard drive Photoshop will use, as you can with memory, it's important to make sure sufficient scratch space is available at all times.

How can I tell how much scratch space has been used?

Use the status bar at the bottom left of the Photoshop screen, which provides a wealth of information about memory and scratch disk usage. You must click on the right arrow next to the status bar and hold down the mouse button to view the available options. The percentage value at the left edge of the bar shows the amount of available RAM that is currently in use, as you can see here:

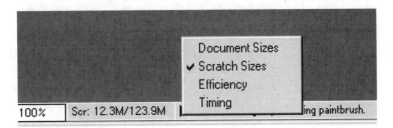

Next to this value is a window that can display information ranging from Document Sizes, Scratch Sizes, Efficiency, and Timing. To see the amount of scratch disk used, choose Efficiency from the fly-out menu. This figure shows the percentage of Photoshop tasks being performed in memory, compared with those that require the scratch disk. If this value is less than 100 percent, your scratch disk is being used.

Then, choose Scratch Sizes from the fly-out menu to see, at left, the amount of memory used by Photoshop for all the open images and Clipboard (less the amount Photoshop must have just to run) and, at right, the total amount of memory available to the program. When the number at left (memory being used) is larger than the number on the right (available RAM), then you can be certain that Photoshop is currently using the scratch disk. Subtract the right figure from the left to determine the size of the current scratch file.

Remember: Photoshop's virtual memory scheme is different from the one used by your operating system. If you run out of memory or fill up your scratch disks, you'll need to pay special attention to how this feature is configured.

OPTIONS FOR MEMORY AND IMAGE CACHING

? **I frequently run several programs simultaneously. How can I keep Photoshop from grabbing all the available RAM on my Macintosh, leaving none for my other applications?**

Windows and Macs differ sharply on how this problem is handled. Here's the Macintosh solution:

1. Using the Finder, locate the Photoshop application icon in its folder and highlight it.

2. Select File | Get Info, or press COMMAND-I to produce the Adobe Photoshop Info dialog box, shown in Figure 2-8.

3. In the Memory Requirements area, make sure at least 8192K is indicated in the Minimum Size field. That allocates about 5MB of RAM for Photoshop itself, and another 3MB for images, which as you might guess, is a bare minimum indeed. In the Preferred Size field, type in a figure that represents as much RAM as you can spare and still run the applications you need.

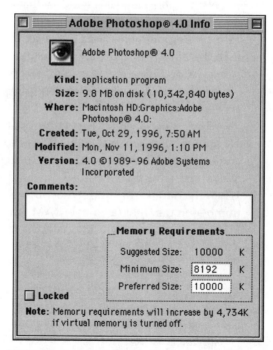

Figure 2-8.   The Adobe Photoshop Info window is used to allocate RAM on the Macintosh.

4. Click the Close box to save the updated information. The Mac OS will try to give Photoshop at least as much RAM as the minimum you indicate, or as much as the maximum, if available.

Note: *Products like RAM Doubler can dynamically reassign RAM among open applications, as well as compress data to stretch your memory even further. At this writing, however, none of these utilities are compatible with Photoshop's own virtual memory scheme.*

? I have the same RAM allocation problem on my Windows machine. How do I handle it?

You can set a Photoshop preference that tells the program how much of your available RAM to grab when it loads. Just follow these steps:

1. Choose File | Preferences | Memory & Image Cache.

2. In the Physical Memory Usage area, shown in Figure 2-9, dial in a percentage of RAM to be used by Photoshop. Both the available RAM and amount to be allocated to Photoshop are shown. You may need to calculate how much memory your other programs use to decide how much to allocate to Photoshop. If you have 64MB to 128MB or more, it's usually safe to let Photoshop grab 75 percent or more. If you have less RAM, you may have to increase

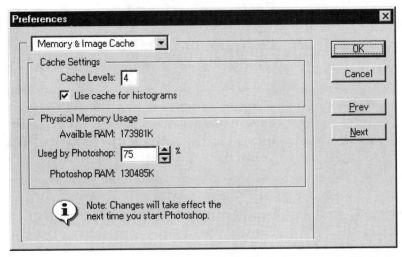

Figure 2-9.   Allocating a reasonable amount of physical memory to Photoshop can leave you with enough to run other applications.

this percentage and be satisfied with running fewer applications at the same time as Photoshop, or accept reduced performance due to increased use of virtual memory.

3. Click OK to save your settings.

❓ I have lots of memory, but don't really work with many huge files. Is there some way I can use this memory to make Photoshop work faster?

Activate or increase the size of Photoshop's Image Cache from the File | Preferences | Image Cache dialog box (Macintosh) or File | Preferences | Memory & Image Cache dialog box (Windows). Set a value of at least four, or as much as eight, depending on how much memory you have to spare and how often you view reduced images.

Explanation? When you zoom a Photoshop image to a larger size, it can do so quickly because the available increments (200 percent, 300 percent, etc.) can be calculated relatively quickly by doubling, tripling, or quadrupling the number of screen pixels used to represent each actual pixel in the image. However, when you view a reduced-size image at 66.7 percent, 50 percent, 25 percent, and so forth, Photoshop must downsample the image to calculate *new* pixels for the smaller representation. That takes more time.

When the Image Cache is activated, Photoshop calculates and remembers these downsampled versions of each image, using RAM or scratch space. An image cache setting of 4 preserves views at 66.7, 50, 33.3, and 25 percent of the original size. A setting of 6 adds 16.7 and 12.5 percent views; the maximum setting of 8 caches views as small as 6.25 percent. If you have a lot of RAM, choose 8; if memory is tight, you might want to change this setting to 1.

Tip: *You can also turn on image caching for histograms, but, unless you refer to them frequently, you won't want to do this. Rather than relying on a less-than-accurate cached copy, you'll get better results if you create a fresh histogram each time you check one.*

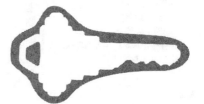

chapter

3 Answers!

Photoshop's Interface, Palettes, and Tools

Answer Topics!

Photoshop's Keyboard Shortcuts @ a Glance

Learn to use Photoshop's keyboard shortcuts. Since Photoshop generally uses the keyboard for commands instead of entering text, (except when you're using the Text tool), it can consider single presses of one of the letter keys as a tool shortcut. The tools and their corresponding keypresses are listed here:

	Tool	Key		Tool	Key
	Marquee	M		Crop	C
	Lasso	L		Magic Wand	W
	Airbrush	A		Paintbrush	B
	Eraser	E		Pencil	Y
	Rubber Stamp	S		Smudge	U
	Blur	R		Dodge	O
	Pen	P		Type	T
	Line	N		Gradient	G
	Paint Bucket	K		Eyedropper	I
	Move	V		Zoom	Z

Remember, you don't need to use the COMMAND/CTRL or OPTION/ALT key—just pressing the designated letter is enough.

GENERAL INTERFACE INFORMATION

? I've modified the settings of some of my tools. How can I return them to the default settings?

Double-click on the tool in the toolbox to bring that tool's Option palette to the front. From the fly-out menu at the right of the palette, choose Reset Tool. To reset all the tools to their defaults, choose Reset All Tools from the fly-out menu.

? I frequently find myself needing more help than Photoshop's built-in Help provides, even after checking this book. Where can I find the most up-to-date information?

You'll need Internet access and a browser to surf to a valuable online resource. Adobe provides the absolute latest information through a built-in online help system that connects to Adobe's Web site. To access this information, shown in Figure 3-1, first log onto the Internet. Then, choose Adobe Photoshop Home Page from the Help menu, or click the Program Identifier icon in the toolbox (it's just above the Marquee and Move tools). Then, when the About Adobe Photoshop splash screen appears, click on the Adobe icon in the upper-left corner. The home page of Adobe's online help system will appear in your default browser.

VIEWING

? I want to clean up some of the clutter from the screen so I'll have more space to view my images. How can I do this?

Photoshop offers several ways to increase the space available to view your images, depending on the platform you are using.

⇨ Close individual palettes completely by clicking their Close boxes. Restore any hidden palette as needed by accessing the Show command for that palette in the Window menu.

⇨ Press the TAB key to show or hide all palettes, including the toolbox. Press SHIFT-TAB to show or hide all palettes *except* the toolbox.

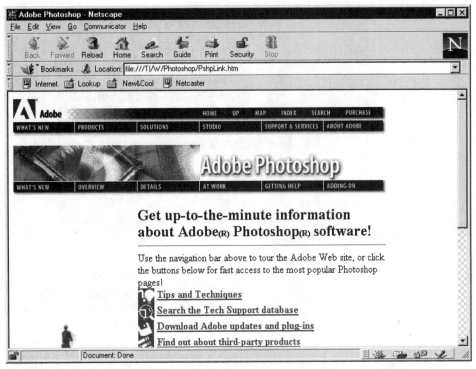

Figure 3-1.   Adobe's online help system

⇨   Minimize the size of the palettes by clicking on the Minimize
button in the title bar of each palette. Its window will shrink to the
minimize size required for access to that palette. The size varies
by the palette itself: the Navigator palette always retains a view of
the currently selected image, while the Actions palette can shrink
down to nothing more than a tab label, as shown in Figure 3-2.

⇨   If you're using a Macintosh, double-click in the title bar or, under
Mac OS 8, click once in the collapse box at the far right of the title
bar to "roll up" a palette using the operating system's window
minimizing capability.

⇨   Press the F key to cycle through Photoshop's Normal display
mode (all menus, toolbox, and palettes showing), full-screen
mode with menu bar (toolbox and palettes also show unless you
hide them), and full-screen mode. In the latter mode there is no
menu bar, but the toolbox and palettes must be hidden. In either
of the full-screen modes, the scroll bars and status lines vanish,

Figure 3-2.   Palettes can be minimized to provide more space onscreen.

leaving you with more screen space for your image. To cycle to the next viewing mode (you'll need to do this to return to the normal screen), press F.

Tip: *Consider changing your video display card's settings to the next highest resolution. That is, if you are using 800 × 600 or 832 × 624 and have a 17-inch or larger monitor, you will probably be pleased with the extra room you gain from the smaller menus and tools provided by 1,024 × 768 resolution.*

❓ Even with my screen space optimized, I still have difficulty displaying all the images I want to see at once. Is there anything else I can do?

Go ahead and load as many images as you like, then move quickly between each of them with a few quick key presses, or array them on the screen so that several can be viewed at once. These techniques apply to the Windows version of Photoshop; there are no equivalent keyboard shortcuts for the Macintosh, although you may size and arrange several images manually. Figure 3-3 shows tiled and cascaded images.

⇨   Hold down the ALT key, then press W followed by W to cascade all the open images in a neat stack. This is a standard Windows key sequence for cascading windows. Cascades are efficient because each panel can be large, yet quickly accessible.

Figure 3-3.   Tiled and cascaded windows allow viewing several images at once, or in turn.

⇨   Hold down the ALT key, then press W followed by T. This is the standard Windows procedure for tiling windows on the screen. A tiled arrangement lets you see two or more images at one time, but each must be of a smaller size.

How can I switch from one open image to another rapidly without having to find it among all stacked and overlapping windows and clicking on it to bring it to the front?

Windows users can press CTRL-TAB to cycle among each of the open images. This works best as a way to move among a cascaded stack of images, since tiled windows can be accessed just by clicking on them.

Is there a fast way to hide or display individual palettes?

Several of the most-used palettes can be accessed and hidden by pressing a function key. Hiding one of these palettes also hides all the palettes they are grouped with.

⇨ Pressing F5 displays the Brushes palette if it is hidden. If Brushes is visible, pressing F5 hides that palette and all the palettes in its group. All will reappear the next time you press F5.

⇨ Pressing F6 hides or displays the Color palette. If it is already visible, it is hidden, along with all the palettes in its group.

⇨ F7 hides or displays the Layers palette and its group.

⇨ F8 hides or displays the Info palette and its group.

⇨ F9 hides or displays the Actions palette and its group.

❓ How can I quickly move from one area of an image to another?

Use the Navigator palette, a new feature of Photoshop that many users overlook. Figure 3-2 shows the tab to click to bring this palette to the forefront. The Navigator allows you to move the active, visible area of a window that is too large to fit on a single screen at the current magnification. This can often be faster than activating the Hand tool. It also can be used to zoom in and out of the image. Here are some tips for using the Navigator:

⇨ The Navigator presents a thumbnail of the active image. To enlarge the thumbnail, drag the sizing box in the lower-right corner of the palette.

⇨ The visible portion of the image is highlighted with a red box. If the entire image is visible on your screen, the box will appear at the borders of the thumbnail. If the image is too large to view all at once (you can tell this by seeing whether the image has scroll bars, which are present only when there is more image to view), the red box will show the visible portion.

⇨ To move the image, drag the red box to the area in the thumbnail that you want visible; or, just click the thumbnail with the mouse. The area viewed will be centered around the point you clicked.

⇨ You can change the thumbnail's area highlight color by selecting Palette Options from the fly-out menu to the right of the palette.

⇨ While the Hand tool can also move the visible area of an image around on the screen, it doesn't provide a preview of the whole image as the Navigator does. That extra capability can make a big difference when working with small areas of large images or at higher magnifications.

? It takes too long to locate the Zoom tool each time I want to magnify or reduce an image. Is there a faster way to do this?

Photoshop offers a whole clutch of different ways to zoom in and out, and each of them has their own advantages and disadvantages. Since this task is performed so often, you should learn these shortcuts:

⇨ To zoom the whole image using one of Photoshop's fixed increments (100, 200, 50, 25 percent, and so forth), hold down the COMMAND/CTRL key and press the plus key on the numeric keypad or number row to zoom in, or the minus key on the numeric keypad (the hyphen on the number row) to zoom out.

⇨ Another way to zoom in and out in the default increments is to click on the Zoom Out icon (a pair of small triangles) on the Navigator palette. Zoom in by clicking the pair of larger triangles.

⇨ If you want to center the enlargement of reduction around a certain point in the image, hold down OPTION/ALT-SPACEBAR or COMMAND/CTRL-SPACEBAR, and the Zoom tool cursor appears. Click in the area you want to center the enlargement/reduction. The OPTION/ALT key sequence reduces the image, while COMMAND/CTRL-SPACEBAR enlarges it.

⇨ To enlarge or reduce an image by an amount that is not one of Photoshop's default increments, type in the value in the percentage field at the lower left of the Navigator palette, then press RETURN/ENTER.

⇨ If you don't know the percentage you want, use the slider in the Navigator palette to zoom in or out until the exact enlargement or reduction you want is shown.

? How can I size an image so that it appears as large as possible on my screen with no scroll bars?

Just press COMMAND/CTRL-0 (zero).

? **I need to be able to see a full image even when I am zoomed in to do some close-up pixel editing. Can Photoshop display two versions of the same image?**

The following steps are the most flexible method, shown in Figure 3-4:

1. Select the image you need to see in two (or more) views.

2. Hold down the OPTION/ALT key.

3. With the key held down, press V, followed by another V (or choose View | New View from the menu bar). Photoshop opens another window showing the same image.

4. Repeat step 3 if you need more than two views of the same image.

5. Resize each window and zoom in or out to get the views you need.

6. Any changes you make to any of the image windows will be reflected on the others. Some workers make a duplicate image when they want to be able to compare the untouched original with the copy they are working on. In addition, the Navigator thumbnail can be made quite large by dragging the palette's sizing box, and then serve as an alternate view. However, the Navigator always shows the full image, whereas you may want a medium close-up of, say, half the image at 200 percent, while zooming in to edit some fine detail at 1600 percent.

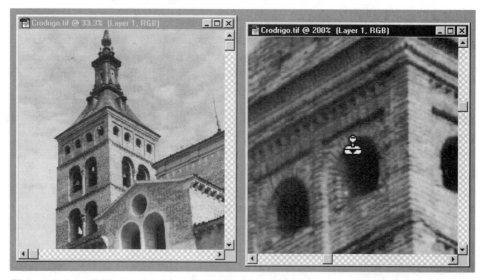

Figure 3-4.   Editing using two views of the same image

GRIDS AND GUIDES

How can I set Guides so they are equally spaced apart?

You can use the image's grid as a measuring tool that's quicker to use than counting ticks on the ruler, as shown in Figure 3-5. Just follow these steps:

1. Press COMMAND/CTRL-R to turn on rulers if they are not visible.

2. If the grid has been turned off, turn it back on by pressing COMMAND/CTRL-" (quotation mark).

3. Turn on Snap to Grid by accessing View | Snap to Grid. A check mark appears next to Snap to Grid. If you know Snap has been turned off, you can toggle it back on by pressing COMMAND/CTRL-SHIFT-" (quotation mark).

4. Drag from the horizontal ruler to position horizontal guides, or from the vertical ruler to create vertical guides.

5. As you move the guides, they will snap to each increment in the grid. Release the mouse button when you've reached the position you want.

6. Repeat steps 4 and 5 to position the guides precisely.

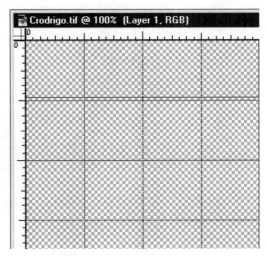

Figure 3-5.   Photoshop's grid can be used to precisely position guides.

? How can I reposition guides?

Select the Move tool, and pass the cursor over the guide until the
cursor changes into a pair of parallel lines with a double-headed
arrow. Then, hold down the mouse button and drag to the new
position. To change a horizontal guide to a vertical guide, or vice
versa, hold down the OPTION/ALT key and click on the guide.

? How can I create diagonal guides?

Photoshop doesn't offer a diagonal guide, but you can fake one fairly
easily, as shown in Figure 3-6. Follow these steps:

1. Press F7 to bring the Layers palette to the forefront, if it is not
   already visible.

2. Click the New Layer icon in the Layers palette. It is shaped like a
   piece of paper with an upturned lower-left corner. A new
   transparent layer is formed.

3. Select the Line tool from the toolbox and draw the diagonal line
   you want to use as a guide. Hold down the SHIFT key as you drag
   to produce a line at a perfect 45-degree angle.

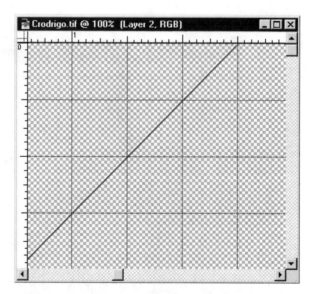

Figure 3-6.   Create a fake diagonal guide with a layer.

4. Although you cannot snap the cursor or objects to this ersatz diagonal guide, you may use it to position objects manually.

5. Turn the "guide" off and on by clicking in the left "eyeball" column of that layer in the Layers palette. Make sure the diagonal guide is turned off when you merge your layers, so it won't end up on the final image.

? How can I use guides to create a perfect circle at a precise point?

Here's how to use a precise point as the center for squares or circles:

1. Set a horizontal and vertical guide so they intersect at the point you want as the center for the object.

2. If you need the object to be exactly some size, place another guide at the position that marks the radius (of the circle) or any edge (of a square).

3. Turn on Snap to Guides if it isn't already active. You may use the View | Snap To Guides menu choice, or press COMMAND/ CTRL-SHIFT-; (semicolon.)

4. Choose the Oval or Rectangle selection tool from the toolbox.

5. Place the cursor at the intersection of your two main guides. It will snap into position automatically.

6. Hold down the OPTION/ALT and SHIFT keys, then press the mouse button and drag the circle or square.

7. If you've set up a radius or edge guide, release the mouse button when the cursor snaps to that guide. Otherwise, let go of the mouse button when the circle or square reaches the desired size.

? How do I remove guides I no longer need?

You have several choices:

⇨ If you just don't want to see the guides on the screen, press COMMAND/CTRL-; (semicolon) and they will vanish from sight. Guides don't print with your image in any case.

⇨ If you need to remove only some of the guides, use the Move tool and drag the guide onto the ruler.

⇨ To remove all guides in a single step, use View | Clear Guides.

THE INFO PALETTE

? **How can I tell what size my image is?**

You have several options:

⇨ Hold down the OPTION/ALT key and press I twice. The Image Size dialog box appears, and shows the size of the current image in pixels.

⇨ Press COMMAND/CTRL-A to select the entire image. If the Info palette is visible, you can read the width and height of the image in the lower-right corner. If the palette is not visible, press F8 to bring it to the front.

? **How can I tell how large a selection is?**

If you just want to see the size of a selection, press F8 and read the size from the Info palette.

? **I find it difficult to move a selection to a precise position in an image. Is there an easy way?**

Follow these steps to move a selection to a precise coordinate point in the image:

1. Press F8 to bring the Info palette to the forefront, if it is not already visible.

2. With any selection tool highlighted, place the cursor at the point on the selection that you want to move to a precise point coordinate.

3. Drag the selection to that point, using the mouse cursor's X and Y readouts in the lower-left corner of the Info palette as a guide.

4. Release the mouse button when the selection has reached the correct position.

BRUSHES

? I tried resetting all my tools, but my Brush palette still displays the custom brushes I created and no longer want. How do I return the Brushes to the default configuration?

Resetting All Tools only changes the options for individual tools. It has no effect on other palettes, including the Brush palette. To change your brushes, as shown in Figure 3-7, you have several options:

⇨ If you think you might need that set of brushes again, choose Save Brushes from the fly-out menu in the Brushes palette, and apply a name to the brush set.

⇨ If you'd just like to delete all the custom brushes, choose Reset Brushes from the fly-out menu.

⇨ The Load Brushes and Replace Brushes options in the fly-out menu allow you to add brushes from a stored library. The Load command adds the new brushes to those already in the Brushes palette, while the Replace Brushes command removes your old brushes and replaces them with the new ones.

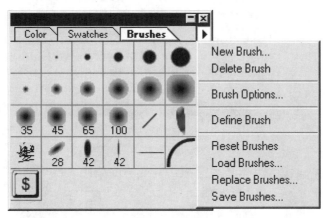

Figure 3-7.   The Brushes palette can be restored to the default configuration, or augmented with brushes from a stored library.

I need a brush that's larger than the 100-pixel brush in Photoshop's Brushes palette. How do I create one?

Follow these steps to create a brush in a custom size:

1. In the Brushes palette, choose New Brush from the fly-out menu. A dialog box like the one shown in Figure 3-8 appears.

2. Select a diameter for the brush using either the slider or by typing a value into the pixels field. Note that you can create brushes up to 999 pixels in diameter, much larger than the largest brush in the default set.

3. Click OK to activate the new brush and place it in the Brushes palette.

Note: *The New Brush dialog box is identical to the Brush Options dialog box. Both let you change the diameter, spacing, hardness, angle, and roundness of the brush. Don't confuse Brush Options with the Paintbrush Options palette, which is used to modify the behavior of the entire tool, rather than brush tips, using factors like opacity, fading, etc.*

Photoshop's soft brushes are too soft, and the hard-edged brushes too hard. I need a brush with a slightly blurry edge, but not too blurry. Can I create a new brush that's a little better suited to my needs?

The Hardness slider in the New Brush/Brush Options dialog box can be used to create or modify a brush with any desired amount of

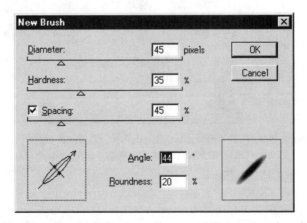

Figure 3-8.   The New Brush dialog box allows creating custom brushes.

fuzziness. Use the New Brush choice in the fly-out menu to create a new brush, or double-click on any existing brush to edit it using the Brush Options parameters.

❓ I need to create a brush that is shaped like an ellipse rather than a perfect circle. How can I do this?

The New Brush/Brush Options dialog box includes Angle and Roundness controls that can create elliptical brushes as well as a whole raft of different effects, as you can see in Figure 3-9. Use these tips to experiment:

⇨ A very low Roundness value produces a thin, tapered brush, while larger values create elliptical brushes until Roundness is set for 100—a perfect circle.

⇨ The Angle control lets you set the brush for any angle, which creates a whole new effect.

⇨ Click in the Wet Edges checkbox in the Paintbrush Options palette to produce another interesting kind of brush stroke.

❓ How can I create dotted lines and other repeating effects with brushes?

The Spacing slider in the New Brush/Brush Options dialog box determines the amount of space between brush strokes. Set the slider to a value from 100 to 999 percent to produce the amount of spacing you need. Figure 3-10 shows some of the effects you can achieve.

Figure 3-9.   Tapered, angled, and wet edges brushes each produce a different effect.

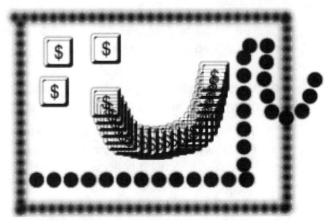

Figure 3-10.   Various dotted-line and other effects can be produced with the
Spacing slider.

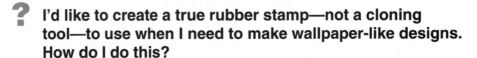 **I'd like to create a true rubber stamp—not a cloning tool—to use when I need to make wallpaper-like designs. How do I do this?**

Photoshop can create a brush from any selection. You can select a random area of your image with the Lasso, or deliberately create a specific brush shape, as shown in Figure 3-11. Follow these steps to produce a rubber stamp:

1. Create an empty transparent layer by clicking the New Layer icon at the bottom of the Layers palette (it's just to the left of the trash can icon), or by selecting Layer I New I Layer.

2. Draw the shape you want to use as a brush on the transparent layer.

3. Select the shape with the Lasso or another selection tool. You don't have to be exact in your selection, because only the image you've drawn on the transparent layer will be captured in your brush.

4. Choose Define Brush from the fly-out menu in the Brushes palette. Your new brush appears in the palette.

5. Select the new brush and create single stamps by positioning the brush cursor and clicking once for each stamp you wish to make.

6. If you'd prefer to leave a "trail" of the stamp image, double-click the new brush and adjust the Spacing field to a value between 100 and 999 percent.

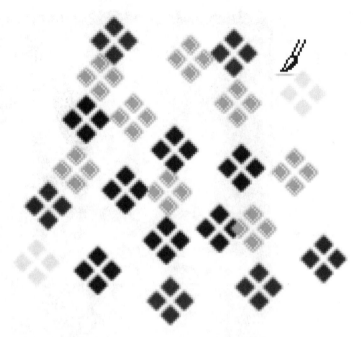

Figure 3-11.   Select an area and choose Define Brush to create a custom brush shape or a rubber stamp.

OTHER TOOLS

? I've tried to create callouts with Photoshop's Line tool, but was not pleased with the arrowheads I got. What did I do wrong?

The most common error is to draw the arrowhead lines with Anti-aliasing turned off. Because even horizontal or vertical callouts include diagonal lines (the arrowheads), the results may look as jagged as a staircase. Follow these steps to create professional-looking callouts, as shown in Figure 3-12:

1. Double-click the Line tool to access the Line Tool Options palette.

2. Click the Anti-aliased box if it is unmarked.

3. Choose a line width. Even a relatively narrow single-pixel callout can look good if Anti-aliasing is turned on, but two pixels or more will look even better.

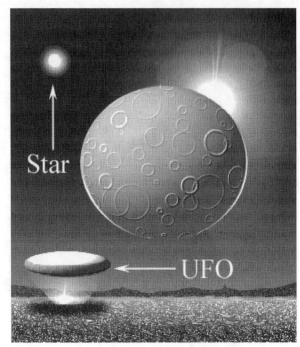

Figure 3-12.   Good-looking callouts are easy to make.

4. In the Arrowheads area, click in either the Start or End boxes. In the former case, the arrowhead will appear where you click to start dragging the line; in the latter, the arrowhead will appear at the point where you release the mouse button. Either option works well—just remember that you want to finish drawing the line at the point that must be most precise (usually the thing being pointed at). Click both Start and End boxes if you need a line with arrowheads at both ends.

5. The default arrow shape has a maximum width of 500 percent of the line's width, tapering down to the width of the line. The default arrow will be 1000 percent the line's width in length. Change the configuration by clicking on the Shape button in the Line Options palette and typing in your own values. You can also modify the concavity of the base of the arrow (making it more arrowhead-like, and less like a triangle) by typing in a value in the Concavity field.

? I want to draw some "graffiti" using a spray-can-like effect. What are my options?

Photoshop's Airbrush tool can simulate a spray can, applying a gradual mist of color to an image, in a much more diffuse way than can be achieved with even the softest brush. Best of all, the Airbrush can fade from the foreground color to the background color, or from the foreground color to transparent (allowing the underlying image to show through), as you can see in Figure 3-13.

Double-click the Airbrush tool, and the Airbrush Options palette comes to the front. You can set several options in this palette:

⇨ The pressure setting determines how quickly the paint is sprayed out of the brush; a low setting provides a fine mist, a setting of 100 percent sprays a wash of color on your image. The longer you hold the airbrush without moving it, the darker the color becomes.

⇨ Click in the Fade box to control how fast the spray fades out from the center to the edges. You may type the number of steps you want from full opaque to a complete transition to transparent or the background color.

⇨ Choose whether the fade should be to transparent or to the background color from the drop-down list.

⇨ If you have a pressure-sensitive pad like those from Wacom, Calcomp, and others, you can activate the Color and Pressure options so you can control these by pressing down harder with the stylus.

Figure 3-13.   The Airbrush produces some eye-catching effects.

?   **I've made some errors in my image, and want some areas to revert back to my previous version. Can I do this and still keep the changes I've made in other areas?**

Photoshop allows you to revert back to the last saved version using the File | Revert command, but as you note, all the changes in the image since the last save are lost. The Magic Eraser allows you to erase only your mistakes, and preserve the portions you want to keep. Just follow these steps to achieve a result like that shown in Figure 3-14:

1. Double-click the Eraser tool in the toolbox to bring the Eraser Options palette to the front.

2. Click in the Erase to Saved box. Any action with the Eraser will replace the image area you're removing with the same image area in the saved version.

Figure 3-14.   The Magic Eraser can selectively restore parts of an image to the previously saved version.

3. From the pull-down list, choose Paintbrush if you want to brush away the error, or Airbrush if you want a more subtle effect. You'd want to use the former option to remove a large, well-defined area, and the latter to blend in the changed portion of the image with the corresponding area in the original.

chapter
4 Answers!

Image Types

Answer Topics!

Image Types @ a Glance

Photoshop allows you to work with two different types of images: *bitmap* (raster) format and *vector* (outline) images. Bitmap graphics can be monochrome (black and white), grayscale, or color. However, it's very important to note that Adobe is in a distinct minority in its usage of the word bitmap. Everywhere you see the word in menus, dialog boxes, or Photoshop help files, Adobe is referring *only* to two-level, binary files. Other kinds of bitmaps are called grayscale or color. It's an unfortunate difference, and has caused more than a little confusion among Photoshop users. Vector graphics are always converted to a raster format after you import them, and color images can be represented in one of several different modes and color models.

Line Art

Line art is any piece of artwork that consists only of areas of a single color (such as black) and white. We usually think of line art only in terms of illustrations that don't use special techniques, such as dithering, to simulate a continuous scale of graytones. Architectural plans, mechanical drawings, and electrical schematics are another sort of line art. The key is that a line of only one density is used to outline the art, although the color of the line can be black or dark blue or any other color.

Because a single density is used to draw line art, such images are called *single-bit, binary images* in most of the world, or, as I noted earlier, *bitmaps* in Photoshop parlance. Unfortunately, *bitmap* has also taken on the secondary meaning of any image drawn with pixels (as all produced by Photoshop are) as opposed to images drawn with lines (as with Adobe Illustrator).

Line art can include patterns or fills, such as the cross-hatching and other effects used to differentiate between adjacent areas. Fills, for example, are often used on bar charts. Because the regular patterns alternate black and white lines, our eyes blur the two to provide a grayish image. Line art may contain only lines and dots of the same density, but still appear to have intermediate tones through the blending of those lines and dots by our eyes. Here is an example:

Grayscale

Another kind of raster image is called *grayscale* because it (ideally) appears to have a continuous scale of shades from pure white to black, with all the grays in between. A black-and-white photograph is a typical grayscale image, often called a continuous tone image by photographers. A single byte, which can contain a value from 0 to 255, is used to store each grayscale pixel, so you can have up to 256 different graytones.

Color

Color images can also have continuous tones, with the added component of hue. In a sense, three-color images like those produced in RGB mode, are simply three grayscale images, each representing 256 different tones of red, green, and blue. You can view these components separately using Photoshop's Channels palette. Because three sets of 256-tone information are needed, color images require three bytes, or 24 bits in all, to represent up to 16.8 million colors. That's the source of both the terms 24-bit color and "Millions of Colors" (the latter is a euphemism used in the Macintosh world). Four-color images, which translate hues into cyan, magenta, yellow, and black, are called 32-bit color for obvious reasons. The number of bits required to store a particular image is referred to as *bit depth*.

Vector/Outline Art

Another sort of image that Photoshop can work with is vector graphics. *Vectors* are the individual lines that make up the image itself. Humans are actually more accustomed to working with the straight lines and curves that compose vector graphics than with the dots used in raster graphics. Many of us were first introduced to vector graphics by the popular Etch-A-Sketch drawing toy.

ADDING VECTOR GRAPHICS TO PHOTOSHOP IMAGES

? I've been given some EPS files to include in an image. What should I do with them?

You can import them into Photoshop using the File | Place command, using the technique described in the next question. Encapsulated PostScript (EPS), used for storing outline images, is the most common of the vector file types (although you can also create EPS files that contain nothing but bitmaps, as you'll see later in this chapter). PostScript is a page description language (PDL) developed by Adobe Systems. Because PostScript uses outlines for fonts and graphics, it allows great flexibility in sizing images, since a description of how to draw the image at any desired size, rather than a map of the bits, is contained within the file. That also means that higher-resolution output devices can take full advantage of their high-resolution capabilities. A 300 dpi bitmap printed on a 1,270 dpi Linotronic imagesetter won't look any sharper. The Lino will simply use four of its smaller dots to simulate each of the larger 300 dpi pixels. However, with a PostScript file, the image can be printed at full resolution.

EPS files are most often simple ASCII files containing the program statements necessary to build an image in the printer's memory. A low-resolution image header, which can be used by the applications program to display a rough approximation of the PostScript image, can be appended.

❓ How do I import these EPS files into Photoshop?

When you use the File | Place command to select and import an image, it appears within a bounding box with sizing handles, as you can see in Figure 4-1. Photoshop can't display vector files directly; you'll see an empty box unless the EPS file has been saved with a rasterized image header file (many programs allow this as an option).

The EPS file inside the bounding box can be resized at will until you press ENTER/RETURN. Then, Photoshop converts the image to pixel format using rasterization. At that point, you can no longer

Figure 4-1.   An EPS file appears as a bounding box that you may resize, until you press ENTER/RETURN and Photoshop rasterizes it.

enlarge or reduce the graphic without suffering the usual problems of upsampling and downsampling.

Why do EPS files take up so much less storage space?

That's not always true. The amount of storage space required for vector graphics isn't measured in pixels or bytes per pixel. Instead, it's related directly to the complexity of the image and the encoding method used to store the file on disk. A drawing that consists of a single straight line can be stored as the start and end coordinates. On the downside, very complex images can take as much storage or more than bitmapped images, and are definitely more complicated for computers to output.

How do I save an EPS file from Photoshop?

Keep in mind that Photoshop cannot save line-oriented versions of its raster files. You can save a raster-only version of a file to include black-and-white, grayscale, RGB, or CMYK images. These files can be imported by applications that can handle EPS.

Follow these steps to save a Photoshop EPS file:

1. Select File | Save As and choose Photoshop EPS from the drop-down Save As list.

2. Click the Save button. The EPS Format dialog box, appears, as shown here:

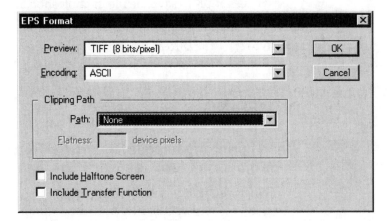

3. In the Preview drop-down list, you may choose None, 1-bit/pixel, and 8-bits/pixel. The last two produce a black-and-white file and

a 256-color TIFF file (respectively) that can be previewed by an application that later imports your file.

4. Choose an encoding method from the Encoding drop-down list:

⇨ **ASCII** is the most widely supported encoding scheme, but produces the largest files. Use this encoding when you're not sure whether the final output device supports PostScript 2 or later versions.

⇨ **Binary encoding** was introduced with PS 2 and produces smaller files that can be sent to the printer more quickly. You can use this format when you know that any output devices and applications that will work with the file support PostScript 2 or later.

⇨ **JPEG encoding** produces the smallest files of all, but often sacrifices some quality and requires PostScript 2 or later printer support. If you've defined a path that will be used to crop or clip the image, select it from the Clipping Path drop-down list. Clipping paths will be explained in more detail in Chapter 5, "Paths, Selections, and Layers."

Do not check the Halftone Screen and Transfer Function boxes. Their functions are explained in Chapter 12, "Output: Printing and Preparing for Prepress."

5. Click OK to save the file in Photoshop EPS format.

Note: *The DCS option appears only when you are saving as a CMYK EPS file. More information on this function can be found in Chapter 12.*

DITHERING

When I print my images, they come out with bands of color that don't look realistic. How can I eliminate them?

When you try to reproduce an image using an insufficient number of grays or colors, similar colors must be lumped together, producing bands and a poster-like look. This phenomenon will be most noticeable in subjects that have large expanses of tone that change gradually from one shade to the next. Pictures with sky, water, or walls typically require more gray or color tones to represent accurately.

Because non-continuous tone printers (which includes most laser and inkjet devices) can print only single-color pixels, additional colors must be simulated by using various-sized dots (in a process called dithering) that the eye blends together to form a full scale of colors. You can see a banded and dithered version of an image in Figure 4-2.

❓ What is dithering, and why do I need it?

Dithering allows you to represent more grays and colors with your output device than the device can produce on its own. For example, if you're using Photoshop on a monitor set for 256-color display, the program must dither the image to simulate full color. When you print a grayscale or color image on a conventional printer, some type of dithering or halftoning must be used to generate a realistic image.

❓ When I change grayscale images to a dithered, monochrome version, they still don't look very good. What am I doing wrong?

Make sure you're selecting the correct mode for the kind of results you need.

The following tips may help improve your dithering. Halftoning will be covered in more detail in Chapter 13.

⇨ You won't need to change grayscale images to a dithered monochrome version when the grayscale image will be output

Figure 4-2.   A banded image (left) and dithered version (right)

directly from Photoshop to most printers. Laser printers and your operating system's printer drivers have built-in dithering routines that produce good results. In addition, many printers have their own algorithms for producing a full range of tones.

⇨ Once you convert a grayscale image to a black-and-white monochrome version (a Photoshop "bitmap"), the image can no longer be scaled up and down; it must be reproduced at exactly the scale it is saved in or else quality will suffer.

⇨ To change a grayscale image to a dithered, monochrome version (to create a pop-art halftone effect, for instance), choose Image | Mode | Bitmap to display the Bitmap dialog box:

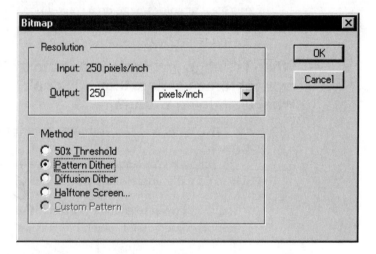

Select one of the Method choices:

⇨ **50% Threshold** All pixels brighter than the middle level (that is, 128 on a scale of 0 to 255) will be rendered as white; all pixels darker than a value of 128 will be converted to black. This produces a very high-contrast image that may be suitable for photographs that were high contrast to begin with. Most of the time, the 50% Threshold choice gives you washed-out images with little or no detail.

⇨ **Pattern Dither** Pixels are arranged in a pattern of dots that simulate grayscales.

⇨ **Diffusion Dither** Pixels are changed to black or white, starting with the pixel at the upper-left corner of the image. The algorithm transfers some of the gray information about each pixel to surrounding pixels so that the errors in converting pixels that aren't pure black or white are spread around the image. The grainy-looking images that result don't suffer from the geometric look of pattern dithered images, and are generally more pleasing.

⇨ **Halftone Screen**   A traditional halftone screen-like pattern is applied to the image. You can select an angle, line frequency, and dot shape. See Chapter 12 for more information on screens.

Examples of dithering using each of the methods discussed here are shown in Figure 4-3.

❓ Can I convert bitmapped images back to grayscale?

Yes, and under certain circumstances you may be surprised at how good the results are, considering the grainy appearance of most bitmapped images. The key is to reduce the size of the original image when you convert to grayscale. Photoshop will take the size of the

Figure 4-3.   Examples of 50% Threshold (upper-left), Pattern Dither (upper-right), Diffusion Dither (lower-left), and Halftone Screen (lower-right)

surrounding black-and-white pixels into account and simulate a decent gray in the reduced image. Follow these steps:

1. Choose Image | Mode | Grayscale. The Grayscale dialog box appears:

2. Choose a Size Ratio of 4 or higher for decent results. Your image will be 25% of its former size, but will contain a fair amount of gray. You may even get passable results with a Size Ratio as low as 2 (50%.) Figure 4-4 shows what you can expect.

3. Click OK to apply the conversion.

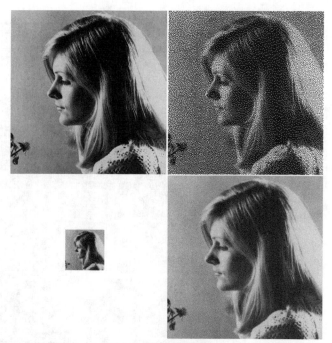

Figure 4-4.   The original image (upper-left), a monochrome bitmapped version (upper-right), a grayscale image created from the monochrome bitmap (lower-left), and the same restored image enlarged 4× (lower-right), back to its original size

? I've been asked to provide a halftone of an image. What kind of format is that?

Halftones are created by a technique that allows printing presses and laser printers to reproduce continuous tone images. Halftones convert the various gray values to black dots of various sizes. The eye merges these black dots with the surrounding white area to produce the perception of a graytone. For instructions on creating halftones, see Chapter 11.

? Can I work with previously halftoned images in Photoshop?

Yes, to a certain extent. You'll find that scanning an image that has already been halftoned reproduces each of the dots in the printed version. While the image may look bad enough on your screen, when it's reprinted it will look even worse. The two sets of dots may produce an interference effect called *moiré*.

To reduce this effect, follow these steps:

1. Select the image.

2. Choose Filter | Blur | Gaussian Blur

3. The Gaussian Blur filter's dialog box appears.

4. Move the Radius slider to the right until the dots begin to vanish, but not so much that the image becomes a hopeless blur. You may have to experiment to find the right compromise. You can also use the Descreen feature of your scanner, if it has one.

? I have a full-color image that must be reproduced with only 256 colors. What can I do?

Use Photoshop's Image | Mode | Indexed Color option, which selects a palette of 256 hues that can best (or perhaps, reasonably) represent your image. With the increasing popularity of Web sites, which often use the GIF file format that supports no more than 256 colors, this sort of conversion has become more frequently needed. You'll find more information about 256-color (and fewer) palettes in Chapter 14, "Photoshop on the Web."

When I convert full-color images to indexed color, I get bad results, ranging from banding to weird speckling. How can I avoid these defects?

You're probably selecting the wrong palette of colors for your particular image. Choose Image | Mode | Indexed Color, and you'll see the following dialog box:

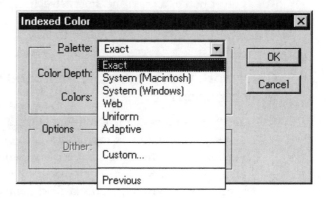

Choose a palette using the following guidelines. Photoshop can create indexed color images in one of several ways:

⇨ The program can examine all the colors in your original image and select a set of 256 hues that best represent those colors. This is known as an adaptive palette. Not all the colors can be included, so some will have to be represented by hues that are close in value. For continuous gradations, this can produce the banding effect I mentioned earlier.

⇨ If Photoshop finds that all the colors in your image amount to fewer than 256 different tones, it can create an Exact palette that reproduces the image perfectly (within the limits of your hardware). You might find this to be the case with images like screen shots. Even though captured in full, 24-bit color, the screen shot may contain only a few dozen distinct colors. When you convert a full-color image to indexed color and an Exact palette can be used, Photoshop defaults to that.

⇨ Photoshop can also use a Uniform palette, one that includes an equal number of all shades. If your image has a heavy concentration of certain colors—e.g., a portrait with lots of pinks and browns in the flesh tones—a Uniform palette won't have enough colors to work with in those areas, and will produce poor results. This kind of palette is best used with images that have a broad range of colors.

⇨ The program can apply one of several predefined palettes. These include the System palettes (one each for Macintosh and Windows), which should be used if you want to ensure that an image contains only colors that can be represented by each platform's 256-color System palette. Photoshop has a Web palette, too, which includes only the 216 colors available within World Wide Web browsers when used in 256-color mode. The other colors are reserved by the system for menus, dialog boxes, and other operating system features.

⇨ Finally, if you have several images and want them all to use the same palette of colors, you may select Previous, which applies the most recently used palette to another image.

❓ When viewing several indexed color images on a 256-color display, I notice that the colors shift. Can I avoid this?

What's happening is that your system is trying to portray two different 256-color images that each use a different palette when only a total of 256 colors are available to do it. You'll need to use a common palette for all of them, such as the Previous palette just described. An alternative would be to view the images on a system with more colors available, as a display set to 24-bit color or even 32,767/65,535 colors ("thousands of colors" in Macintosh parlance, or 15-bit and 16-bit color (respectively) everywhere else) should have no trouble displaying images with several different 256-color palettes.

❓ No matter which palette I choose, the image still has color bands that look terrible. Is there anything else I can do?

You can use diffusion or pattern dithering, described in the preceding grayscale discussion, to tell Photoshop to use a pattern of dots to simulate the colors that can't be included on the palette, exactly as it simulates gray. In this case, the dots will not only vary in size but in hue as well, so that many more colors can be shown. You'll find the pattern choices available in the Options drop-down list in the Indexed Color dialog box.

RESOLUTION

❓ What resolution should I use when working with an image? More is better, right?

Actually, unneeded resolution produces large file sizes and wasted time in printing, copying or uploading those files. A general rule of thumb is that you don't need any more resolution than your final output device, and can often get by with much less. If you're going to be printing line art on a 600 dpi printer, there's no need to scan at more than 600 samples per inch. For a 1,200 dpi output device, you'll rarely need more than 1,200 spi. Grayscale images that will be printed using halftoning techniques can get by with even lower resolutions, typically 1.5 to no more than 2.5 times the line screen that will be applied to the photograph. That is, if a grayscale image will be printed with a 133-line halftone screen, no more than about 300 spi is required. The extra detail would be lost in the halftone dots, anyway.

❓ I'm trying to reproduce postage stamps, but the fine lines exhibit jaggies or staircasing. How can I avoid this?

Nonphotographic postage stamps and currency are engraved, and have many fine details within a relatively small area. You can see that a 4 × 5-inch piece of line art scanned at 300 spi yields almost two million pixels of information, while a 1 × 1-inch stamp captured at 300 spi generates only 90,000 pixels. Print a 4 × 5 image of the stamp, and it's easy to understand why the 4 × 5 original will appear 20 times sharper than the stamp at the same size. Because small originals are generally printed in a larger size, higher resolutions are needed. Use the highest resolution you can when scanning such originals.

❓ I have only a 300-dpi scanner. How can I get the resolution I need?

It's more correct to refer to samples per inch—spi—than dots per inch, since a scanner doesn't produce dots. The net effect is the same, however: how many samples/pixels/dots per inch are used to resolve the image. Strictly speaking, Photoshop doesn't use dots per inch, either—it works with pixels per inch. The term *dpi* is correctly applied to output devices like your laser printer. Regardless of the terminology, there are several methods for getting higher resolution out of your scanner.

One good way is to use interpolation. Photoshop and your scanner both include algorithms that can simulate higher resolutions by examining surrounding pixels and calculating a value for new pixels. Interpolation may not work well for line art images like engraved postage stamps, because all pixels are either one color or another (black/white, blue/white, green/white, or whatever). The amount of information that can be used to estimate whether the new pixel should be black or white is limited. The trick is to scan in grayscale mode and convert to a bitmap. Follow these steps and you'll see why:

1. Set your scanner to its maximum optical resolution, whether it's 300 spi or 600 spi. You may have to check the scanner's specifications in the back of the manual to determine this, because vendors have been known to confuse the issue by emphasizing the maximum interpolated resolution the scanner is capable of.

Tip: *HP ScanJet models, while honestly rated by the vendor, cloud things by making it tricky to set a specific resolution within the DeskScan scanning software. You may have to create a custom print path, and set the horizontal and vertical resolution for that path manually.*

2. Scan the line art in Grayscale mode.

3. Within Photoshop, select the Image | Image Size function.

4. In the Width units list, choose Percent. Then, type in a value of **400** percent.

5. Make sure the Resample checkbox is marked, and that Bicubic interpolation is selected.

6. Click OK to direct Photoshop to upsample the image.

7. Convert to a bitmap using Image | Mode | Bitmap and the 50% Threshold option.

8. Click OK to make the conversion.

If you compare the bitmap original image, enlarged four times, with the resampled grayscale image converted to a bitmap, you'll see the version that started out as a grayscale image appears much sharper, as you can see in Figure 4-5. What happened here?

Photoshop was able to make some better guesses about whether a new pixel should be black or white because the grayscale image

Figure 4-5. The original line art enlarged 400 percent (left), and the same line art (right) converted to grayscale, enlarged 400 percent, and converted back to a bitmap

provided valuable extra information specifically—whether a pixel was located on the edge of a line or in the center. The edge pixels appear lighter compared to the center pixels, and Photoshop's bicubic algorithm picks up on this, resulting in a "sharper" interpolation.

? I'm not scanning line art; I'm working with grayscale images and need more resolution because I plan to crop a small section out of the original. Is there any trick I can use?

When working with photographs, the simplest way to give yourself a resolution boost is to have your photo lab make a larger version of the image and scan that. Recognize that larger prints may enlarge the grain of a smaller (say, 35mm) piece of film, so this trick works best if you start with a 120-format or 4×5-inch original. Then, you can grab the image at your scanner's top resolution and capture the film (or dye) grains in the print if you like.

Tip: *Don't forget to apply Photoshop's Unsharp Masking filter to your line art and grayscale scans to sharpen them up a little. This filter is discussed in Chapter 7, "Retouching and Compositing."*

I have an 800 × 600 pixel image that I need to fit in a 640 × 480 pixel window. How can I change the size of this image?

Before you go off resampling the image and possibly losing some resolution, double-check to see if you need to resize it at all. You may be able to fit all the image information you really require in the smaller window. Here's a quick way to check:

1. Press CTRL-A to select all of the 800 × 600 image.

2. Press CTRL-C to copy the image to the Clipboard.

3. Use File | New to create a new, empty image with a width of 640 pixels and a height of 480 pixels.

4. Select the new file, and press CTRL-V to paste down the 800 × 600 pixel image. Use the Move tool to slide the image around in this smaller window to see if a satisfactory cropping is possible. If so, save the image and don't bother with changing the size.

I need to fit *all* of an 800 × 600 image into a 640 × 480 window. What's the deal, here?

No problem, since 640 × 480 has the same aspect ratio as 800 × 600— only at 80 percent scale. Just follow these steps:

1. Choose Image | Image size.

2. Make sure the Constrain Proportions box is checked.

3. In the Width field, type in **640**. Because the Constrain Proportions box is marked, the Width and Height fields are joined by a chain to show they are linked. When you type a new value into either field, the other one changes automatically to provide the same proportions as before.

4. Make sure the Resample Image box is marked and that Bicubic shows in the drop-down list next to it.

5. Click OK to resize the image.

? **I have an image that must measure exactly 700 pixels wide. The height isn't critical. What do I do?**

Follow the preceding steps. The image will be resized to fit your 700-pixel requirement, keeping the same aspect ratio as before. If you need to have an image of a particular height, and don't care about the width, type the height into the Height field.

? **I need an image that's 34 percent smaller than the one I have. How do I do this?**

Follow the preceding procedure, but select Percent in the Width or Height field and type in the percentage of the original size the resized image must be.

? **I need to change the resolution of an image without changing its pixel dimensions. Is this possible?**

It can happen! You may have an 800 × 600-pixel image scanned at 600 spi. Left alone, it would print at a minuscule 1.33 × 1-inch size on a 600-dpi printer. While printer drivers can scale an image up or down, and Photoshop lets you specify a print size independent of the resolution of an image, other applications may not have that feature. Instead, you can reduce the resolution to increase the size the image will be printed at. Follow these steps:

1. Choose Image I Image Size.

2. Uncheck the Resample Image box if it is marked. Immediately, the Width and Height fields are locked, and the Print Size width, height, and resolution become linked with the Chain icon.

3. Change the resolution of the image to 100 pixels/inch. The Print Size changes to 8 × 6 inches.

4. Click OK to convert the image to the new resolution.

? **I have an abstract texture image that measures 300 × 400 pixels. I'd like to take the entire image and make it fit a 400 × 400 pixel square. Can I do this?**

It helps that your image is abstract. If the image lends itself to a little stretching in one direction or another, you might be able to change the aspect ratio without causing noticeable visible distortion. Just follow these steps:

1. Choose Image | Image Size.

2. Uncheck the Constrain Proportions box.

3. Change the 300-pixel width to 400 pixels in the Width field.

4. Click OK to resample the image in the new aspect ratio.

? **Why do file sizes grow so quickly as I increase resolution?**

The higher the resolution, the sharper the image will appear to be, at a cost of four times as much disk space each time you double the samples per inch. Compare 150 × 150 samples per inch (22,500 pixels) with 300 × 300 samples per inch (90,000 pixels) to see what's going on.

? **What's a quick way to see the dimensions of an image?**

Here are two fast ways:

⇨ Hold down the OPTION/ALT key and press I, followed by I again. The Image Size dialog box appears, with the dimensions showing in the Width and Height fields.

⇨ Press F8 if the Info palette is not visible, followed by COMMAND/CTRL-A. The entire image is selected, and its dimensions appear in the lower-right corner of the Info palette.

? **There isn't enough space in my current image for some modifications I want to make. How can I enlarge it?**

Choose Image | Canvas Size, and type in the new dimensions for your image. Extra space will be added around your original image, which remains at its original size, as shown in Figure 4-6.

Figure 4-6.   Enlarging the working area with the Canvas Size facility

? I only want to add extra space at the right side of the image. Can I do that?

Use Image | Canvas Size, as just described, type in the new width, then click the middle box in the left column of the Anchor preview. The new space will be inserted to the right of the original image, which is represented by the white box. You can move this box to any location in the preview to add the additional space to any part of the canvas you like.

chapter

5 **A**nswers!

Selections and Paths

Answer Topics!

Selections and Paths @ a Glance

Selection is a feature that allows you to copy, edit, fill, or otherwise manipulate only part of an image. The selected portion of the image is contained inside a selection border, which appears as a series of dotted lines that appear to move or crawl in a clockwise direction. Selections can be defined by one of several tools, including the Rectangular, Elliptical, and Polygonal Marquee tools, as well as the Lasso and Magic Wand. You may also create selections by painting onto a mask, or by accessing one of the commands in the Photoshop Select menu. Selections are most often a single area in an image, but you may add discontinuous portions by holding down the SHIFT key while selecting more of the image.

Once you've made a selection, you can perform actions like these on the selected area:

⇨ Edit a selected area with any of the Editing tools.

⇨ Change the size or shape of the selection by scaling, rotating, or distorting it.

⇨ Paint or fill the selected areas with color or a pattern using any of the painting tools.

⇨ Paste images copied to the clipboard into the selected area.

⇨ Invert a selected area to protect it so you can work on the rest of the image without changing what is contained in the selection.

⇨ Apply a filter to only a selected area (or to only the rest of an image, after inverting).

⇨ Save selections in channels or layers so they can be used more than once.

⇨ Convert selections to line-oriented paths.

⇨ Selections may have hard edges, be feathered so that the selected area gradually fades out into the surrounding image, or be Anti-aliased so that edges are smoother. Selections created as masks can be completely opaque, semitransparent, or graduated in opacity.

⇨ The Magic Wand selects all pixels that touch each other that are similar in hue and value to the pixel you first clicked on.

⇨ The tolerance of the tool is a parameter that sets how close in value to the original pixel an adjacent pixel must be to be included in the selection.

⇨   The higher the tolerance, the wider the range of pixels selected; low tolerance will select many fewer pixels.

⇨   Paths can be open—a line—a closed shape, or a series of lines, shapes, and combinations of lines and shapes. All these are created using line segments, which connect two anchor points. To create a path, select the Pen tool, then click in your document to set an anchor point. Release the mouse button, then click somewhere else in your document. A line is drawn between the two points, creating a simple path. The currently selected anchor point is darkened, while all other points are shown in a lighter shade.

⇨   You may add new anchor points to lengthen the path.

SELECTING AREAS

?   I find choosing a selection tool from the fly-out menus clumsy. Is there a faster way to activate the tool I want?

Just press the shortcut key for the selection tool you want multiple times. Repeatedly pressing M, for example, cycles among the available modes for the Marquee tool. Pressing L cycles between Lasso and Polygon selection tools. You can choose the Rectangular, Elliptical, Cropping, and Single Line selection tools by holding down the OPTION/ALT key and clicking on the Marquee icon in the Tool Box. Each time you click, the icon for the next mode for that tool appears. Both these shortcuts work for any type of tool that includes multiple modes in a fly-out menu.

?   How can I place an elliptical or rectangular selection exactly where I want it?

Follow one of these options to place the selection at a certain point. You can also use grids and guides (explained in Chapter 3) if you need to put a selection at a precise set of coordinates.

⇨   To place a corner, a rectangle, or the circumference of an ellipse at a desired point, click the point with the mouse button and drag down and to the right to position the upper-left corner of the circle there; up and to the right to position the lower-left corner at that spot; up and to the left to place the lower-right corner; and down and to the left to place the upper-right corner.

⇨ To center a rectangle or ellipse around a certain point, click at the point and then hold down the OPTION/ALT key while dragging.

⇨ To create a perfect square or circle, hold down the SHIFT key while dragging.

? How can I add or subtract from a selection?

Use any of the selection tools and hold down the SHIFT key while you create the additional selection. The original selection will remain and the new area is added to that selection, even if it is not contiguous. Figure 5-1 shows a single selection that encompasses multiple areas.

Figure 5-1.   A single selection can encompass multiple areas.

Note: *You might think that holding down the* SHIFT *key when an area is already selected will create a square selection. That's not true. Once any area is selected, holding down the* SHIFT *key while selecting adds the new area to the selection, but the Rectangular and Elliptical selection tools are not constrained to produce squares or circles.*

When I try to add a perfect square or circle to a selection, the SHIFT key only adds the selection—it doesn't constrain it to a square or circle. What can I do?

There are two ways to add circles or squares to an existing selection. If you want multiple circles and/or squares, these steps are the fastest way to do what you want:

1. Choose the first selection tool you want to use and apply the selection in the usual way.

2. When you're ready to add the circle or square, using the Marquee Options palette, choose Constrained Aspect Ratio from the drop-down Style list, as shown in Figure 5-2. Make sure a value of 1 appears in both the Width and Height fields.

3. Create the next selection. It is not necessary to hold down the SHIFT key, as the style you've selected forces Photoshop to create only squares and circles of any desired size.

4. You may turn the Constrained Aspect Ratio style on when you want to create circles or squares, or change it to Normal when you want to select other shapes.

The second way takes a bit of coordination, but you can master it with a little practice:

1. Choose the first selection tool and apply the selection in the usual way.

2. Choose the Rectangular or Elliptical selection tool, depending on whether you want to add a square or a circle.

3. Hold down the SHIFT key and drag. A rectangle or ellipse is added to the current selection.

4. *With the mouse button still held down,* release the SHIFT key, then press it again. The selection changes to a square or circle. The "long" dimension of the rectangle or ellipse is reduced to the same

Figure 5-2.   The Constrained Aspect Ratio style makes selections using fixed proportions.

size as the "short" dimension. Remember this so you can add squares and circles in the size you want.

5. *With the* SHIFT *key still pressed down,* release the mouse button. Then you may release the SHIFT key and the selected square or circle will remain. If you release the SHIFT key before the mouse button, the selection returns to its original shape.

? The Constrained Aspect Ratio feature is great when I want to create circles or squares. What can I do if I want to constrain the Elliptical or Rectangular selection tools to some other proportions?

You can type any ratio of height and width into their respective fields. Entering **4** into the Width field and **1** into the Height field will make the selection four times wider than it is high. The numbers represent a ratio, not a particular width and height (as they do when you choose the Fixed Size style).

? **When I make multiple selections, I sometimes accidentally click without holding down the SHIFT key, and lose all the selections I've made so far. How can I avoid this?**

If you *immediately* press COMMAND/CTRL-Z (Undo), Photoshop will restore your selection. If you accidentally do something else after that first click, your selections will be lost. If this happens often, you might want to consider saving intermediate selections to your hard disk and adding the new selections to the saved version. You'll need to take a couple extra steps. Follow these directions:

1. Create the first selection.

2. Choose Save Selection from the Save menu. The Save Selection dialog box appears, with the New Channel checkbox marked. (Selections are one kind of channel.)

3. Click OK to return to the image editing window.

4. Click anywhere outside the selection. It will disappear.

5. Holding down the SHIFT key, create the next circle or square selection.

6. Use Select | Save Selection again.

7. This time, in the Channel drop-down list, choose the channel that holds the original selection. If you haven't saved any selections prior to this for this image, it will be named #2 for a grayscale image, #4 for an RGB image, and #5 for a CMYK image. If other selections are already present, your most recent selection will be the bottom one on the list.

8. In the Operation area, click the Add to Channel radio button. Click OK. Your selection now contains both areas.

? **Can I give a selection a name to make it easier to find than remembering channel numbers?**

Just do this:

1. Using the Channels palette, double-click on the channel containing your square selection.

2. The Channel Options dialog box will appear. Type in a name for the selection, such as "**Squares**," then click OK to return to your

image. You'll see the selected area represented in white, surrounded by the unselected area in black. Photoshop defaults to showing you the channel you just named.

3. To get back to the Normal display, click in the box at the top of the left column (it will be named Black, RGB, or CMYK) until the Eyeball icon appears, indicating that that channel is visible.

4. Click in the left column next to your renamed channel until the Eyeball vanishes. Figure 5-3 shows named selections.

How can I see exactly what area is included in a selection I've saved?

Using the Channels palette, click in the left column next to the saved channel. A red mask overlay appears showing the selected and unselected areas, as shown in Figure 5-4.

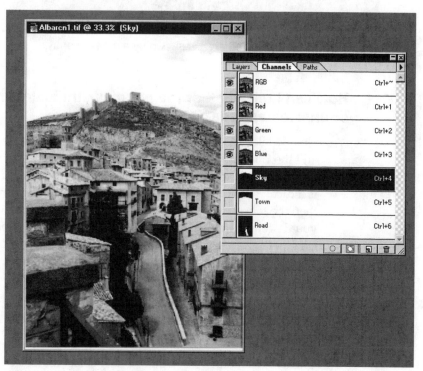

Figure 5-3.   Named selections

Figure 5-4.   The selected area is shown by a mask overlay.

❓ How can I tell whether the red mask indicates the selected or unselected area?

Double-click in the saved selection's name in the Channels palette, and the Channel Options dialog appears. In the Color Indicates area, if the Masked Areas radio button is marked, then the unselected area is indicated by the colored tone. If the Selected Area button is marked, then the tone indicates (think fast!) that the selection is colored. If you'd prefer a mask color other than red, click the Color patch in the Channel Options dialog box and choose a new hue from the Color Picker that pops up. If you'd like the mask to be denser or more transparent, type in a value in the Opacity field.

❓ When I want to create a new selection, how can I deselect the area currently selected?

Click anywhere in the image with any selection tool. If you're not using a selection tool, select one and click before creating the new selection. You can also press COMMAND/CTRL-D to abandon a selection. This is faster if you're not currently using a selection tool and just want to continue with the tool you have.

Tip: *If you're using the Magic Wand tool and want to start over with a new selection, either click in the area you now want to select with the Magic Wand, or press COMMAND/CTRL-D. Because the Magic Wand can take some time to calculate the area it is selecting, you'll waste time waiting if you don't click where you actually want the new selection.*

How can I move a selection?

To move the selection itself (and not the contents of the selection), choose any selection tool (it doesn't have to be the one that created the selection) and place the cursor inside the selection. You may then drag the selection to any part of the image you like. You can also move a selection in small increments with Photoshop's Nudge feature. Choose any selection tool, then press the cursor arrow keys to move the selection a pixel at a time in that direction. Hold down the SHIFT key to move the selection by five pixels with each nudge.

How can I select a single row or column of pixels?

Use the Single Row or Single Column tools from the fly-out menu in the Marquee tool. These modes select, as you might guess, a single row or column of pixels extending from the point you click to the edges of the image. To select multiple single columns or rows, hold down the SHIFT key. If you've turned on Snap to Grid, you can create rows and columns that are aligned with your grid.

Can I create a rectangle or ellipse of a particular size?

Yes. You may want to do this to create an object of a particular size, or to select a specific amount of your image. If you need a selection of a particular pixel dimension for a desktop publishing program, this is an easy way to accomplish that. Just click the Marquee tool and choose Fixed Size from the Style drop-down list. Type in the height and width (in pixels) that you want. Thereafter, when you click with the cursor, a selection of the size specified appears.

ADJUSTING YOUR SELECTIONS

? **When I use Fixed Size the corner of the selection always appears at the position I click. I can't get the selection centered by pressing the OPTION/ALT key. What can I do?**

Photoshop's thrown you a curve ball here. You must follow these steps to do what you want:

1. Click with the mouse at the position you want the selection centered around. The selection appears, but offset from that position.

2. Without releasing the mouse button, *now* press the OPTION/ALT key. The selection appears centered around the point you clicked. Don't release the OPTION/ALT key yet!

3. With the OPTION/ALT key still pressed down, release the mouse button. You can then release the OPTION/ALT key, and the selection will be centered around the place you selected.

? **Can I create a selection that is a row or column two pixels wide?**

Yes, but you can't use the Single Row or Single Column selection tools. Instead, use the Rectangular marquee with the Style set to Fixed Size. Type in a value of **2** as the value for the dimension you want to select (you can make the "row" or "column" 3, 4, 8, or as wide/tall as you want). Then make the other dimension any size that is larger than your image, say 5,000 pixels. Your selections will then be of the thickness you desired, and as wide or as tall as the boundaries of your image.

? **I want to blend my image into the background. Can I do this?**

You can apply feathering to a selection border to soften the transition between the inside of the border and the background. You can feather all selection tools except the Magic Wand. Click the tool in the Tool Box to bring the Options palette to the front. Then type the number of pixels you want to use to fade the selection in the Feather field. The value is called the Feather Radius, which is misleading; feathering doesn't actually begin in the center of the selection but, rather, at a point half the Feather Radius value towards the center of the selection.

With feathering activated, any selection you create with that field will be softened. Figure 5-5 shows a blended image.

Note: *Thanks to a bug in Photoshop, you can apply feathering to Single Row or Single Column selections, but if the value is higher than zero, you'll be unable to make a selection at all!*

? I made a selection with feathering turned off in the Options palette. Is it too late to feather this selection?

You can apply feathering to your current selection by choosing Select | Feather, or by pressing SHIFT-COMMAND/CTRL-D and entering the number of pixels you want for your feathering zone into the Feather Radius dialog box.

Figure 5-5.   Feathering a selection border helps blend an image into the background.

? **When I select a rectangular area and pull down the Image menu to crop the photo to that size, the Crop choice is grayed out. What am I doing wrong?**

Set Feathering to 0 pixels in the Marquee Options palette. Photoshop cannot crop to a feathered rectangular selection.

? **Can I choose which way the blending is applied?**

When you select an area and apply Feather, the feathering is applied equally on either side of the selection border. That is, if you've chosen a feathering value of 60, feathering will begin 30 pixels inside the original border, and progress to its maximum effect 30 pixels beyond the border. If the idea confuses you, Figure 5-6 makes the concept a little clearer. At left is the original selection. In the middle, the selection has been feathered by a value of 60 and then filled with black. At right, the same feathered selection has been inversed, then filled with black.

? **The edges of my selection are too rough. Can I soften them?**

Anti-aliasing will do the trick. Anti-aliasing blurs the edges of hard diagonal lines by using a gradation of gray pixels to make the lines

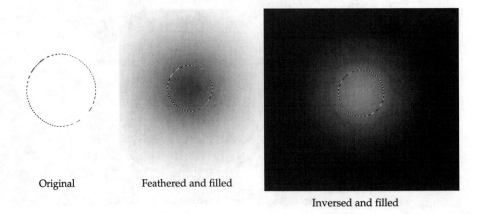

Original   Feathered and filled

Inversed and filled

Figure 5-6.   Examples of feathering

appear smoother. You can blur the edges of any selection tool that creates diagonal lines, plus objects drawn by the Line and Type tools, but excluding Rectangular Marquee selections. Just mark the Anti-alias checkbox in that tool's Options palette. Figure 5-7 shows a diagonal line both unaliased and anti-aliased.

❓ I need to select an odd-shaped portion of my image. How can I do that?

The ability to accurately select exactly the portion of an image that you want is one of the fundamental skills of the Photoshop expert. The first thing you need to do is learn how to use the Lasso tool to make freehand selections. Here are some tips for using the Lasso and its mate, the Polygon selection tool:

⇨ To select with the Lasso, drag the cursor around the area you want to select while holding down the mouse button. When you

Figure 5-7.   At left, a diagonal line with its "jaggies" showing; at right, an anti-aliased version

release the button, the beginning and ending points of the line connect and close the selection.

⇨ To create an odd-shaped selection border with straight lines, hold down the OPTION/ALT key and the mouse button as you touch key points along the perimeter of the selection. The Lasso will stretch and contract like a rubber band so you can create a selection border with straight lines.

⇨ When you're ready to resume drawing the selection border in freehand mode, release the OPTION/ALT key, but leave the mouse button depressed. You can alternate between freehand and straight line modes.

⇨ When you release the OPTION/ALT key and the mouse button, a straight line will be drawn between the beginning and ending points of the selection border, creating a closed selection.

❓ I use the OPTION/ALT key with the Lasso very often, but often accidentally release the mouse button before I am finished selecting. Is there a quicker way to select using straight lines while avoiding this problem?

Select the Polygon selection tool (press L until a nonelliptical Lasso icon appears) and use that to select with straight lines. Release the mouse button each time you want to set a point to begin a new straight line (the selection won't close itself as it will with the Lasso). If you need to select Freehand momentarily, press the OPTION/ALT key. This tool works exactly the opposite of the Lasso. When you're finished selecting, double-click anywhere and the selection will close itself, or click on the beginning point of the selection.

❓ I was tediously drawing a selection border with the Lasso, and accidentally released the mouse button before I was done. How can I undo this mistake?

You can't. COMMAND/CTRL-Z (Undo) undoes your entire selection. Be very careful when selecting with the Lasso. You can avoid this problem by making your selection using a Quick Mask instead.

? I find the selection border distracting. Can I turn it off?

You can toggle the selection border's visibility on or off by pressing COMMAND/CTRL-H. When the border is turned off, the selection is still active.

 Tip: *If you are trying to apply a tool and can't get it to work, you may have an active selection you've forgotten about, and can't see because the border has been turned off. Press COMMAND/CTRL-H to make this selection (if any) visible.*

? I tried to select a solid-color background with the Magic Wand, but instead selected a spotty patchwork of pixels. What's wrong?

Your solid color background isn't as solid as you thought, and you probably set the tolerance of the Magic Wand too low. In the Magic Wand Options palette, set Tolerance to a higher number; if it's currently smaller than 32, try using 32 or 48 as a value. If you want smooth edges to your selection, click the Anti-aliasing box as well.

USING THE MAGIC WAND AND COLOR RANGE

? How do I select an area that's even in tone with the Magic Wand?

If an area is absolutely even in tone, a tolerance of 1 or 2 will select it. If not, move the tolerance upwards in increments of about 8 until all or most of the area is selected.

? How do I select an area that has a variety of tones?

To select as much as possible of an area with a variety of tones, zoom in on the image and use the precise cursor to click on a pixel that looks like it represents a middle value among the tones you want to select. Choosing pixels with the Magic Wand is often a trial-and-error effort.

? **How does the Magic Wand determine which pixels are selected?**

The Magic Wand uses the Sample Size set in the Eyedropper Options palette. Choose Point Sample if you want to select the exact pixel you click on. The 3×3 and 5×5 Average settings use the value of a 9-pixel and 25-pixel grid, respectively, centered around the point you click. The latter two settings are useful if the image you are trying to select has pixels of many different shades/colors evenly spread throughout and it would be difficult to find one in the middle range that you want.

? **How do I add pixels to a selection using the Magic Wand?**

Hold down the SHIFT key while clicking multiple times to add pixels to your selection without changing the tolerance.

? **I'm having problems selecting an area with many different shades with the Magic Wand. It's surrounded by areas of fairly uniform color. Can I select that area instead?**

You've almost answered your own question. Follow these steps:

1. Select the surrounding area(s) with the Magic Wand.

2. Add any other areas in the image that are *outside* the area you want to select to the current selection. Press down the SHIFT key and use the Lasso or another selection tool to add the rest of the image.

3. Use Select | Inverse or press SHIFT-COMMAND/CTRL-I to invert the selection.

? **After selecting with the Magic Wand, I find that all the pixels I want aren't included because I set the tolerance too low. Can I add more pixels without losing the current selection or making another trip back to the Magic Wand's Options palette?**

Use Select | Grow. Photoshop takes the highest and lowest gray or color values in the currently selected portion, then takes the tolerance value you originally specified and applies it to the values of the highest and lowest pixels already selected. This step "grows" the tolerance level to encompass both brighter and darker adjacent pixels.

The results can sometimes be unpredictable, particularly when working with color images, but it's worth a try.

? I have a landscape photo and want to select all of the sky, including the gaps between leaves and branches on trees. Do I have to click with the Magic Wand in each tiny area?

No, Photoshop's Select | Similar command will work great in this situation. Make your initial selection, then choose Similar from the Select menu. Photoshop grabs pixels throughout the image with tones similar to those you just selected.

? I need to change the color of just the red pixels in my image. How can I do that?

Use Photoshop's Color Range feature, which works similarly to the Magic Wand, except that only color is used to select pixels. Best of all, you can add or subtract colors until you get the exact selection you need. Just follow these steps to select by a single color:

1. Choose Select | Color Range from the menu bar. A dialog box like this one appears:

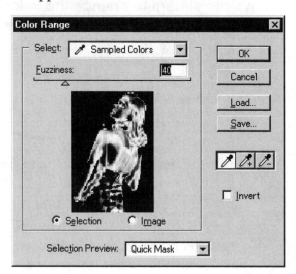

2. Choose Reds from the Select drop-down list (you can also choose sample colors, plus green, blue, cyan, magenta, yellow, or three levels of gray).

3. Click OK. You'll be returned to your image window, with all the red pixels selected.

4. Choose Image | Adjust | Hue/Saturation. You'll see the following dialog box:

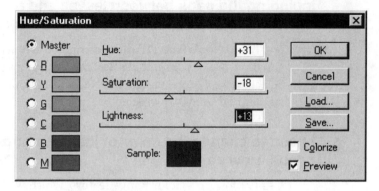

5. Move the sliders to make your color change. The Hue slider modifies the color, the Saturation slider changes the richness of the color (from drab to full), while the Brightness slider makes the colors in your selection brighter or darker.

? Move the sliders to change the color? Isn't there an easier way to choose the colors that will be selected?

Yes. Just follow these steps, to produce results like those shown in Figure 5-8:

1. Choose Select | Color Range.

2. Choose Sampled Colors from the Select drop-down list. The cursor changes into an Eyedropper.

3. In the preview window, click in an area containing the color you want to select. Pixels selected will be shown in white in the preview.

4. To add additional colors, click the Eyedropper-plus icon, then click in the preview window in areas containing the additional colors.

5. To remove colors, click the Eyedropper-minus icon, then click in the colors to remove.

6. If you're selecting or deselecting too many pixels with each click, move the fuzziness slider to the left to reduce the selection

Figure 5-8.   Selecting by color range

range of each click. Move the slider to the right to increase the Eyedropper's tolerance.

 Note: *The higher the fuzziness, the fewer samples you'll need to take. With a lower fuzziness, you must take more samples to grab the area you want.*

? I want to eliminate the fuzzy edges of my selection. How is that done?

Once you've made your selection, you can change it slightly using the Select I Modify menu choice, which offers four options: Border, Smooth, Expand, and Contract:

⇨ **Border** creates a selection from the periphery of your current selection, using a pixel width you specify.

⇨ **Smooth** rounds off sharp edges of your selection, using a pixel radius you enter.

⇨ **Expand** and **Contract** move the selection border inward and outward, respectively, by the number of pixels you request.

Figure 5-9 shows the results of each of these.

Border   Smooth

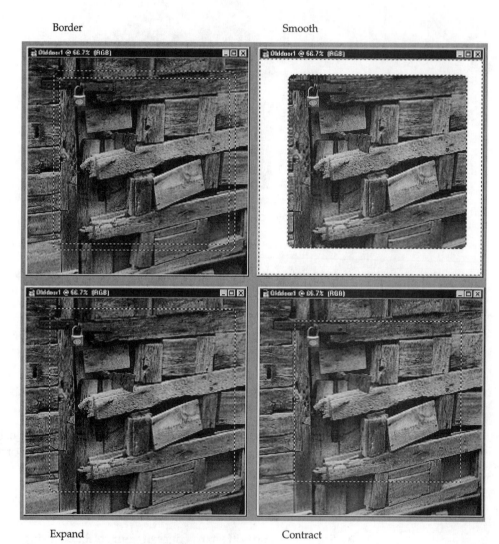

Expand   Contract

Figure 5-9.   Modifying a selection

WORKING WITH PATHS

? What are paths?

Paths are line-oriented objects that consist of one or more segments, usually created with the Pen tool. However, you can also create a path by converting a selection into a path. Paths can be added to or edited with the Pen tool, filled with color, outlined (stroked), and then converted into a selection. Paths exist on a separate plane—an invisible layer, so to speak—and do not affect the underlying pixels in any way.

? I need to select a smoothly curved object. None of the elliptical selection shapes work, and neither freehand nor polygon lassos do the job. What are my options?

Use the Pen tool, a versatile resource that makes it easy to create smooth lines and shapes, edit their curvature, and then use them as selections. Follow these steps, illustrated in Figure 5-10:

1. Press the P key until the Pen tool is visible in the Tool Box.

2. Double-click the Pen tool's icon to bring the Pen Tool Options palette to the front if it is not already visible.

3. Mark the Rubber Band checkbox. This will make the potential path you are tracing visible before you click the next anchor point. You'll find it easier to follow the outline of the object you are tracing.

4. Outline the object by clicking around its periphery with the Pen tool. Close the shape when you've gone all around the object by clicking in the first point you created.

5. Hold down the OPTION/ALT key while clicking on the Pen icon to switch to the Convert Anchor Point tool. Click on anchor points at either end of any curved lines you want to adjust to change those points to a curve point.

6. Hold down OPTION/ALT and click the Pen icon in the Tool Box to change to the Arrow tool. Drag the anchor point to adjust the position of the curve, or the curve handles to adjust the curve of each line segment until they match your original object closely.

Figure 5-10.   Selecting with paths

7. Choose Make Selection from the fly-out menu on the Paths palette to convert your path into a selection.

How do I add or remove anchor points?

Add or remove anchor points using the Add Point and Remove Point tools represented by a Pen-plus or Pen-minus icon on the Pen fly-out menu in the Tool Box.

How do I create a curve?

After setting an anchor point, if you hold down the mouse button while dragging with the Pen tool, you'll create a curve. The shape of a curve is determined by the direction line that appears when you click on an anchor point with the Pen arrow tool. At each end of a direction line is a curve handle. Drag the anchor with the arrow tool to change the position of the anchor point. Drag either curve handle to change the slope of the curves located between that anchor point and the anchor points on either side of it.

❓ Can I change a corner point to a curve point, or vice versa?

The Convert Anchor Point tool (an open arrow) changes an anchor point from a corner (straight line) point to a curve point, and back again.

❓ I want to change a selection to a path and edit it. Can I do this?

Make your selection, then choose Make Work Path from the fly-out menu in the Paths palette. Choose a tolerance level to adjust how closely the path will follow the curve of your selection. A higher number will reduce the number of points and the accuracy of the path's shape compared to your selection, but will make your path smoother.

❓ My curved path is too rough looking. How can I fix it?

You may need to remove anchor points using the Pen tool with the minus sign. Just click on a point to remove the unneeded point. Then, drag the anchor point and curve handles to produce a smooth curve.

❓ Can I move a path I've created to another position on the screen or create a duplicate of a path?

Yes. Choose the Arrow tool, then drag a rectangular shape around the path as if you were using the Rectangular marquee. Then, drag any of the points in the path to move it to the new location. Hold down the OPTION/ALT key to duplicate the path as you drag it.

❓ I know I can save a selection once I've converted a path to a selection. However, I'd like to save the path itself so I can edit it in another session. How is this done?

By default, any path you create is given the name Work Path in the Paths palette. Choose Save Path from the fly-out menu in the Paths palette, and give the path a name.

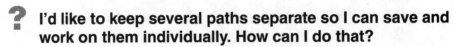

I'd like to keep several paths separate so I can save and work on them individually. How can I do that?

By default, paths are created in the same plane, even after you save a path with a name. The new shapes and lines are automatically saved to that named path when you exit the image document. To create a path on a new "layer," use the New Path command in the Paths palette's fly-out menu. You can switch back and forth between each set of paths by clicking on the path name in the Paths palette.

Can I copy a path from one image or path layer to another?

Just select the whole path as if you were going to move it. Then press COMMAND/CTRL-C to copy the path, move to the second image document or path layer (you'll need to create a new layer first, if none exists), and press COMMAND/CTRL-V to paste it down. You can also copy a path to a new layer directly by choosing Duplicate Path from the fly-out menu. If you want to *move* a path instead of copy it, use COMMAND/CTRL-X to cut the path from its original location.

Channels and Layers

Answer Topics!

Channels and Layers @ a Glance

You learned a little about channels in earlier chapters of this book, but we haven't delved into layers yet. The easiest way to start to understand what channels and layers are is to visualize them as editable copies of all or part of the original image, stacked on top of each other like a set of translucent overlays. Channels are grayscale representations, while layers are full-color representations. Each is used for a separate purpose within Photoshop.

⇨ Each color in a full-color image is assigned a channel of its own. An RGB image, for example, contains separate red, green, and blue channels. Those channels show how much of a particular color is present. In the red channel, for example, the lightest areas contain the most red, while the darkest areas contain the least amount of red. A CMYK image contains four color channels, one each for cyan, magenta, yellow, and black. (K is used to represent black instead of B, to avoid confusion with blue.)

⇨ As you learned in Chapter 5, additional channels may be assigned to store selections. Up to 24 channels can be allocated in a single image, plus one more channel per layer that is used for a layer mask for that channel. Channels used to store selections are also called alpha channels.

⇨ *Mask* is another term for a saved selection, since the selection can be used to block off, or mask, the nonselected portion from editing changes. A layer mask is a selection that is applied only to a single layer. Other masks/selections are channels that apply to all layers that are visible.

⇨ Layers are full-color overlays, which, like channels, masks, and selections, can be made visible or invisible. A layer can be a copy of all or some of an original image that you can work on separately, or an entirely new image. When you're finished editing layers, they can be merged to produce a single image.

⇨ To make a channel or layer visible, click in the column to the far left of the channel or layer's name in the Channel or Layers palettes. An Eyeball icon appears when that channel or layer is visible. You must always have at least one channel visible at all times, but layers can all be switched on or off, as you wish.

⇨ Using layers is an excellent way to keep various components of an image separate, so you can more easily see or undo the effects of your editing.

MANIPULATING COLOR AND ALPHA CHANNELS

? **Why would I want to edit color channels?**

As you'll learn in Chapter 10, you can work with individual color channels to reduce or enhance the amount of color only in a certain area of an image. Color channels can also be manipulated to apply brush strokes or other effects only to particular hues in your image. You'll want to edit color channels at times when you want to work specifically with one color, or to apply effects only to one color of your image.

? **I want to edit individual color channels of my image. How can I modify only one channel at a time?**

To edit only the red channel, for example, in the Channels palette, click in the Eyeball icon next to the green and blue channels to make them invisible. The eyeball next to the combined or *composite* RGB channel at the top of the Channels palette will automatically turn off to show you're working with only some of the channels of an image. The visible, editable channel will be highlighted to show it is active.

? **Can I edit more than one color channel at a time?**

Just SHIFT-click in the right, or named, column of the additional channel. Its Eyeball icon will become visible, and the channel will also be highlighted.

? **I have two channels visible, but my editing appears on only one of them. What have I done wrong?**

You probably made the second channel visible by clicking in the left column to make its Eyeball icon visible. Channels are editable only when highlighted, even if they are visible. SHIFT-click in the right column to make the second channel visible *and* editable.

? **I want to see the effects of my editing on a full-color image, yet edit only one or two channels at a time. Can I do this?**

Make all three channels visible, but SHIFT-click only in the channels you want to edit. To make a visible, editable channel noneditable but still visible, SHIFT-click in that channel's right column until it is unselected, then click the Eyeball icon to make it visible.

? Is there a shortcut for switching among channels quickly?

Press COMMAND/CTRL-~ (tilde) to switch to the combined RGB or
CMYK channel. Press COMMAND/CTRL-1, -2, -3, or -4 to switch to the
red, green, blue or cyan, magenta, yellow, and black channels.

? Can I duplicate a channel?

You can copy any existing channel, but cannot create new color channels
without changing modes (e.g., from RGB to CMYK). If you duplicate a
color channel, it simply becomes an alpha, or selection, channel.

? How do I add a channel?

To create a new, empty alpha channel (that is, one with nothing
selected), click on the Create New Channel icon at the bottom of the
Channels palette, shown in Figure 6-1. You can also select New
Channel from the Channels palette's fly-out menu.

To copy a channel, right-click on the name of the channel you
want to duplicate in the Channels palette and choose Duplicate
Channel. (Macintosh users should CTRL-click—not COMMAND-click—
on the name of the channel. Macs have both CTRL and COMMAND keys,

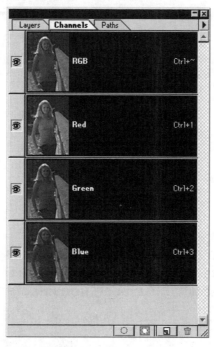

Figure 6-1.   The Channels palette

but the CTRL key is most often used in dual-platform programs to mimic a right-click in Windows applications.) You may also select Duplicate Channel from the Channels palette's fly-out menu.

? What good is a new, empty alpha channel? That just means nothing is selected.

You can paint in the new channel by making it visible and editable. Your strokes become a selection. Because Photoshop doesn't have brush-like selection tools, this method or the Quick Mask alternative are the only ways you can "paint" a selection.

? I don't want to create a new saved selection. Can't I simply "paint" a selection onto my existing image?

If you need to paint a selection that won't be reused, Quick Mask is faster:

1. Double-click the Quick Mask icon immediately below and to the right of the Color Controls boxes. You'll see the Quick Mask Options dialog box, shown here:

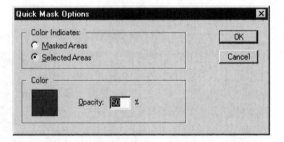

2. Check the radio box for Selected Areas to tell Photoshop to show areas that have been selected in the color overlay that appears as you paint.

3. Click the Standard Mode icon to turn off Quick Mask, and the painted area is a selection.

? I don't like the way the Quick Mask overlay obscures the area I am selecting. Can I have the Quick Mask strokes show what has been nonselected instead?

Double-click the Quick Mask icon, and check the Masked Areas radio button instead. The selection will be shown without a color overlay, and the masked area will be covered instead.

? **How can I see more detail in the area covered by the overlay in Quick Mask mode?**

Double-click the Quick Mask icon and choose a percentage lower than the default 50% value. You can also click in the color box and choose a new overlay color from the Color Picker.

? **Are the Brush tools the only tools I can use while in Quick Mask mode?**

No, you can use any painting or selection tool in Quick Mask mode. You might want to apply a feathered selection using the airbrush, or select part of the image to protect part of the Quick Mask from your strokes.

? **I try to use Quick Mask on an alpha selection channel to add to the selection, but when I return to Normal mode, only the new selection is added. What am I doing wrong?**

Quick Mask always creates a new, temporary channel and treats an alpha channel as just another channel or layer, rather than as a selection. As you've discovered, if you use Quick Mask on a selection channel and then return to Normal mode, only the Quick Mask-painted area is selected. To add to (or subtract from) a saved selection using Quick Mask, you must activate the selection first, *then* switch to Quick Mask mode. When you turn Quick Mask off, both the original and new selections will be active. Because Quick Mask's effects are temporary, you must save the new selection as a channel if you want to preserve it.

? **Is there a faster way to save a selection as a channel than using the Select|Save Selection dialog box?**

Yes. Click the Save Selection as Channel icon at the bottom of the Channels palette (second from the left).

? **Is there a faster way to load a selection than using the Select|Load Selection dialog box?**

Absolutely. Just COMMAND/CTRL-click on the selection channel you want to load in the Channels palette. You can also highlight a channel and click the Load Channel as Selection icon in the Channels palette.

If you want to do this using nothing but keyboard commands, determine the number of the channel by looking at the Channels palette, then press COMMAND/CTRL-OPTION/ALT-#, replacing # with the number of the channel you want to load as a selection.

❓ My image has many similar selections. Is there an easy way to tell them apart?

You already learned how to double-click in a channel's name column to apply a name to the selection using the Channel Options dialog box. (Channel Options can also be chosen from the Channels palette's fly-out menu.) Another good way of differentiating channels is to make the preview window (the middle column) larger and easier to view:

1. Choose Channels Palette Options from the fly-out menu.

2. Select a thumbnail preview size from the options shown:

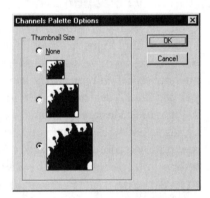

If you'd rather not see a preview, check None instead.

❓ I have a complex image and find that Photoshop won't let me create as many channels as I need. Is there anything I can do about this?

If you run up against Photoshop's 24-channel limit, your best course of action is to copy some of the channels that you won't be needing right away to a new document. You can then delete them from your original image to make room for others. Because each channel increases the memory and hard disk requirements of an image, moving channels temporarily can make working with your image both faster and easier. To move a channel, just follow these steps:

1. Make the channel selection you want to move active, using one of the techniques described earlier.

2. Choose Select | Save Selection from the menu. The Save Selection dialog box appears:

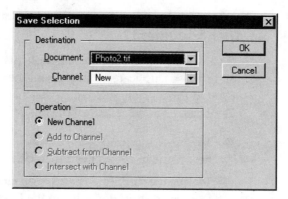

3. In the Destination area, the Document field will already have the current document's name filled in. Choose the name of any open document *of the same dimensions* from the drop-down list, or, if you'd like to create a new document to store the selection, choose New and apply a name. Click OK to save the selection.

4. To remove the channel, drag it to the Trash Can icon at the bottom of the Channels palette.

   Keep the following points in mind:

   ⇨ As I mentioned, the open or new document must be the same size as the original so Photoshop can save the selection at the appropriate coordinates.

   ⇨ This method allows you to duplicate a saved or unsaved selection in the second document. If you want to duplicate a saved selection, use the quicker method described in the question that follows.

   ⇨ If you create a new document to store your selection, it is created as a multichannel image, rather than as a grayscale image.

⇨ Once you've saved more than one channel in a multichannel image, you can convert it to grayscale, if you like. The first channel becomes the grayscale image's black channel, and the second channel becomes an alpha/selection channel.

⇨ If you've saved three channels in a multichannel image, you can convert it to RGB. Each of the channels becomes a red, green, or blue channel, respectively.

? Is there a faster way to duplicate a saved selection in another document?

If you've already saved the selection, just highlight the channel name and choose Duplicate Channel from the fly-out menu, or right-click (CTRL-right-click on the Mac) in the channel name and choose Duplicate Channel. Then follow one of these steps:

⇨ To save a duplicate of the channel in the current document, type a new name in the As field, then click OK.

⇨ To save the duplicate in a new document, choose New from the Document drop-down list in the Destination area of the dialog box. You can type in a name for the new channel if you wish to, but it isn't mandatory.

⇨ To save a duplicate of the channel in an open document of the same size, choose the document's name from the Document drop-down list.

In all three cases, click OK to finish the process.

? How do I copy a selection from another document into my image?

You can copy a selection from another document *of the same size* into your image by following these steps:

1. Choose Select I Load Selection.

2. In the Source field, choose the document to be copied from the Document drop-down list.

3. Select the name of the channel from the Channel drop-down list. You can choose any numbered or named alpha channel. You can

also choose Selection from the list, in which case any current selection in the source document will be copied.

4. You may choose New Selection, Add to Selection, Subtract from Selection, or Intersect with Selection to determine how the copied channel/selection will be added to your document.

5. Note that the loaded selection is made active in your document but is not saved as a selection channel. Click the Save Selection as Channel icon in the Channels palette to preserve the selection.

❓ Can I combine channels?

Yes. Photoshop allows you to merge several channel selections in a variety of ways. You'll need to use the Select I Load Selections menu choice to produce the Load Selection dialog box to merge the channels in a variety of different ways. Here are your key options with this dialog box:

⇨ To add the current selection to a saved selection channel, make your new selection and then use the dialog box with the Add to Selection radio button checked, choosing the saved selection you want to add to the current selection.

⇨ To subtract a saved selection from the current selection, check the Subtract from Selection radio button and choose the name of the selection you want removed from the current selection.

⇨ To create a selection that includes only the area that overlaps between two selections, check the Intersect with Selection radio button.

The selections you are combining can be from the same document, or another one chosen in the Source I Document field. The new, merged selection is not automatically saved as a new channel; you must do that yourself. Figure 6-2 shows the results of merging two selections in these various ways.

❓ Why can't I just drag and drop a channel between open documents?

You can. When you drag a channel between two documents, Photoshop centers the selection in the middle of the other document. If both are the same size, the channel will be identical to the one in the original. If the destination document is larger than the original,

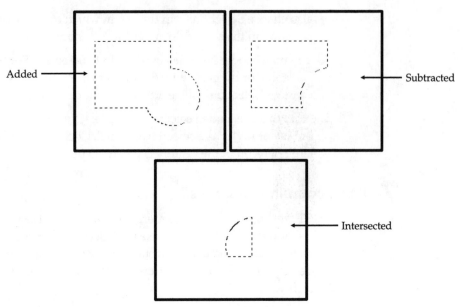

Figure 6-2.   Selections can be merged in different ways.

additional selected area will be produced outside the centered selection. If the destination is smaller than the original, some of the selection will be lost. Figure 6-3 shows what happens in both cases.

? Can I copy a selection that hasn't been saved between two open documents?

Yes. Just make your selection, and with any selection tool chosen, drag the selection from the source document into the second one. You can place the copied selection anywhere you like in the destination.

? But I want the copied selection to be in the exact same location as in the first image. Is this possible?

Follow these steps carefully:

1. Click in the selection to be moved with any selection tool. Hold down the mouse button.

2. Without releasing the mouse button, press the SHIFT key.

3. Drag the selection from the source document to the destination.

4. Release the mouse button first, then the SHIFT key.

Figure 6-3.   Dragging a channel between open documents

If both documents are the same size, the selection will be placed in the exact location it was in the original. If they are not the same size, the selection will be centered. Note that if you press the SHIFT key *before* clicking the mouse button, you'll create a new selection added to the first one, instead of moving the original selection as you intended.

LAYERS

? Layers have changed drastically since Photoshop 3.0x. Why has Adobe made things so difficult?

The biggest change made with the advent of Photoshop 4.0 is the heavier reliance on layers as separate entities. With earlier versions, for example, you could paste into any layer, float the selection to any location you wanted, then defloat it to merge it with that layer. Now, just about anything you do with pasting, copying, or entering text creates a new, separate layer that you must merge manually. That may seem like extra work, but what Adobe has done is free you from having to remember which layer you've pasted where. The risk of merging a component somewhere you didn't want it is reduced. Now that layers are automatically created, you have to try really hard to goof things up. Of course, if you create 10 or 20 different lines of text and find that each one is on a separate layer, you may not think so—until you discover a typo in one of those layers at the last moment, and discover how easy it is to delete.

? An object on one layer obscures another object. How can I "stack" them the way I want?

All the layers and their stacking order are displayed in the Layers palette, shown in Figure 6-4. Click on the icon or name of any layer and drag it to the new position in the stack. If you give the layers names, it will be easier to pick them out and place them in the right order. For example, if you were sketching out an elevated view of a kitchen, you might name one layer "Stove," another layer, "Frying Pan," and a third layer "Lid." You could then stack the Stove on the bottom, Frying Pan on top of that, and Lid in the topmost layer.

You can also change the stacking order of layers using the Layer | Arrange menu and its options: Bring to Front (moves to the top of the stack), Bring Forward (moves the layer up one level), Send Backward (moves the layer down one level), and Send to Back (moves the layer to the bottom, except if the Background layer is italicized—and therefore can't be dislodged from its bottom-most position).

The shortcut keys for Bring Forward and Send Backward are COMMAND/CTRL-] and COMMAND/CTRL-[, respectively. To Bring to Front or Send to Back, use SHIFT-COMMAND/CTRL-] and SHIFT-COMMAND/CTRL-[, respectively.

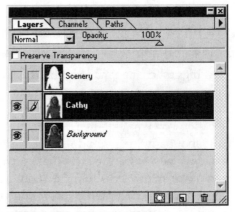

Figure 6-4.   Stacked layers in the Layers palette

? I can't move the Background layer to a new position. What's wrong?

Photoshop makes the first layer (Layer 0) the *Background*, using italics to show that it was the original Background layer. The italicized Background layer cannot be moved. However, you can convert it into a regular layer by double-clicking, then renaming it in the Layer Options dialog. You can even use Background as the new name if you like. The new name will be nonitalicized and completely restackable.

? When I create new layers, Photoshop gives them names like Layer 1, Copy of Layer 1, Layer 2, Copy of Background, and so forth. Can I give the layers descriptive names?

When you create a layer using the Layer | New Layer menu or Layer | Duplicate Layer, the Layer Options dialog box appears and you may type a name. When you create a layer by pasting a selection, Photoshop just applies the next available number and gives it a generic Layer 2, Layer 3, or similar name. To name one of these layers, or rename any layer, double-click the layer's preview thumbnail or name and type in the new name in the Layer Options dialog box.

? Is there a quicker way to duplicate a layer?

Just drag a layer on the Layers palette to the Create New Layer icon. A duplicate will be made. You can also select everything in the layer by pressing COMMAND/CTRL-A, then duplicate it by pressing COMMAND/CTRL-J. Finally, you can choose Duplicate Layer from the Context menu when right-clicking with a PC mouse, or CTRL-clicking with a Macintosh mouse.

? I've created several lines of text. As you noted, each was placed on a separate layer. Can I combine them into a single layer?

You can merge any group of layers into a single layer. Just make those layers the only ones that are visible (as with channels, just click in the far-left column to turn the Eyeball icon on), then choose Layer | Merge Visible, or use the keyboard shortcut command/CTRL-SHIFT-E.

? **I just want to merge two layers from the many in my document. Is there a way to do that without bothering to make all the others invisible? (I'll just have to make them visible again when I finish merging.)**

Make sure the two layers you want to merge are stacked one on top of the other. Select the uppermost layer, then choose Merge Down or press COMMAND/CTRL-E. The top layer will be merged down into the one below.

? **I'd like to copy some of my image as it appears on several layers without merging them first. How do I do that?**

Ordinarily, several layers may be visible at once, but you can copy only from the active layer. If you want to copy from several layers, you must merge them, or use this technique:

Make only the layers you want to copy from visible, then choose Edit I Copy Merged from the menu, or press COMMAND/CTRL-SHIFT-C.

? **I want to fill a selection with an image area I've copied from a layer. Can I do that?**

Follow these steps:

1. Select and copy the area to be pasted from its layer.

2. Highlight the layer that contains the area you want the copy to be pasted into, and select the new area.

3. Paste the image on the clipboard into the selection, using Edit I Paste Into or SHIFT-CTRL/COMMAND-V. A new layer will be created, but it will contain only the image area that fits inside the selection.

? **Can I copy a layer from one document to another?**

Yes, you can do this using any of the options for copying channels, including the following:

1. Select the portion of the layer you want to move (or all of it using COMMAND/CTRL-A).

2. Use the Move tool to drag the image area to the new document.

    A new layer will be created. If the source selection or layer is smaller than the one in the destination, you may drag the image content of the layer to any location in the destination document you like. If the source layer or selection is larger, it will be centered in the destination document.

3. Click in the selected image area or the layer name or preview in the source document, then hold down the SHIFT key when dragging to a document of the same size to produce a perfectly registered copy of the layer.

❓ I want to fade one layer into another. Can I do that?

Make sure the layer you want to fade is placed above the underlying layer in the Layers palette. Then move the Opacity slider until the top layer has faded to the degree you want.

❓ I only want part of a layer to fade. What's the easiest way to make it happen?

You could copy the part you want to fade to a new layer and fade that, but if you want a smooth transition between the faded and unfaded part, it's better to use a layer mask. These masks are grayscale channels that determine how transparent a layer is. You can paint on the layer mask to adjust transparency, use gradients, or other effects. Follow these steps to create a simple layer mask:

1. Click the Add Layer Mask icon in the Layers palette (the one on the left) to create a layer mask. An additional preview thumbnail will appear to the right of that layer's original thumbnail.

2. Click in the layer mask thumbnail to make it editable. A Layer Mask icon will appear in the second column from the left of that layer, showing you can now paint on the layer mask.

3. Using the Gradient tool, add a gradient from left to right. If you're working with a color image, the foreground and background colors of the gradient don't matter: the layer mask is a grayscale channel, and only monochrome hues can be painted on it.

4. When finished editing the layer mask, click the layer's thumbnail. A paintbrush will appear in the second column from the left, indicating that layer can be modified again.

The layer mask fades in the layer it is applied to with the one below, using the gradient you just created. If you hold down the OPTION/ALT key when you click on the Add Layer Mask icon, the layer mask is inverted; that is, anything you paint will *hide* rather than *reveal* the image in that layer. Select one mode over the other depending on whether your mask will be doing more hiding or more revealing. That way you'll end up with the smallest, most easily managed layer mask. (These Layer commands can also be accessed from the Layers menu, but this method is much faster.)

? I want to see how my layer looks without the layer mask. How do I temporarily turn it off?

SHIFT-click on the layer mask's preview. A large X will appear over it, showing that it is not currently being applied to that layer. Click in the thumbnail again (SHIFT-click is not required) to turn the layer mask back on. You may also use the Layer | Disable Layer mask from the menu.

? I'm ready to combine some of my layers into a final image. How is that done?

To make the best use of layers, follow these steps:

1. Make sure the layers are in the order you want.

2. Save the image as a Photoshop-format file. This will create a copy with the layers preserved, in case you need to edit them later on to produce a different version.

3. Turn off any layers you want to discard.

4. Choose Layer | Flatten image. The image will be saved as a single layer, using all the visible layers. If you have hidden layers, Photoshop will ask you to confirm that you want to discard them.

5. Use File | Save As to save the flattened file under a new name. If you have no alpha channels (saved selections), you may save the file under any graphic format that supports the current mode (i.e., you can't save in GIF, which requires no more than 256 colors, if you have a 24-bit color image). If you have saved

selections, Photoshop will suggest you use one of the formats that support them (PSD, TIF, PICT, PIXAR, PNG, RAW or TARGA). Only the first two are frequently used in the Windows world, while Mac users often rely on the third format, PICT, which is the Mac's native vector/raster graphics format.

? What can I do if I want to save a copy of a file without including any of the alpha channels?

You could always discard the channels first, but Photoshop gives you an easier way. Use File | Save A Copy. The dialog box that pops up includes checkboxes for Flatten Image (combining all the layers) and Don't Include Alpha Channels, which discards saved selections. These boxes appear only if you choose a format that supports layers and/or alpha channels. If you select a format that can't use either, such as JPEG, layers and channels will be discarded automatically.

? Can I apply some kinds of modifications only to particular layers?

Yes. A Photoshop feature called Adjustment Layer lets you manipulate the Levels, Curves, Brightness/Contrast, Hue/Saturation, Color Balance, Selective Color, Invert, Threshold, and Posterize effects. You can apply these to any layer or group of layers you want, and change them at any time; since only the effect is shown, the layers themselves are not modified until you flatten the image. We'll look at more applications for Adjustment Layer in Chapter 7.

chapter

7 Answers!

Retouching and Compositing

Answer Topics!

Retouching and Compositing
@ a Glance

Given the right techniques, Photoshop can merge two or more images seamlessly to generate a new one—whether it's rearranging the Pyramids of Egypt to produce a better photographic composition (as National Geographic did for one of its covers), or sending one Hollywood icon out for a date with another, even though the two of them have never met. Compositing and retouching also have more mundane applications that involve nothing more than blending several photos, or correcting defects in the original image.

The key tools used in combining and retouching photographs are

⇨ **Tonal control** One of the most common defects in a photograph is improper balance of light and dark areas of an image.

⇨ **Lightening/darkening/blurring/sharpening** Along with blending, you also need to learn how to adjust the tone and texture of images to help editing merge invisibly.

⇨ **Rubber Stamp** Photoshop's Cloning tool is indispensable for copying image material from one part of an image to another part, or to another image entirely, to provide detail that isn't available in the original.

⇨ **Blending** You must be able to blend pasted elements seamlessly so your final image doesn't scream FAKE!, and merge retouched portions smoothly with the untouched part of the picture.

⇨ **Selections** You must be able to select the exact area you want to work on, while leaving the rest of the image alone. Selection techniques were covered in Chapters 5 and 6.

⇨ **Cutting and pasting** Successful compositing and retouching requires skillful cutting and pasting of portions of an image.

⇨ **Transformations** These let you rotate, skew, scale, distort, or add perspective to a selection.

TONAL CONTROL

? My photograph is too dark. Should I fix this by adjusting the brightness and contrast controls?

Probably not. Photoshop's Image I Adjust I Brightness/Contrast applies its changes to your whole image. It's more likely that you'll need to lighten shadows while keeping the lighter portions (highlights) of the image the same. Try Image I Adjust I Auto-Levels (or press SHIFT-COMMAND/CTRL-L) to let Photoshop automatically examine your image and change the tonal balance to suit. Fairly good results can be achieved in this way.

? **"Fairly good?" I tried Auto-Levels and got some bizarre results. In one photo, the color balance of the image has been thrown completely off. In another, the tonal changes were applied only to part of the image. What's wrong here?**

What happened is that Photoshop used Auto-Levels correction only on one color channel in the color picture, and only on an alpha channel selection in the grayscale image. You must make sure the program operates only on the "main" channel (black with grayscale images, and the RGB or CMYK composite channel with color images). To ensure this, if you're working with a grayscale image, check the Channels palette and make sure the Black channel is highlighted. With a color image, the RGB (or CMYK) channel should be used. In the case of color images, a drop-down list appears in the Levels dialog box that allows selecting one of the channels

? **OK, I used Auto-Levels on the correct channel this time, but "fairly good" isn't good enough. I still don't like the way my photo looks after Auto-Levels has been applied. Is there another technique I can use?**

You can apply Levels adjustments manually and fine-tune your image that way. Access the dialog box shown in Figure 7-1 using Image | Adjust | Levels, or by pressing COMMAND/CTRL-L.

The "mountain-shaped" graph is called a histogram. It consists of 256 vertical lines, each representing the relative number of pixels at each particular graytone within the image. Pictures with lots of dark shadows will have a clump of tall lines at the left (black) end of the histogram; images with detail in the highlights will have tall lines at the right end of the histogram. Because there are only 256 different tones that can be used to represent a grayscale image (or each red, blue, or green hue of a full-color image), it's important to make sure that none of these tones are wasted. Follow these steps:

1. With the Levels dialog box in view, examine the histogram. Notice that the black triangle at the left side marks the darkest tone currently used by Photoshop to present the image. The white

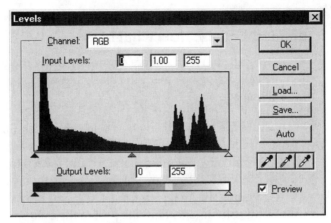

Figure 7-1.   The Levels dialog box

triangle at the right represents the lightest highlight tone. The gray triangle in the middle represents the midpoint, which Photoshop uses to represent the middle graytones of your image.

2. If the Preview checkbox is unmarked, click in it. This will provide a preview of your changes in the main document window.

3. If the histogram shows there are no pure black pixels or pure white pixels at the left and right ends, respectively, move the black and white sliders toward the center, as required, so they now mark the limits of the actual graytones used in your photograph. If you're working with a color composite channel, the relative lightness and darkness of all three colors will be modified at the same time, preserving the color balance.

4. Examine the histogram again. Most likely it will not show a bell-shaped distribution of tones. Instead, you'll often find a preponderance of lines at one end or point. You can move the center gray triangle towards the clump to provide additional graytones to represent those pixels. Don't worry about interpreting the histogram yourself. Just slide the gray triangle (actually called the gamma slider, because it alters midtones—the gamma—of an image without changing highlights and shadows) back and forth until your preview looks good to you.

5. Click OK to apply the tonal changes to your image. Depending on your image, you have succeeded in giving your shadow areas or highlight areas a larger allocation of the 256 different tones, so one (or the other) can present more detail.

? **The image still isn't good enough after I've manually applied Levels. Now what?**

You can gain a little more control by using the Eyedroppers in the Levels dialog box to set the black and white points precisely. Follow these steps:

1. In the Levels dialog box, select the Black Eyedropper (it is half-filled with black tone) and move it around your image, watching the Info palette. Values from 0 to 100% will be shown in the K (black) area of the Info palette if you're working with a grayscale image, or from 0 to 255 in the RGB area if you're using a color image. Find the part of the image with the lowest number (you may not find anything darker than 20 or 30 RGB, or 5% in monochrome). Click to select that black point.

2. Select the White Eyedropper (half-filled with white) and move it around, looking for the highest number—100% in grayscale, or 255 in color. You probably won't find those maximum numbers. Click when you locate the brightest point.

3. Now, move the gray gamma triangle under the histogram to adjust the contrast and brightness of your image.

4. If you need to do some additional fine-tuning, experiment with the Output Levels sliders at the bottom of the dialog box. This control compresses the tonal range of the image into fewer than 256 grays. This has the effect of decreasing the overall contrast of the image.

? **I want to be able to vary the amount of tonal control over a particular layer, rather than setting it once. Can I do this?**

This is a perfect application for an Adjustment Layer. Follow these steps:

1. Choose Layer | New | Adjustment Layer.

2. When the dialog box pops up, choose Levels from the drop-down Type list. You can apply a label to the layer in the Name field if you like.

3. Click OK to create the layer. The Levels dialog box appears. Make any adjustments you want, then click OK once more.

The Levels changes you specify apply to all levels below an adjustment layer. So, to apply it only to certain layers, move the other layers above the adjustment layer. Any time you wish to change the Levels settings you've made, double-click the adjustment layer's name in the Layers palette.

COMMON DEFECTS

? **I have portrait photos in which the subject's eyes appear dull and lifeless. Can I fix this with retouching?**

Your subjects probably don't have any catchlights in the eyes—the little twinkles that result from a light source reflecting from the eye's front surface. This can happen when the illumination comes from above, or is bounced evenly around the room so that it doesn't come from any one strong source. A related problem is multiple catchlights, which can happen when there is more than one strong light that can be reflected by the subject's eyes. To fix this quickly on full-length or ¾-length photos, use the Eyedropper to sample a light white tone, then use a small, fuzzy paintbrush to dab in a catchlight in each eye. Make the catchlight in the same position on each iris, and if there is more than one person in the picture, make them all match. For multiple catchlights, sample some of the eye color with the Eyedropper and paint out the extras in each eye. Figure 7-2 shows a portrait with and without catchlights.

? **When I paint catchlights into head shots and close-up portraits, they don't look realistic. What can I do?**

In close-ups, you can often distinctly see the reflections off the corneas of the eyes, especially the shapes of the light source itself. Generic round catchlights don't always work. Try this more precise method, instead:

1. Use Layer | New Layer or click the New Layer icon in the Layers palette to create a new layer.

2. Sample a light color and use a small, hard-edged brush to create a catchlight in each eye.

3. Select the Eraser tool, and choose a much smaller hard-edged brush.

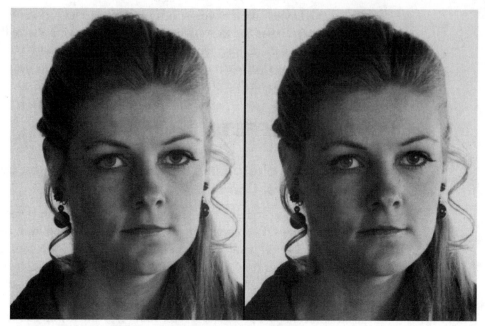

Figure 7-2.   With (left) and without (right) catchlights

4. With the eraser, take a little nip out of each catchlight in the same place.

5. In the Layers palette, adjust the opacity slider until the catchlight's brightness is realistic.

6. You can merge these two layers now, or when you finish your retouching.

❓ My portraits have eyes sunk deep in shadows, so they are much darker than the rest of the face. What can I do?

As you may already know, the eyes, nose, and mouth are the features we use most to identify other humans. They *must* be represented accurately, or else the portrait won't look "right." Dark circles are one of the worst defects you can discover in a portrait. Fix them by following these steps:

1. Click the Toning tool, holding down the OPTION/ALT key until the Dodge tool (it looks like a lollypop) appears.

2. Next, double-click the tool to bring the Toning Tool Options dialog box to the front.

3. Choose Shadows from the drop-down list if the dark shadows are very dark, or Midtones if they are only a little darker than the skin tones.

4. Move the exposure slider to about the 15 percent mark.

5. Choose a fuzzy brush that's about the same size as the dark circle under the eyes.

6. Paint over the dark circle carefully. Each pass will lighten the area a tiny bit. Be very careful that you don't lighten the dark area too much. (You might want to duplicate the layer and work on that rather than the bottom, background layer.)

Figure 7-3 illustrates this technique.

RETOUCHING

❓ What can I do when I need to remove a person, a tree, or some other object from a photograph?

You'll want to master Photoshop's Clone feature, called the Rubber Stamp tool, which duplicates part of an image you select, pixel by pixel, in a new location of your choice. The stamp analogy isn't very good, however, since you're actually drawing with a brush that you can size and control in other ways—transparency of the new image laid down, or some other behavior.

Figure 7-3.   Getting rid of dark shadows is a snap.

Dodging and Burning

While most prints are made by automated means these days, when color or black-and-white prints are made by exposing photosensitive paper under an enlarger, the darkroom worker can modify how the image appears. That's done by giving extra exposure to some areas of the print and holding back other areas so they don't receive as long of an exposure.

The image is visible in negative form on the paper as the exposure is made, so the process is relatively simple. An area, such as a shadow, that would appear too dark on the finished print can be made lighter by inserting an object between the lens and the paper. This casts a shadow, which prevents that portion of the image from being exposed for the full length of time. A portion of the image that has been *dodged* in this way will appear lighter than if the entire image were exposed evenly.

Sometimes, the darkroom worker will use a hand to obscure large areas of the image, but more frequently a dodging tool is used. Often handmade from coat-hanger wire and a piece of cardboard, the dodging tool looks something like an all-day sucker like Photoshop's Dodge tool (but can actually take any shape). The tool is waved around over the area being dodged so that the handle doesn't show up and the edges of the dodging effect are feathered.

The opposite procedure, called *burning*, is also used to give additional exposure only to areas of the image that need it, such as highlights that would appear too light or *burned out* in the final print. The most common tool for this effect is a pair of hands like Photoshop's Burn tool: a roundish opening between them can be varied in size to burn more or less of the image, as desired.

Cloning can be used to copy portions of an image to another location in the same or a different image. If your desert scene is too sparse for you, a single cactus can be multiplied several times or even copied from a different desert altogether. You may add a window to the side of a building by "painting" one from another building using the Clone tool.

To use the Rubber Stamp, position the cursor in the place you want to copy from, hold down the OPTION/ALT key, and click. That point will be selected as the source for your cloning. Then, paint with any brush size in the destination. The image source will be copied to the new place.

? When I clone an area, each time I release the mouse button and begin painting, Photoshop starts painting from the original source area rather than continuing where I left off. What's wrong?

You're probably using Clone (unaligned) by mistake. From the Rubber Stamp Options dialog box, select Clone (aligned) from the drop-down list. Then, once you determine the origin point, the Clone tool maintains a fixed spatial relationship between it and the destination portion of the image, no matter how many times you apply the brush. This will be easier to visualize if you examine Figure 7-4. Once you select an origin point, brushing with the Rubber Stamp always applies more pixels copied using that *fixed spatial relationship*. That is, if you move the tool over an *inch to the right* and start painting again, you'd apply pixels copied from an area an *inch to the right* of the point of origin. Cloning an aligned image makes it easy to duplicate objects from one portion of an image (or from a different image), since you can use multiple brush strokes to copy the same object.

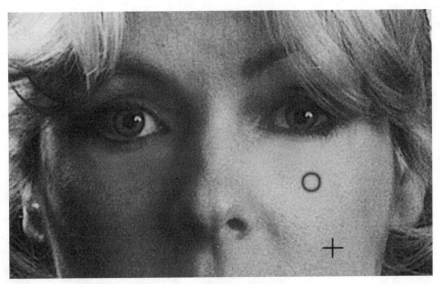

Figure 7-4.   Cloning source and destination

? **The area I want to cover with cloned strokes is bigger than the area I am cloning from. I have to keep redefining my source point. Can I avoid this?**

This is a good application for Clone (unaligned), especially if you're copying a texture, such as a wall or sky, rather than a specific feature. Once you see you're reaching the limits of your source area (a special crosshair appears at the source point to show you where you're cloning from), release the mouse button and press it again to resume cloning from the original source. For best results, choose a point in the center of the source area as your starting point.

? **I make mistakes while cloning and have to revert to the last version of my image. Can I save myself this trouble?**

Duplicate the layer you're working on, and apply the cloning to the copy so you can always change your mind and go back to the unaltered version without losing the other edits you've made since the last time you saved the file. It's always a good idea to release the mouse button from time to time, check your work, then resume cloning. That way, if you make a mistake, you can press COMMAND/ CTRL-Z (Undo) and reverse only the most recent strokes. Otherwise, you'll have to go back to the original version of the layer and lose all the changes you've made.

? **I want to undo more than just the most recent strokes. How can I change various portions of the image—but not all—back to the way they were when I last saved the file?**

The Clone (From Saved) mode, selected from the drop-down list in the Rubber Stamp Options dialog box, can save your neck when you discover you've cloned too much of an image, or have made any sort of other error that needs correction. The point of origin is automatically set to the equivalent pixel position in the last saved copy of the file, so, in effect, you can paint over a changed portion of the image with the original version. Use this option when you have done considerable work on a file since you saved it and only want to cancel out some of the changes you've made. The Magic Eraser technique can also change portions of an image back to its previous state. Simply hold down the OPTION/ALT key while using the Eraser.

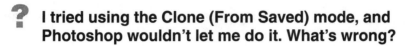

I tried using the Clone (From Saved) mode, and Photoshop wouldn't let me do it. What's wrong?

The saved version used to restore your image must be the exact same size and pixel resolution as the working image. If you change the size of the image (using, say, Image | Image Size), you'll find that neither Clone (From Saved) nor the Magic Eraser trick will work.

I don't want to clone from the original saved version of my image. Sometimes I need to replace part of an image area with the same area after I've done some editing. Can I do that?

Use Edit | Take Snapshot to store a snapshot of your current image in a special buffer area. If the image has more than one layer, Take Snapshot captures only the currently active layer. To grab all the visible layers, use Edit | Take Merged Snapshot. Then, you can select the Clone (From Snapshot) choice in the Rubber Stamp Options dialog box to use your snapshot instead of the originally saved version of the image. Keep in mind that your snapshot is not stored on your hard disk and is lost when you exit Photoshop, and only one snapshot can be available at a time.

I want to apply a pattern to an image, using part of another image as my pattern. How can I do that?

Photoshop allows you to use any open window or any visible layer as the source for cloning, so this is easy. However, you will want to use Clone (unaligned) to create a free-form pattern with any spacing between the duplicate images you desire. If you want a more regular pattern, use the Pattern (aligned) option, which repeats the pattern as contiguous, uniform tiles, even when you stop and resume painting several times. The Pattern (nonaligned) option also produces a regular pattern, but centered on the Rubber Stamp pointer each time you stop and resume painting. To use either Pattern options, you need to define the pattern first by selecting an area with the Rectangular Marquee tool, then choosing Edit | Define pattern to apply it as the current pattern.

? I get ugly, repeating patterns when I clone. How can I avoid this?

The source point for your current cloning brush stroke moves as you move the mouse. If you start to copy from an area that has already been modified by cloning, you'll repeat the area, producing a fish-scale kind of effect. To avoid this, create a duplicate of your original image and clone from that. Figure 7-5 shows how you can tell when you've applied this effect by accident.

? Sometimes I have photographs that have light or dark areas. Can I restore the lost detail without cloning over them completely?

You can use one of Photoshop's blending modes while cloning to darken or lighten areas. Photoshop has a series of blending modes, which it uses to calculate how pixels should interact with each other when superimposed. In Normal mode, each pixel cloned from another image completely replaces the pixel it is painted on top of. If you change the Opacity slider in the Rubber Stamp Options dialog box, the cloned pixel becomes transparent, allowing some of the underlying pixel to show through. Neither of these effects are what you want.

Figure 7-5.   Fish-scaling from repeated cloning

Instead, choose Darken (or Lighten) in the Rubber Stamp Options dialog's drop-down list to the left of the Opacity slider. Then, clone from a similar area elsewhere. As you paint, Photoshop compares each pixel from the source area to the destination pixel. Any pixels in the destination that are already darker (or lighter, depending on which mode you selected) will be left alone. Any pixels that are lighter (or darker, if you're using the Lighten mode) will be replaced by the cloned pixel.

? I want to clone the image from several layers at once, without flattening the image. Can this be done?

Make each of the layers you want to clone from visible, then check the Sample Merged checkbox in the Rubber Stamp Options dialog box. Photoshop will clone from all the layers you have showing.

Photoshop's Blending Modes

Photoshop's blending modes are often ignored by beginning and intermediate-level users because they seem difficult to understand, and are referred to as Modes, Calculations, or other terms that can be confusing. Blending modes are simply ways of specifying how each two corresponding pixels duke it out for supremacy when you're merging layers, cloning image areas, or painting. There are 18 different modes in all. The most commonly used are

⇨ **Normal** Each pixel is applied just as it was originally, except for other effects you may be using, such as Opacity.

⇨ **Darken** Pixels in the selection, layer, or cloned area are applied only if they are darker than the pixels in the destination image or layer. When used with color images, the color balance can change.

⇨ **Lighten** Pixels in the selection, layer, or cloned area are applied only if they are lighter than the corresponding underlying pixel. When used with color images, the color balance can change.

⇨ **Multiply** Mixes the tones or colors of the selection and original image, producing a darker image with the combined values of both. The Photoshop manual compares this effect to superimposing two color transparencies on a light table. Visualize two color slides and the areas that overlap: a medium gray and another medium gray would produce a darker gray (or black), while a medium blue and a medium red pixel would combine to produce a darker magenta pixel.

⇨ **Difference** Chooses the pixel (either source or destination) that has the greatest brightness, and subtracts that value from the other to produce a new value.

⇨ **Dissolve** Atomizes the pixels in the feathered edges of the selection, producing an interesting edge effect.

Other modes allow comparing of the pixel pair's hue, saturation, color, luminosity, and other attributes, or basing the pixel calculations on other exotic factors.

COMBINING IMAGES

? **I want to copy from an image that has several layers. Can I copy from all the layers without flattening the image?**

Yes. Make the layers you want to copy from visible, then use Edit I Copy Merged or press SHIFT-COMMAND/CTRL-C.

? **I've completely goofed up my editing session and want to start over. How do I do this?**

Use File I Revert to return to your last saved version of the image.

? **How can I paste an object into a particular area of my image?**

Use Photoshop's Paste Into facility, in which the clipboard's contents are pasted into the selected area only. Portions that don't fit are obscured by the original image. Follow these steps:

1. Put the object in a layer of its own, or in a separate document, then copy it to the clipboard.

2. In the destination image or layer, use Quick Mask to paint the area you'll be pasting into. Use a fuzzy brush if you want to blend the pasted object in smoothly.

3. Exit Quick Mask. You might want to save this selection if you think you might want to reuse it later.

4. Choose Edit | Paste Into (or press SHIFT-COMMAND/CTRL-V) to paste the object into the selection.

5. Use the Move tool, if necessary, to adjust the position of the pasted object.

6. Merge the two layers when you're satisfied.

? I want to paste a selection *behind* another object in my image. How can I do this?

Earlier versions of Photoshop had a Paste Behind command. Now, the simplest thing is to follow steps 1–3 in the preceding answer, then use Select | Inverse (or press SHIFT-COMMAND/CTRL-I) to invert the selection before pasting. The object you paste will be visible everywhere *except* the area you just selected.

? Can I control how the object being pasted is merged with the underlying image?

Earlier versions of Photoshop had a Paste/Composite Controls command, because selections were pasted as floating objects above the image. Now, everything pasted is placed into its own layer, and you can use the Layers palette's Opacity slider or the blending modes to preview how your image will look when the layers are combined, making any changes you like before merging them.

? How can I make an object I am pasting into an image merge smoothly?

Try selecting the object, then using Select | Feather (or pressing SHIFT-COMMAND/CTRL-D) to feather the selection. Experiment with values like 10 or 20 pixels. Then copy the selection and paste it down. Figure 7-6 shows an object pasted with feathering.

? I get a fringe around the outside of a selection I have pasted, making it very noticeable. Can I eliminate this?

Use Layer | Matting | Defringe to remove a small quantity of the selection at the outer edges. If you find you have a distinct black or white fringe (because they were Anti-aliased against a black or white background), use Layer | Matting | Remove Black Matte or Layer | Matting | Remove White Matte, respectively.

? The selection I've pasted is a little too large. Can I reduce it without going back and modifying the size of the original?

Yes. Use Layer | Transform | Scale. Handles will appear around the selection. Drag them to adjust the size of the selected image. Hold

Figure 7-6.   Feathering smooths the transitions between objects.

down the SHIFT key if you want to constrain your resizing to retain the original proportions; otherwise, you can scale horizontally or vertically separately. You can use this technique with any selection or layer, not just one that has been pasted. Note that if you scale a selection larger than the image canvas, Photoshop doesn't clip off the extra image until you flatten the layers, so you can resize to smaller dimensions later on using the entire selected image.

TRANSFORMATIONS

How can I flip the selection I've just pasted?

Use Layer | Transform | Flip Horizontal or Layer | Transform | Flip Vertical. You can also rotate the selection clockwise or counterclockwise in 90 degree increments.

I need to rotate a selection just a smidge. Can I do that?

Use Layer | Transform | Rotate. Drag the handles that appear to rotate the image. Hold down the SHIFT key to rotate in 15 degree increments. Press ENTER when satisfied to confirm the rotation, or press ESCAPE to cancel.

When I rotate an object, it no longer fits on my image canvas. How can I make the canvas larger?

Use Image | Canvas Size. Type the new height or width you want into their respective fields. Click on one of the nine boxes in the Anchor preview to position your original image in relation to the new canvas.

Can I rotate all the layers at once?

Yes. Use Image | Rotate Canvas, and choose from 180 Degrees, 90 Degrees Clockwise, 90 Degrees Counter-clockwise, Flip Horizontal, Flip Vertical, or Arbitrary (by the number of degrees you specify).

Can I distort a selection?

Photoshop offers Skew, Distort, and Perspective commands. Select them from the Layer | Transform menu, and drag the handles to get the effect you want. Press ENTER (to confirm) or ESCAPE (to abandon) your changes. The three produce the following effects, shown in Figure 7-7:

⇨ **Skew** Slants an image in one direction or another, moving only the handle you drag and the two closest to it.

⇨ **Distort** Only the handle you drag moves, distorting the image.

⇨ **Perspective** Creates a 3-D effect by moving two of the selection handles in opposite directions, making the outer borders converge on an imaginary vanishing point elsewhere in the image. When you drag a handle, the handle opposite to the direction you are dragging moves in the opposite direction.

？ I want to scale and distort a selection at the same time. Can I do that?

There are two ways to do this. For freehand changes, use Photoshop's Layer | Transform | Free Transform option. All the key presses required to achieve a specific effect can be confusing, but are worth learning since you can apply these transformations without moving from one mode to another. Use one of these techniques:

⇨ To move the selection or layer, place the pointer inside the bounding border and drag.

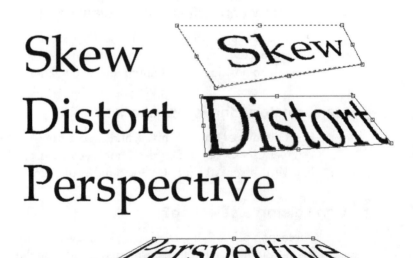

Figure 7-7.   Skew, distort, and perspective control

⇨ To change the size of the selection, drag a handle, holding down the SHIFT key to scale proportionately.

⇨ To rotate, move the pointer outside the bounding border and drag.

⇨ To distort freely, press COMMAND/CTRL and drag a handle.

⇨ To distort around the center of the selection, hold down the ALT/OPTION keys and drag a handle.

⇨ To skew the selection, hold down the SHIFT-COMMAND/CTRL keys while dragging a handle.

⇨ To adjust perspective, press COMMAND/CTRL-OPTION/ALT-SHIFT and drag a corner handle.

Remember to press ENTER when finished to apply your transformation.

❓ I want to scale or distort by a precise amount. Is that possible?

Photoshop's Numeric transformations are the second way to apply more than one transformation at once. Use Layer | Transform | Numeric, and type the values you want into the dialog box. Click OK when finished to apply the transformation.

chapter

8 Answers!

Using Filters and Special Effects

Answer Topics!

Filters and Special Effects @ a Glance

Filters transform a dull image into an Old Masters painting with delicate brushstrokes, or create stunning, garish color variations in a mundane photograph. Filters allow you to add some subtle sharpness or contrast to dull or blurred areas, or produce undetectable changes that make a good image even better.

Photoshop-compatible plug-in filters are actually miniature programs in their own right, designed in such a way that they can be accessed from within an image editing application, to manipulate the pixels of a file that is open in the parent application. You'll find most filters in the Filters menu, but some can be located in the File menu under Import and Export.

Filters may remove pixels entirely, or shift them around in an image in relation to others that remain in place. The programs that make up filters can be very simple, or extremely complex and require no user input or have complex dialog boxes using slider controls, buttons, preview windows, and other features. There are nine different types of filters and plug-ins:

⇨ **Acquire/Import/Export modules**   These allow Photoshop to import images (e.g., with a scanner) or export them in formats not normally supported by the Save As dialog box. For example, the GIF89a module allows creating transparent and/or interlaced GIF files.

⇨ **Production modules**   These are non-Adobe add-ons that must be purchased at additional cost if you need special help in streamlining color correction and separation.

⇨ **Image Enhancement filters**   These filters improve the appearance of images, while leaving the basic appearance alone. These include Blur, Sharpen, Unsharp Mask, Dust, and Scratches.

⇨ **Attenuating filters**   These are filters like Noise, Grain, Texturizer, and others that superimpose a texture on your image.

⇨ **Distortion filters**   These filters actually move pixels from one place in an image to another, providing mild to severe distortion. They can map your image to a sphere, immerse it in a whirlpool, or pinch, ripple, twirl, or provide distortion to some or all of an image.

⇨ **Pixelation filters**   These filters also add texture or surface changes, like attenuating filters, but take into account the size, color, contrast, or other characteristic of the pixels underneath. They include Crystallize, Color Halftone, Fragment, and Mezzotint.

⇨ **Rendering filters**   Rendering filters create clouds, lens flares, lighting effects, and textures, sometimes using part of the underlying image and sometimes not.

⇨ **Contrast-enhancing filters**   These work with the differences in contrast that exist at the boundary of two colors in an image, like sharpening filters, but with more dramatic effects. They include Find Edges, Glowing Edges, Accented Edges, Poster Edges, Ink Outlines, and Emboss.

⇨ **Other filters and plug-ins**   You'll find many other kinds of filters available from third parties, such as Alien Skin's versatile Eye Candy and MetaCreations' all-purpose Kai's Power Tools.

GETTING STARTED

? **I've applied a filter, but find it too strong. What can I do?**

Using the Filter | Fade command was important enough to make Chapter 1's Top Ten list. However, there are other things you can do. First, it's always a good idea to copy the layer or image area you'll be working on to another layer, then apply the filter to that layer. Even if you change your mind much later, you can just make the layer invisible and merge the others to undo your change. In addition, you can use the Layers palette's Opacity slider to fade a filter's effects.

? **It's difficult to experiment with filters because it takes so long for Photoshop to apply them. I don't want to wait two or three minutes just to decide to redo a filter with different parameters. How can I speed things up?**

You have several alternatives. Photoshop is optimized with internal code that makes the most of the horsepower of Power Macintosh,

Pentium MMX, and dual Pentium Pro/Pentium II systems. Complex filters that perform multiple calculations on each pixel can seem to crawl when applied with a 680x0-based Mac or Windows 486 (or slower) machine. If you can't upgrade to a faster computer try these tips:

⇨   Select a small, but representative portion of the overall image and apply the filter to that. If you're working with a portrait, select only the face. You can often gauge an overall effect from a limited section of the image.

⇨   Consider creating a smaller, lower-resolution version of an image, and applying the filter to that. Low-res images won't provide a perfectly accurate representation of what a filter will do at a higher resolution, but they will give you a good idea.

⇨   Use Photoshop's Edit | Quick Edit facility to import only a small portion of an image at once; you can work faster with this portion of the document, yet do the same editing you would perform on the full image.

? What's the best way to preview the effects of a filter?

Many filters, like Unsharp Mask, can apply their effect to your main document window as you adjust parameters in their dialog box. Move the filter's dialog box to the side so you can view the main window. If you open a second view (View | New View) that has been zoomed in, you can examine the image from two perspectives. Also, learn to use the Preview window most filters offer. You can click the Plus and Minus buttons under the preview to zoom in and out, and place the cursor inside the preview (it becomes a Hand tool) to move the window around on your image. This is a great solution with filters that work too slowly to apply themselves to your entire image as a preview.

? How can I apply the same filter to a new selection without accessing the filter's dialog box?

COMMAND/CTRL-F applies the last filter, using the same parameters. If you need to change settings, you can use the OPTION-COMMAND/ALT-CTRL-F shortcut to go directly to the last filter's dialog box.

SHARPENING AND BLURRING YOUR IMAGES

? **I have lost the negatives for some photos I must use. I have only very small prints and a few darkroom contact sheets. Can I get sharp images from these?**

If the prints were made with a good-quality lens, or the contact sheets were made with the emulsion (image) side of the 35mm negative placed in direct contact with a sheet of photosensitive enlarging paper, you can get surprisingly sharp images. Scan at the highest resolution your scanner allows, then use the Unsharp Mask filter to sharpen them up.

? **I can never decide whether to use Sharpen, Sharpen More, or Sharpen Edges. What's the difference between them?**

The difference between the basic Sharpen tools and Sharpen Edges is easy to see. Sharpen and Sharpen More increase the contrast between all the pixels in an image. It's as if there were a huge number of tiny edges everywhere in the picture. Sharpen/Sharpen More finds these myriad edges and darkens or lightens the pixels at them. Sharpen Edges, on the other hand, looks only for grosser, or larger, edge boundaries and enhances the contrast only between them. The broad range of tones between these edges are not modified. Figure 8-1 shows an example of each kind of sharpening.

? **I heard that Sharpen More is roughly the equivalent of using the Sharpen filter three times in a row. Is that true?**

No. In my tests, I found that multiple passes with the Sharpen filter gave different results than the Sharpen More filter, probably because sharpening an image that has already been sharpened is different from performing a greater degree of sharpening on the same image one time. You'll find that Sharpen applied twice provides a little less of the effect than Sharpen More, while three applications gives you a much coarser texture. Remember that Sharpen filters increase contrast, so you may not need that extra contrast boost you'd planned on.

Unsharpened photo   Sharpen

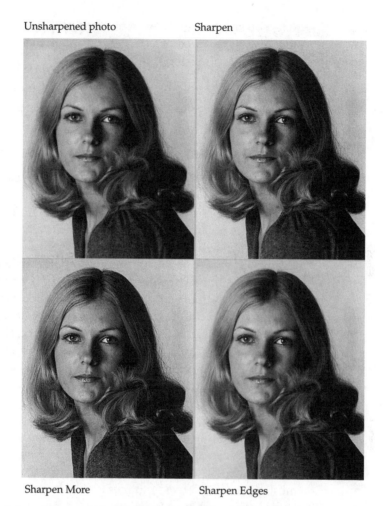

Sharpen More   Sharpen Edges

Figure 8-1.   Effects of Photoshop's sharpening features

❓ Why would I want to use Sharpen Edges?

Sharpen Edges sharpens only the significant edges—it doesn't produce the grainy effect that results when the image or selection is made crisper in its entirety. Most of your image will remain as smooth, or blurry, as it was, but by sharpening the edges it may look quite a bit sharper. You'd want to try this filter out on buildings and other heavily textured objects, which contain many fine details that could benefit from overall sharpening. People and faces often look better with only the edges enhanced. With most portraits, the outlines of eyes and other features should look sharp, but you don't want every flaw in the skin to be accentuated. Use Sharpen Edges.

? Why doesn't Unsharp Masking make an image unsharp?

Despite the conclusion you might draw from the name, Unsharp Masking is used to make images *sharper*. The technique was first applied to images made on sheet film, in sizes from around 4×5 to 8×10 inches or larger. To produce the effect conventionally, a film positive is made from the original film negative (a negative of the negative, so to speak). The positive is slightly blurred, which spreads the image slightly. When the positive and negative are sandwiched together and used to expose a new image, light areas of the positive correspond very closely to the dark areas of the negative, and vice versa, canceling each other out to a certain extent. However, at the edges in the image, the blurring in the positive produces areas that don't cancel out, resulting in lighter and darker lines on either side of the edges. This extra emphasis on the edges of the image adds the appearance of sharpness.

It's fairly easy for a computer to simulate the blurry positive mask and then mate it with a negative image of the original picture—with an added advantage. We can have greater control over the amount of blur in the mask, the radius around the edges that are masked, and a threshold level (relative brightness) at which the effect begins to be applied. The Unsharp Mask filter is similar in many ways to the Sharpen Edges filter—but with this enhanced control.

? How do I use the Radius slider in the Unsharp Mask dialog box?

This slider determines the width of the edge that will be operated on, measured in pixels, with valid values from 0.1 (very narrow) to 250 pixels (very wide). You should adjust the range to take into account the resolution of your image. Low-resolution images (under 100 dpi) can't benefit from much more than one to three pixels worth of edge sharpening, while higher-resolution images (300 dpi and up) can accommodate values of 10 or more. You'll know if your values are set too high—you'll get thick, poster-like edges that aren't realistic, accompanied by a high degree of contrast. You may, in fact, like the weird appearance, but you've left the realm of sharpening and ventured into special effects at this point.

? What is the Threshold slider in the Unsharp Mask dialog box used for?

This control is used to set the amount of contrast that must exist between adjacent pixels before the edge is sharpened. Values from 0 to 255 can be used; a very low value means that edges with relatively small contrast differences will be accentuated. High values mean that the difference must be very great before any additional sharpening is applied. Normally, you'll need the Threshold slider only when the default value produces an image with excessive noise or some other undesirable effect. To be honest, in my tests, changing the Threshold setting produced effects that were hard to predict because they varied widely, depending on how the other two controls were adjusted and the nature of the image itself. Your best bet is to set the Amount and Radius settings first, then experiment with Threshold to see if you like the results any better.

? Why would I want to blur an image? Isn't blur a kind of defect?

You'll find many instances where an image contains excessive noise or visible dust and scratches, or where transitions from one portion of an image are too abrupt. If the details in that image area are unimportant, you can benefit from some blurring. Figure 8-2 shows how dust can be obscured by careful blurring.

? How do I get the most control over blurring effects?

Blur and Blur More work like Sharpen and Sharpen More, only in reverse. They decrease the contrast between pixels, and operate directly without a dialog box. Use Gaussian Blur if you want to fine-tune the amount of blur applied. The only control you really need to worry about with the Gaussian Blur filter is the radius setting, from 0.1 pixel to 250 pixels. The higher the radius setting, the more pronounced the blurring effect.

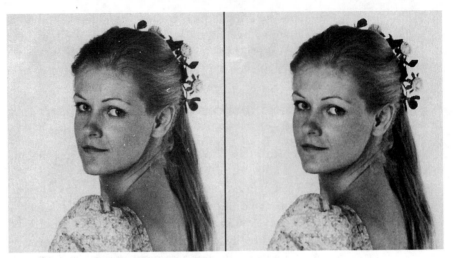

Figure 8-2.   Blurring dust to make it less noticeable

What's Radial Blur?

Radial Blur is a special effect that simulates the image a zoom lens produces when it is zoomed in and out during an exposure—or the effect you'd get by photographing an object on a circular, spinning platter. (Imagine photographing a picture as it moves around on a phonograph.)

How can I remove dust and scratches from photographs?

By an amazing coincidence, Photoshop has a Dust & Scratches filter, which selectively blurs areas of your image that contain dots, spots, scratches, and other defects. When the filter is applied, Photoshop examines each pixel in the image, moving outward radially to look for abrupt transitions in tone that might indicate a dust spot on the image. If a spot is found, the dusty area is blurred to minimize the appearance of the defect. It has Radius and Threshold sliders, with the same functions as those in the Gaussian Blur filter.

The Dust & Scratches filter tends to make my image too blurry. Is there some way I can reduce dust and other artifacts without ruining the sharp detail in the edges of my photos?

The Despeckle filter decreases the contrast in all of the selection *except* for the edges. The edges end up with relatively more detail than the rest of the image.

Keep the following points in mind:

⇨ If your image has dust spots in random locations and you don't need edge enhancement, use Dust & Scratches.

⇨ If your image is already relatively sharp, to the point where there is objectionable detail or noise in the image areas, use Despeckle to provide a blurring effect that doesn't mask edge detail.

⇨ If your image doesn't contain excessive noise, use Sharpen Edges to sharpen it up a bit without introducing an undesirable texture.

? How can I simulate a fast-moving racing car or an accelerating object?

Use the Motion Blur filter, as it duplicates the blurring you get when a fast-moving subject races across the field of view when a photograph is taken with a shutter speed that is too slow to freeze the action. You can adjust the direction of motion of the subject and the amount of blur. This filter works best when it's applied to individual objects in an image, such as a guitar player's hands, or a racing car's wheels.

? When I am combining images from two different photographs, I find they don't "match" when there is more grain or other roughness in one than in the other. What should I do?

Use the Add Noise filter, which adds texture to areas that are too smooth, or the Grain or Photographic Grain filters. This is one situation in which the Filter | Fade control comes in very handy. Fade the amount of noise or grain you are adding until your two images match in texture.

TRANSFORMING IMAGES

? I want to warp an image onto a sphere. How do I do that?

Photoshop's Spherize filter can do that. The Spherize filter maps your image or selection onto a sphere, represented by the wireframe shown on the grid in the dialog box. You can specify an "outward" bulge from 0 to 100 percent, or an "inward" indentation of 0 to -100 percent. The Spherize filter also lets you distort your image around a vertical or horizontal cylinder by clicking on the Horizontal only or Vertical only radio buttons. Figure 8-3 shows an image mapped to a sphere.

Figure 8-3.   Wrapping an image around a sphere

? Can I create a sphere with realistic shading?

Sure. Just try this trick: select a circle and fill it with a radial gradient. Position the center of the gradient up and to one side of the circle. Use Filter | Render | Lens Flare to make the surface even more realistic. Then, apply the Spherize filter. Presto! One ball-shaped object, ready to roll.

? What if I want a black hole effect instead of a sphere?

Make your image look like it is being sucked down a black hole with the Pinch filter. Like Spherize, it's a pixel mover that distorts your image, so you should use it with care. The Pinch filter squeezes an image towards its center or pushes it out toward its outer edges. You can pinch the entire image or just a selection. The only control you have available is an Amount slider, which can be varied from 0 to 100 percent (to pinch inward) or from 0 to -100 percent (to push outward). Photoshop applies the filter to an elliptical section of the selection—the largest ellipse that will fit inside the square or rectangle. The effect is feathered into the rest of the selection, providing a smooth transition.

If your selection is round, elliptical, or irregular in shape, or if it consists of discontinuous multiple selections, the Pinch effect will be applied to the largest ellipse that can fit inside, but there will be an abrupt boundary at the selection border. To avoid this, make your selection first, then choose Select | Feather and specify five pixels or more as your feather radius. The pinching effect will be applied to the entire selection, gradually tapering off in the feathered portion.

❓ I need some rippling water effects. How do I do this?

Don't try Photoshop's Ripple filter, which has a deceptive name. You'll get better results with the Zigzag filter, instead. You can specify an amount of distortion from −100 to +100, reflected in the grid in the dialog box. The number of ridges (1 to 20) can also be specified. You may select from the following:

⇨ Pond ripples: which Adobe defines as ripples that progress from the upper left or lower right (depending on whether you've entered a positive or negative number).

⇨ Out from center: ripples that are generated from the center of your image or selection.

⇨ Around center: whirlpool-like ripples that revolve around the center of the image or selection, first in one direction, then in the other.

❓ I want to simulate the effect you get by swirling pigments in a paint mixer. Can I do that?

Sure. Use the Twirl filter, which makes the pixels in the center of your image or selection move more drastically than those on the periphery, which lag behind. The effect is quite striking. Your only control is the slider that specifies degrees of twisting; you can use from −999 to +999 degrees. (Any twisting more than 360 degrees produces multiple spirals.)

❓ I need some random wave effects. What's the best way to produce these?

The Wave filter is extremely versatile, with 13 different controls you can use to specify how your image is stirred up. You get three kinds of waves, can specify the number, size, and frequency of the ripples, and even randomize things if you want a natural appearance. You can spend a lot of time figuring out how Wave works but, on the plus side, you can achieve effects that are unlikely to be duplicated. The key controls are as follows:

⇨ **Number of Generators**   The number of points where waves are created. Up to 999 different little wave generators can be entered, but that's far too many for most images—the effect is so muddled that each wave may be only a pixel or two wide. In my tests, high numbers ended up producing areas with plain tones, and no waves at all! You'll want to use from five to twenty, tops.

⇨ **Wavelength Minimum/Maximum**   This parameter sets the distance from one wave crest to the next. In this case, wavelength minimum and maximum (from 1 to 999) refer to the number of individual waves produced by each generator.

⇨ **Amplitude Minimum/Maximum**   Height of the waves, also settable from 1 to 999.

⇨ **Horizontal/Vertical Scale**   How much distortion you get per wave can be set here, with values from 1 to 100 percent.

⇨ **How Undefined Areas Are Filled In**   You can have pixels wrap around from one side to another, or just stretched from the edge to fill the empty spaces.

⇨ **Type of Wave**   Choose from smooth sine waves, pointy triangle waves, or chunky square waves (which are more blocks than waves to my eye).

⇨ **Randomize**   If you just want waves and don't care what they look like, click on this button to supply random values. Keep clicking until you find an effect you care for.

PAINTING WITH PHOTOSHOP

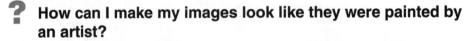

How can I make my images look like they were painted by an artist?

Photoshop has several filters that will do the job. Try one of these:

⇨ **Chalk & Charcoal**   This filter gives you the effects of a mixed-media drawing using rough chalk to express the midtones and highlights and charcoal for the shadows. If Photoshop's default colors (black and white) are used, the charcoal will be black and the chalk white.

⇨ **Sponge** A filter that allows you to paint with a sponge-like texture.

⇨ **Sumi-e** Simulates using a wet brush, loaded with ink, drawing on a highly absorbent rice paper.

⇨ **Water Paper** Looks like water-based paints applied to wet paper.

⇨ **Paint Daubs** Offers six different brush types, a selection of brush sizes, and some sharpness controls. You can choose from simple, light rough, dark rough, wide sharp, wide blurry, or sparkle brush types.

⇨ **Ink Outlines** It produces an image with the outlines and edges enhanced, but without losing the original colors. You can use it to create a cartoon-like appearance, or combine with other filters to generate a more painterly effect.

⇨ **Conté Crayon** Simulates the soft, smudgy, atmospheric effects of Georges Seurat.

⇨ **Crosshatch** adds a cross pattern of pencil-like strokes to your image, adding texture without destroying all the original colors and detail of the original. It's a good, arty effect with an unusual degree of control. Not only can you specify the stroke length and sharpness, but the number of times in succession the filter is applied. The more repetitions, the stronger the effect.

⇨ **Sprayed Strokes** This filter uses angled, sprayed strokes of wet paint. You can adjust the stroke length, direction, and radius of the spray emitted.

⇨ **Rough Pastels** This filter transforms your image into a rough chalk drawing, using the default canvas texture as a background; or an alternate texture such as brick, burlap, sandstone; or your own file. The least amount of texture is applied to the brightest areas, while darker areas take on more of the underlying texture. You can picture how this filter works by imagining a canvas with chalk applied: the thicker the chalk, the less of the canvas texture shows through.

⇨ **Watercolor** Watercolors produce their distinctive pastel effect because the pigments that dissolve in water are typically not as strong or opaque as those that can be carried in oil or acrylic paints. In addition, watercolors tend to soak into the paper, carrying bits of color outside the original strokes as the water spreads.

⇨ **Smudge Stick**   Another painterly effect you should try, which resembles chalk smudged with the fingers.

⇨ **Spatter**   Produces a look you might get from a sputtering airbrush, using the Radius slider to adjust the number of pixels covered.

⇨ **Fresco**   Produces short, jabby strokes, as if colors were applied to wet plaster.

⇨ **Graphic Pen**   The Graphic Pen filter obliterates the detail in your image with a series of monochrome strokes that can be applied in right or left diagonal directions as well as horizontally and vertically.

⇨ **Dark Strokes**   This filter has two effects on your image. First, it reduces the number of different tones in the image through a posterization-like effect that combines similar tones in an unusual way. Instead of grouping similar colors together, Dark Strokes makes dark tones darker and light tones lighter, increasing contrast. At the same time, each tone is rendered using diagonal brush strokes—short strokes for dark tones and longer strokes for light tones.

⇨ **Dry Brush**   This filter mimics a natural-media effect—stroking with a brush that's almost devoid of paint—in a fairly predictable way. It doesn't obscure as much detail as the typical watercolor, stipple, or impressionistic filter found in most image-editing applications, but still has a distinct painted look. Dry Brush posterizes your image, but produces more distinct banding than Dry Strokes.

⇨ **Craquelure**   Produces the effect of paints applied to canvas after they've cracked, providing an Old Masters patina.

Figure 8-4 shows some painterly effects.

BREAKING UP IMAGES

❓ Can I reduce the detail in an image in an artistic way?

Photoshop has several filters that break up an image in interesting ways, without producing a brushstroke or pen effect like the filters described above. Try one of these:

⇨ **Crystallize**   This filter converts your image or selection to random polygons, each with a maximum cell size that you specify, from 3 to 300 pixels.

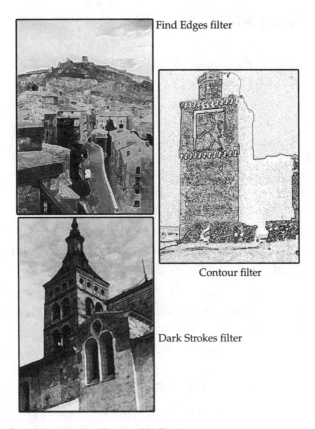

Figure 8-4. Some painterly effects with filters

⇨ **Facet** This filter changes blocks of pixels that are similar in color to one tone, producing a faceted effect like the face of a diamond. The effect becomes more pronounced with repeated applications. Just use COMMAND/CTRL-F to apply the filter several times until you get the look you desire.

⇨ **Mezzotint** This filter provides a stroke or dot effect similar to a Mezzotint filter used in prepress operations.

⇨ **Mosaic** Generates the pixelated effect used in court television shows to obscure the faces of witnesses. It's great for creating an abstract image of a subject that screams "computer-generated!"

⇨ **Diffuse** This filter divides your image or selection up into four-pixel elements (you can't control the size of the cell), then moves pixels towards the edges or higher-contrast areas of your image. This tends to smudge the image in a pleasing way, producing a very nice artistic effect.

3-D EFFECTS

? Can I produce an embossed effect that simulates the rich look of stationery?

Photoshop has an emboss filter that will do exactly what you want. It raises the edges of your image above its imaginary surface, much like an address embosser presses a 3-D version of your name, address, or monogram into stationery or an envelope. This digital filter more or less discards most of the colors in your image, providing a stamped-metal effect. You can modify the angle of the light source, height of embossing, and amount of embossing.

? Can I produce an effect that looks like my image was made up of stacked boxes?

Use Extrude, which seemingly combines the Mosaic filter with Emboss. Choose rectangular or point pyramid blocks, and adjust the size, depth, and whether the faces of the box are plain or carry some of the original image.

? I want a different embossed look. What can I do?

Try the unusual Note Paper filter, which creates the look of embossed paper, but with a flatter image than you get with Emboss or Bas Relief. It really does look as if the image was created out of paper. There are three controls at your disposal: image balance, graininess, and relief. The key to using Note Paper is the Image Balance slider. Very small changes with this control make dramatic modifications to how much of your image appears embossed.

? Can I produce a stone-carved look?

Yes. Use the Bas Relief filter, then apply a sandstone texture using the Texturizer filter.

? How can I apply textures to surfaces?

Consider the Texturizer filter your basic tool. You can select from brick, burlap, canvas, and sandstone textures, or your own texture file. Textures are applied more strongly in those areas of your image where the brightness changes, so the results are not identical to what you'd get if you merged your image with another layer containing the texture.

? Can I create glass-like textures?

The Glass filter is a multipurpose plug-in you can use to produce glass-block effects, warping, watery ripples, and dozens of other looks. The flexibility comes from the multitude of combinations you can achieve using several controls, including the amount of distortion, smoothness of the glass, and scaling. Figure 8-5 shows a glass effect from this filter.

Figure 8-5.   Glass effects applied with a filter

Tip: *When experimenting with 3-D effects, don't forget the psychology of lighting: humans expect objects to be lit from above, and, usually from one side or the other. You'll get the most realistic raised effects if you position the light source at top, top left, or top right. Move the light underneath, and you'll get anything from a "horror" effect to a reversal of the 3-D look—your image may appear to be depressed into the surface rather than raised above it.*

SPECIAL EFFECTS

How can I accentuate the edges of images in an artistic way?

Photoshop has several different filters you'll want to experiment with. These include the following:

⇨ **Find Edges**   Produces effects like drawing with colored pencils.

⇨ **Trace Contours**   Like Find Edges, but allows you to change the brightness level used to accentuate the edges.

⇨ **Accented Edges**   This filter works a little like the Find Edges filter, but you have extra control over the width, smoothness, and brightness of the edges located in your image.

⇨ **Glowing Edges**   Adds wild colors to the edges of your image, producing a strange, abstract, mask-like effect that you can enhance further by inverting the image, increasing the brightness and contrast, and with other tweaks. This filter is similar to the Find Edges plug-in, but with a great deal more control over the results.

Photoshop's Wind filter gets old very fast. Are there any tips to using it in new ways?

There are several secrets to using Wind effectively:

⇨ First, choose your images carefully. When you have a picture with an empty or dark area that the Wind effect can smear your image into, the results are much more impressive. It also helps if your subject can be enhanced by the streaky effect. A house may look pretty blah when streaked, but adding a Wind effect to a baseball player sliding into second base raises the action level several notches.

⇨ You're not limited to left and right wind directions, regardless of what you may think from the dialog box. Rotate an image, apply Wind, then rotate it back to its original orientation. Instead of a gust of wind from the left or right, you end up with a dripping effect. You can even rotate the image in other than 90-degree increments to create interesting smearing.

⇨ Streak your image from two different directions to create a wild wet-paint, splotchy look that looks a lot more like something created by a real artist than most of the filters discussed in this chapter. Figure 8-6 shows this effect.

❓ How can I achieve a metallic effect?

Use the Chrome filter, which adds a slick metallic effect. You'll rarely, if ever, want to apply it to an entire image. Your best bet is to select some object in the image, isolating it from the background. If there is not sufficient differentiation between the gray tones of an image or selection, Chrome turns the whole thing into a featureless gray mass. In that case, beef up the contrast using Image I Adjust I Brightness/

Figure 8-6.   Mimicking splotchy paint with the Wind filter

Contrast, and give the filter some meaty details to work with. You might also want to try the Plastic Wrap filter, which you can think of as a Chrome filter that's transparent.

❓ I want to transform my image into a poster. How is this done?

Use Poster Edges, which converts full-color or grayscale images into reduced-color versions by combining similar colors into bands of a single hue, then outlining all the important edges in your image with black. In many cases, the finished photo looks as if it were an original drawing that was hand-colored in poster fashion.

❓ I need to add a romantic look to a photograph. It has quite a few defects. Can I disguise them while adding the atmosphere I want?

You need the Diffuse Glow filter, which can produce a radiant luminescence in any image that seems to suffuse from the subject and fill the picture with a wonderful luster. At the same time, this plug-in softens harsh details. It's great for romantic portraits, or for lending a fantasy air to landscapes. Diffuse Glow works equally well with color and black-and- white images, as you can see in Figure 8-7. Use these controls:

⇨ The Graininess slider adds or reduces the amount of grain applied to an image. A large amount obscures unwanted detail and adds to the dreamy look of the image.

⇨ The Glow Amount control adjusts the strength of the glow, as if you were turning up the voltage on a light source. The higher the setting, the more glow spread throughout your picture.

⇨ The Clear Amount slider controls the size of the area in the image that is not affected by the glow. You can use this control with the Glow Amount slider to simultaneously specify how strong a glow effect is produced, as well as how much of the image is illuminated by it.

⇨ The current background color becomes the color of the glow. That's an important point. Beginners sometimes forget this, and then wonder why their glow effect looks weird. If you want a glowing white effect, make sure the background color is white. Anything else will tint your image. You can use this feature to good advantage by selecting background colors with a very slight tint of yellow, gold, or red to add a sunny or warm glow to your image.

Figure 8-7.   Diffuse Glow adds a romantic look

RENDERING IMAGES

? Can I add clouds to some barren skies in my images?

Certainly. Select the sky area using the Magic Wand or another
favorite selection technique, then apply the Clouds filter. Opaque
clouds are created using fractal algorithms, producing a highly
realistic effect. Clouds uses the current foreground and background
colors to generate its cloud effects. You can select a blue and white
tone to produce realistic clouds.

**? I accidentally applied clouds using black and white colors.
Can I color them?**

Use Image | Adjust | Hue/Saturation. When the dialog box pops up,
click on the Colorize button, then move the Hue slider to a sky
color you like.

? Can I create fog?

Just use the Clouds filter, then use Filter | Fade Filter to adjust the
opacity of the clouds so the other parts of your image show through.

? **I'd like to incorporate my image into the clouds themselves. Can that be done?**

Use the Difference Clouds filter, which uses information about the current image in the scene to calculate the difference in pixel values between the clouds and the underlying image. The end product is an image that is a combination of clouds and a weird, negative image.

? **I want to add a bright sun to my daylight, outdoors image. How do I go about it?**

Lens Flare can duplicate this effect nicely, and also produce spotlights in your onstage concert photos. The flare is generated inside your image or selection using a center point you can specify by dragging the crosshair in the Preview window. The amount of flare can be adjusted using the Brightness slider, from 10 percent to 300 percent. The Lens Type radio buttons let you choose the particular type of photographic lens that will be simulated. Figure 8-8 shows the effect of lens flare.

Figure 8-8.   Producing lens flare

? **Can I simulate studio lighting in a photograph?**

Yes, and you'll get a nice 3-D effect with Photoshop's Lighting Effects filter.

This filter allows you to define up to 16 different light sources to "illuminate" your image from any angle you choose in the picture's original 2-D plane. Figure 8-9 shows how lighting effects can look.

Not only can you specify the direction and type of light source with Lighting Effects, but you can add textures and perform other magic.

There are several factors that govern how lighting affects an image:

⇨ **Light type**   Spotlight, omni light, and/or directional light. Each has distinct characteristics.

⇨ **Light intensity**   Brightness. Photoshop lets you set a negative or darkening intensity.

⇨ **Light focus**   An adjustment of the spotlight from narrow to wide.

⇨ **Light color**   The color of the light source.

⇨ **Highlights**   Gloss—matte or shiny.

⇨ **Reflector material**   Either plastic or metallic.

⇨ **Exposure**   The intensity of the light as it reaches the surface of the object.

Figure 8-9.   Lighting effects

⇨ **Ambience**   The amount of existing light in the room before you add extra lights.

⇨ **Number of lights**   You can use up to 16 different lights by dragging the Light Bulb icon in the dialog box to the picture preview area.

? Can I add texture along with lighting effects?

Yes. The Texture Channel controls can be used to apply a texture to the area illuminated by your light sources. You can choose from Red, Green, Blue channels in RGB mode, or Cyan, Magenta, Yellow, and Black in CMYK mode, or None if you prefer not to add a texture. You can also apply texture only to selections, and specify the amount of 3-D effect of the texture.

Answer Topics!

Type @ a Glance

⇨ Unlike word processors, Photoshop doesn't allow you to enter type directly onto your document. Instead, you'll use the Type Tool's dialog box, which has options for choosing letterspacing, amount of spacing between lines, type size, font, and alignment. You may also choose styles, such as Bold, Italic, Outline, Underline, Strike-Through and Anti-aliased (smoothed). Photoshop can use any font installed on your system.

⇨ Text is entered into a preview area at the bottom of the dialog box. You can press ENTER to create a new line. An upper limit of about 32,000 characters can be entered into the dialog box at one time, although in practice you'll rarely need to enter that much text into Photoshop.

⇨ The preview can show your text in a generic font and size (roughly 12 points), or present it using the exact font and size you've specified. When you click OK in the dialog box, the text is changed into pixels and placed into its own layer. You can't correct typos in text that has been placed into a layer, although you can change the spacing used by selecting characters and then using the Move tool. To fix text, delete a layer or make it invisible, and enter corrected text into a layer of its own.

⇨ Photoshop also has a Type Mask tool that creates a selection in the shape of the text you type, on whatever layer you choose. You can fill the selection with color, or use it to copy part of the image area to a new layer.

THE BASICS

? **When I try to add type to a layer as I did with Photoshop 3, Photoshop 4 creates it in a separate layer. How can I prevent this?**

Here's the quickest way to create type within a layer:

1. Choose the Type Mask tool from the toolbox.

2. Click in the layer you want to augment with type.

3. Choose the font, size, and other parameters, from the Type Tool dialog box.

4. Enter the type you want included, then click OK. Photoshop creates a selection in the layer you chose.

5. To fill the type mask/selection with color, do one of the following:

⇨ If the type is not on a transparent layer, press DEL to fill it with the background color, or OPTION/ALT-DEL to fill it with the foreground color.

⇨ If the type selection is located on a transparent layer, you can fill it with the foreground color by pressing OPTION/ALT-DEL. However, pressing DEL makes anything within the type selection transparent, rather than filling it with the background color. In this case, press X to switch the foreground and background colors, then press OPTION/ALT-DEL.

The way Photoshop now handles type is a major improvement once you get used to it. Instead of having to keep type floating in a layer until you've positioned it, you can leave it in a layer of its own, then move it, add color or special effects, stack it on top of or below another layer, and perform other tasks at any time until you flatten the image. If you really want to place text on a particular layer immediately, place the type layer above the other layer in the Layers palette, then use Layer I Merge Down from the menu bar, Merge Down from the fly-out menu on the Layers palette, or press COMMAND/CTRL-E. If you've merged layers and then discover a typo you need to correct, you'll see the value of Photoshop's new method.

Tip: *To add a type mask selection to a selection you already have, SHIFT-click while using the Type Mask tool. To remove a type mask selection from a selection you already have, OPTION/ALT-click using the Type Mask tool.*

❓ How can I use type as a cookie cutter to fill letters with part of my image?

It's easy. Follow these steps to get the results you can see in Figure 9-1.

1. Switch to the layer you want to "cut" some image area out of using the type as a mask.

2. Choose the Type Mask tool and enter the type you want to cut with.

3. With any selection tool chosen (including the Type Mask tool you are using), drag the selection to where you want to cut out part of the image.

4. Press COMMAND/CTRL-C to copy the image within the type selection.

5. Press COMMAND/CTRL-V to paste it down into a new layer. The type will be filled with the image area you selected.

? How do I add several lines of type at once?

Just press ENTER to add a hard return between the lines. Photoshop will end each line at the point you specify. Choose one of the alignment radio buttons to center your type around the point you clicked with the mouse, or to left- or right-justify it around that point.

Figure 9-1. Using a type selection as a cookie cutter on an image

WHIRLING YOUR WORDS

? **I want to display some type upside down, but when I use the Layer | Transform | Flip Vertical command, the type is reversed as well, so I have to use the Layer | Transform | Flip Horizontal command as well. Isn't there a faster way to do this?**

You can rotate type in Photoshop just as you can rotate any object or selection. Enter the type in the normal fashion, using the center or left- and right-justify radio buttons. Then use Layer | Transform | Rotate, and then hold down the SHIFT key as you rotate the text. An even faster way is to press SHIFT-COMMAND/CTRL-T, and when the Numeric Transform dialog box appears, type 180 into the Angle field of the Rotate area. Click OK, and your text will be rotated upside down. You can also type in some other angle, such as 90 degrees, 45 degrees, and so forth, to rotate your type by another angle.

? **I want my type rotated 90 degrees, but displayed centered around a certain point. Can I do that?**

Use the second column in the Type tool's Alignment area. These choices align center, or left- or right-justify, text at the point you select, but rotate it 90 degrees clockwise.

POLISHING THE LOOK OF YOUR TYPE

? **My type doesn't look very sharp. What am I doing wrong?**

Make sure you've checked the Anti-aliased box in the Style area of the Type Tool dialog box. Because Photoshop creates type using pixels, diagonal and curved lines in any characters you enter will appear jagged unless you use Anti-aliasing. Figure 9-2 shows unaliased and Anti-aliased type.

? **I prefer the sharp type effects I get from my illustration package. Can I reproduce those effects in Photoshop?**

No, but you can import type created in Adobe Illustrator, CorelDraw, and other illustration software by saving the type in Encapsulated

Unaliased
Unaliased

Figure 9-2.   Unaliased (above) and Anti-aliased type (below)

PostScript format, then using File | Place and choosing the EPS file. Drag the handles that appear around the box enclosing the type until it is the size you want, then press ENTER. Photoshop then turns the type into pixels (which means you can no longer resize it without suffering the normal vagaries of up- and down-sampling). Before you do this, however, consider whether this type needs to be imported into Photoshop in the first place. For many desktop-published documents, you can import both illustration-program artwork and Photoshop raster files, and place them in their native formats.

GETTING THE MOST OUT OF PHOTOSHOP'S TYPE FEATURES

No matter what font I choose from the Type Tool dialog box's drop-down list, the preview shows it in a generic font. What's wrong?

In the Show area at the bottom of the dialog box, make sure the Font box is checked. Photoshop will then use the font you've selected to provide a preview.

The type in the preview is too large to see. Can I fix this?

You're probably using a large font and have checked the Size box in the Show area at the bottom of the dialog box. Photoshop is displaying your type in the actual size to be used in your image. Uncheck the box and Photoshop will use a smaller font (approximately 12 points) to show your preview.

? Can I create outlined text?

The Type Tool dialog box includes an Outline style you can select to create an outlined version of your text. The type will be created on a new layer, using the foreground color as the outline and with a transparent center. Figure 9-3 shows an example of outlined text.

FINE-TUNING YOUR TYPE

? Photoshop won't let me choose the Underline style. What's up?

When you're using the vertical alignment options in the right column of the Alignment area, Underline is disabled. Photoshop can't automatically underline text created in this way. Instead, create the text in Normal mode and rotate it.

? How can I adjust the space between lines of type?

If you've already created the type, just select a particular line by itself and use the cursor arrows to nudge it to where you want it. If you want consistent line spacing, you're better off specifying it before you create the type. Use the Leading field to enter the amount of spacing between lines. The spacing is measured from baseline to baseline, using the same unit as the type (points or pixels), so if you're using 22-point type, leading of 22 points would space each line 22 points apart. This may be more spacing than you need, since most of the type probably won't be 22 points high. Instead, use so-called *negative leading* (e.g., 20 points for 22-point type) to squeeze the lines closer together.

Figure 9-3.   Outlined text

? **Can I adjust the space between characters?**

You can do this automatically by entering a Spacing value in the Type Tool dialog box. The values are the same as the unit you're using to create the type; e.g., if you're using points, a value of 1.1 adds 1.1 points to the space between each character, on top of the default spacing that would normally be used. Negative values bring type closer together.

? **Can I adjust the space between characters for type that's already been created in my image?**

Yes. If the type is in its own layer, select the characters you want to adjust, then press M to select the Move tool, and either drag the characters to a new position or nudge them with the ARROW cursor keys.

DRAMATIC EFFECTS

? **I want to give my type some perspective, similar to the opening of that famous space shoot-em-up movie. How can I do that?**

Enter the text, then use Layer | Transform | Perspective to add the right slant. Figure 9-4 shows an example.

Figure 9-4.   Perspective added to type

❓ How can I create a dropped shadow?

You'll be surprised at how easy that is, as you can see in Figure 9-5. Just follow these steps:

1. Open an empty document in Photoshop.

2. Press D to make sure the default foreground and background colors are used.

3. Choose the Type tool and click where you want the text to appear.

4. Type in your text in the font and size you want. Click OK in the Text dialog box.

5. Press COMMAND/CTRL-A to select the text you just placed in a separate layer.

6. Press COMMAND/CTRL-C to copy the text, then COMMAND/CTRL-V to paste down a second copy of the text.

To make a "hard" drop shadow:

1. Click the Layers palette and make sure Preserve Transparency is checked. The layer with the text you just pasted should be highlighted.

2. Click the Swatches palette and choose the color you want as the foreground over the drop shadow.

3. Choose File I Fill and fill the text with color you've chosen.

4. Use the Move tool to move the colored text over the drop shadow.

5. Use the cursor ARROW keys, if necessary, to position the text over the shadow precisely.

6. Use Layer I Flatten Image to flatten the text and drop shadow.

Dropped Shadow

Figure 9-5.   Drop shadows added to type

To make a "soft" drop shadow:

1. Follow steps 1 through 3 above to fill the text with the color you want.

2. Click the Layers palette and select the layer below the layer you are working with—this should be the first text you pasted down, which is "underneath" the colored text.

3. Make sure Preserve Transparency is NOT clicked.

4. Choose Filters | Blur | Gaussian Blur and move the slider to blur the drop shadow. A value of 2 or 3 should be about right.

5. Use the Move tool to move the blurry shadow up under and offset slightly from the text.

6. Use Layer | Flatten Image to combine the layers.

? Can I apply a gradient to type?

Yes. Just create the type in its own layer, then click the Preserve Transparency box in that layer before applying the gradient.

? How can I create glowing text on a dark background?

You can easily create a "radioactive" effect like the one shown in Figure 9-6 with a black background or any dark color. The eerie glowing text is a little hard to read, so you'll want to use this haunting effect for logos and other large graphics. Just follow these steps:

1. Choose a thick, sans-serif font. These look better than feathery typefaces with serifs, as they tend to get washed out in the glow.

2. Next, select a bright color for the radiance effect. Magenta, bright yellow, or red look good.

3. Enter your text into a blank, transparent image, using the dark color you want for the final background.

4. Immediately copy the text to the clipboard; you'll need this original version later.

5. Next, make sure Preserve Transparency is unchecked.

Figure 9-6.   Glowing text

6. Use Filter | Gaussian Blur to blur the text.

7. Check the Preserve Transparency box.

8. Fill the blurred text with the color you've selected for the glow.

9. Press COMMAND/CTRL-V to paste the text copied to the clipboard on top of the blurry glow.

10. Use the Move tool to position the text, if necessary.

❓ Can I make type cast a shadow?

Yes. You'll often want to use drop shadows and other shadowing effects. The following technique uses two different tricks to produce an interesting look, as you can see in Figure 9-7.

1. Enter the text into a blank transparent image, using any color you want.

2. Press COMMAND/CTRL-C to copy the text to the clipboard.

3. Press COMMAND/CTRL-V to paste it down into a separate layer.

4. Use Layer | Transform | Flip Vertical to flip it upside down. (It will be reversed, but that's what we want.)

5. Make sure Preserve Transparency is checked.

6. Fill the text with a dark shade, such as black.

Shadow

Figure 9-7.   Type casting a shadow

7. Use Layer | Transform | Perspective (or Distort or Skew) to angle the shadow so it appears to have been cast by the original letters.

8. Uncheck Preserve Transparency and use Gaussian Blur to blur your shadow, if you want.

9. Press COMMAND/CTRL-V to paste down the text previously copied, then once more fill it with black (don't forget to check Preserve Transparency).

10. Use the cursor ARROW keys to nudge the text to produce a 3-D or drop shadow effect.

❓ Can I create text that looks like it was bent from tubing?

Yes, this is an easy effect to achieve. Just follow these steps to produce the result shown in Figure 9-8.

1. Choose a sans-serif font with thick strokes, like VAG Rounded.

Tubes

Figure 9-8.   Tubular text

2. Select a medium-dark hue as your foreground color.

3. Create your text on its own layer.

4. Choose the Darken version of the Toning tool.

5. From the Brushes palette, select a fuzzy brush about a third the width of the major strokes of the text.

6. Darken the outer edges of the text using the Darken tool. You don't have to be precise; a little variation in your strokes makes the text look more organic and realistic.

7. Choose the Lighten variation of the Toning tool and lighten the center of each stroke. You'll end up with a cool tubular effect without much work at all.

? Can I create text that looks like graffiti?

Sure, as you can see from Figure 9-9. Use a handwriting font, or just draw the characters yourself using a fuzzy brush. Then, make sure the Preserve Transparency box is unchecked and apply Gaussian Blur until your text looks like graffiti. You can also get a similar effect using the Airbrush, although you may find it a little harder to control.

Figure 9-9.   Do-it-yourself graffiti

Answer Topics

Color Models and
Color Balancing @ a Glance

Most Photoshop work is done in RGB and grayscale modes, which represent two "models" that present images in the same way your monitor screen does, by adding different shades of light together. CMYK represents the colors used in the printing process, and you would use that color model when using Photoshop to make color separations used for printing, or to preview how an image might look printed. L*A*B color was developed as a device-independent international standard that theoretically should look the same whether output by a monitor, a printing press, or another device. Photoshop uses it as an intermediate mode when changing from one color system to another.

⇨ *Hue* refers to a predominant color, saturation is how pure the color is, luminance is the lightness or brightness of a color, and chroma is a combination of hue and saturation. Tint is a color produced by adding white to a pure hue; shades are generated by adding black, and tones by adding both black and white.

⇨ Images can be color-corrected—within limits—by adding or subtracting colors in highlights, midtones, or shadows, fixing problems that can be caused by a list of errors ranging from mixed light sources to bad photofinishing. Photoshop's Variations mode is a quick way of correcting color and density using a ring of comparison photos you can choose from.

⇨ Switching from one color mode to another, such as RGB to CMYK, or from RGB to Indexed Color, must be done with care to ensure that no important colors are lost during the process. When creating 256-color images, you can choose various color palettes—called Color Lookup Tables—and reapply them to other images, or edit them.

THE BASICS OF COLORS

？ I understand RGB and grayscale, but what are those other choices that appear in the Image|Modes menu?

You'll almost always use RGB and grayscale for most work, since they represent two "models" that present images in the same way your monitor screen does—by adding different shades of light together. CMYK represents the colors used in the printing process, and you would use that color model when using Photoshop to make color separations used for printing, or to preview how an image might look printed. L*A*B color was developed as a device-independent international standard. Duotone is a way of creating livelier grayscale or monochrome images with a richer span of tones by using two different colors of ink. Indexed color is simply color that uses no more than 256 different hues or shades.

? I'm confused by terms like hue, saturation, lightness, brightness, luminance, and chromacity. What do they all mean?

Each of these terms has a technical definition, but often you'll find them used in other ways. Hue, for example, represents the predominant color of a particular mixture of light waves, but is commonly used just to mean color. Saturation is the strength or purity of a color. Luminance is also referred to as lightness or brightness, and represents the intensity of a light source. Strictly speaking, however, lightness is defined as the combination of saturation and brightness, but you'll often see it used interchangeably with brightness alone. Chromacity, or chroma, is a property that's a combination of hue and saturation. According to Photoshop's own help file, saturation and chroma mean the same thing (although Adobe says that saturation is sometimes called chroma). You may find these terms confusing, but as you work with these properties, their characteristics will become second nature to you.

? OK—how about tints, shades, and tones?

You'll often see light colors referred to as tints, and any gradation of color or black and white as a shade or tone. However, a tint is produced by adding white to a pure hue, desaturating it like white pigment poured into a can of blue paint. Adding black to a pure color produces a shade, while tones are generated by adding both black and white. In practice, you'll rarely need to know the names for these distinctions.

Where Color Models Come From

⇨ **RGB** Your CRT can generate red, green, or blue, and creates other colors by a combination of two or more of those hues. All three together equal white; no color at all equals black. Grayscale images are made of equal amounts of all three colors in varying intensity levels. So-called *additive* colors (because they are made from light itself) can encompass an enormous range of tones. Very bright colors that still manage to hold detail can be generated by using a bright light source; dark tones with detail can be generated by reducing the light level.

⇨ **CMYK** Printing inks work in the opposite way from additive colors: they start with white light and absorb part of the spectrum, reflecting the remainder back to the eye. Because light is removed, this color model is called *subtractive* color. Inks are always the complements of their additive counterparts: cyan (which absorbs red), magenta (which absorbs green), and yellow (which absorbs blue), with a fourth color—black—added to add snap, contrast, and detail in the darker areas. Subtractive colors have a narrower range and can produce fewer colors than additive systems, because there is a limitation on how much light that paper or another substrate can reflect back to our eyes.

⇨ **L*A*B** The L*A*B color model, developed by the Commission Internationale d'Eclairage (CIE), builds colors using a luminance (L) channel (adjustable from 0 to 100), plus A and B channels to represent colors from along a red-green axis and blue-yellow axis (−120 to +120) respectively. Don't try to picture how this works: it's basically a mathematical way of looking at color. This system can reproduce all the colors available in both the CMYK and RGB models, so you can convert images from either of these into L*A*B and back again without losing any tones (which can happen when switching from RGB to CMYK or vice versa). This makes L*A*B perfect for very tricky color-correction feats, such as when you need to vary the luminance of a color independently of its hue and saturation to create a smooth gradient. L*A*B also is good for printing to color PostScript Level 2 or 3 devices, which also support L*A*B. Even if you don't use L*A*B, Photoshop uses it as an intermediate step when switching between color models.

⇨ **Other color models** Photoshop supports other color models, at least in part, including HSB (hue-saturation-brightness) and HSL (hue-saturation-lightness), showing up in the Color Picker, the Hue/Saturation dialog box, and a few other locations. In HSB/HSL, colors are represented as they are in a rainbow, as a continuous spectrum. This kind of model probably more closely represents the way humans think about color than RGB and CMYK, which correspond more closely to the ways in which mechanical devices like monitors and printing presses must reproduce color.

CORRECTING COLOR

⁇ My image is too red. How can I fix that?

If an occasional image is too red, you can probably fix it easily in Photoshop, as long as sufficient amounts of the other colors in the image are available. If most of your images have this defect, you should investigate one of the common causes of recurring color balance problems in the following sidebar.

To fix a reddish image (or an image that is noticeably too strong in any one color), choose Image | Adjust | Color Balance (or press COMMAND/CTRL-B) to display the Color Balance dialog box:

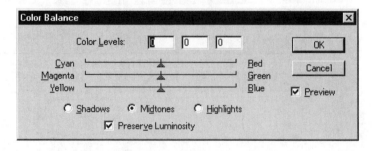

Then follow these steps:

1. Make sure the Preview box is checked, so you'll be able to see the results of your changes in the original image as you work.

2. Choose whether the shadows, midtones, or highlights need adjustment, and click in the appropriate radio button. If you're unsure, start with the midtones setting.

3. Move the color sliders to adjust the balance of your image, following these guidelines:

   ⇨ If the image is too red, subtract red by moving the red/cyan slider towards cyan (which is red's complementary, or "opposite," color).

   ⇨ If the image is too green, subtract green by moving the green/magenta slider towards magenta.

   ⇨ If the image is too blue, subtract blue by moving the blue/yellow slider towards the yellow.

   ⇨ If the image is too cyan, magenta, or yellow, move the appropriate slider to the right, toward that color's complement.

Causes of Bad Color in Photographs

⇨ **Incorrect light source**   Color films are balanced for a particular color of light, called color temperature. Daylight at noon has a color temperature in the 5500- to 6000-degree range. Indoor illumination is around 3400 degrees. The higher the number, the bluer the light. If a photograph is exposed indoors under warm illumination using film balanced for cooler daylight, the image will appear much too reddish. If you were using a slide film, you would get reddish slides. The photoprocessing lab can add some blue while making prints from "daylight-balanced" color negatives exposed under this warm light, though, giving you well-balanced prints. A few professional films are balanced for interior—tungsten—light sources, but most of the time you'll be working with daylight films. You can prevent bad color by using a filter indoors to correct daylight film for tungsten illumination; or, if you're using print (negative) film instead of slide film, let your color lab make the correction.

If your photolab consistently delivers bad color, consider switching to another lab.

⇨ **Fluorescent lights** While tungsten illumination and daylight differ chiefly in how warm the light source is, some types of fluorescent tubes produce light that is severely deficient in just particular shades of a color, such as red. You can't compensate for the resulting greenish tone by adding all tones of red, either digitally or with a filter, but must instead use a filter specifically designed for that kind of fluorescent light. Your camera store expert can help you choose the right filter for the light source you'll be using.

⇨ **Bad photofinishing** Automated photofinishing equipment is quite sophisticated, and can differentiate between indoor and outdoor pictures, photos with a lot of sky or ocean, or other unusual situations. However, sometimes the sensors go awry and you get pictures that are too light, too dark, or off-color. If this happens, ask that your prints be reprinted, or try to salvage them in Photoshop. If it happens often, switch to a different finisher.

⇨ **Mistreated film** Storing a camera in a hot glove compartment or trunk is a surefire way to get prints with a purple cast, rainbow flares, or other defect caused by heat-driven fogging of the film. There's no cure for film ruined in this way, so your best course is to avoid the situation entirely by storing your camera in a cool place between uses.

⇨ **Mixed illumination** Bounce your flash off a colored wall or ceiling, or take a photo partially illuminated by daylight and interior light, and you'll end up with photos that have mixed colors. You can make some fixes using Photoshop's Variations dialog box, or you can plan on turning the picture into an arty piece of creative expression. There's no easy solution once you've gotten into this fix.

⇨ **Faded color** All dyes change in color over time, and change faster when exposed to strong light or heat. Prints, slides, and negatives will even change when kept in the dark for long periods of time (20 years or more). You can sometimes make a new print from the original negative, if you can find it and it has not also faded. You can sometimes fix images within Photoshop by reducing the amount of other colors to match the hue that's faded.

Tip: *If you do much color correction using this method, learn to recognize the difference between colors: cyan and magenta in light shades are often confused with blue, green, and red. Pale yellow may look like pale green, as well.*

I have a whole collection of photos, all of them off-color by the same amount. Is there a faster way to correct them?

Yes. When you adjust colors for the first image using the Color Balance dialog box, remember the values shown in the Color Levels fields after you've made a correction. The values will range from 0 to +100 percent or –100 percent. Then, press COMMAND/CTRL-B for each successive image and type those values into the corresponding fields for the other images. Applying the same amount of correction to a group of similar images may not provide exact color balance, but you should get pleasing results. You can also automate the step further using Photoshop's Actions palette, discussed in Chapter 12.

Try to make your correction using a single slider, if possible. You should be aware of the possible interactions when you move more than one slider. For example:

⇨ Adding the same amount of any two colors from a particular color model (e.g., RGB or CMY—ignoring black for the moment) is the same as subtracting the third color, and vice versa. That is, when you add equal amounts of cyan and magenta, that's the same as subtracting that amount of yellow. Adding equal amounts of blue and green is the same as subtracting that amount of red.

⇨ If you add or subtract all three colors from the same color model, you'll add or subtract a neutral (or gray) component that you probably don't want to add or subtract. For example, adding +25 Red, +25 Green, and +25 Blue produces no color shift at all. Adding +25 Red, +50 Green and +25 Blue produces a color shift of +25 Green, since +25 of each color cancels each other out.

? How can I be adjusting cyan, magenta, and yellow if I am working with an RGB mode image?

Even though red, green, and blue are the primary colors for your image, it will still contain combinations of those hues. Equal amounts of red and green produce yellow, equal amounts of red and blue produce magenta, and equal amounts of green and blue produce cyan. If you have more of one RGB primary color than another, the result will be an in-between shade. The RGB and CMY sliders in the Color Balance dialog box just give you a fast way of adjusting the amount of red, green, blue and green-blue (cyan), red-blue (magenta), and red-green (yellow) hues. The dialog box has the same choices when you're working with an image using the CMYK color model, too.

? When I try correcting the color of an image, I get a grayish picture that still has the objectionable color cast. What's wrong?

To be fixable, an image must have *too much* of a color, some of which can be removed with the Color Balance controls. When that color is subtracted (or the other colors added in) the picture becomes properly balanced. However, if a photo is too far off-color (say, it's faded from sunlight to a ripe magenta), you'll be unable to add colors that aren't there. Subtracting magenta from a photo without significant cyan and yellow tones leaves nothing behind but gray.

? My image isn't off-color, as such, but has faded colors. How can I fix this?

You probably need to use the Image | Adjust | Hue/Saturation dialog box. You can press COMMAND/CTRL-U to get to this box quickly. Move the middle, Saturation, slider to the right or left to add or subtract richness from the color.

Note: *Saturation is the property that indicates how much of the hue is composed of the pure color itself and how much is diluted by a neutral color, such as white or black. Think of three cans of paint in red, white, and black. Pure red paint is fully saturated. As you add white paint, the color becomes less saturated, until you reach various shades of pink. Add enough white, and the red is completely overpowered, leaving you with a white image (in Photoshop, a completely desaturated image will look like a black-and-white photo). Add black paint and the colors also lose saturation by becoming darker.*

? I have a black-and-white photo I'd like to colorize. Can I do that?

Yes. The process was mentioned briefly in Chapter 8 as a way of adding color to black-and-white clouds. The technique works just as well with entire photos. Just follow these steps:

1. Use Image I Mode I RGB Color to change the grayscale image to RGB color.

2. Select Image I Adjust I Hue/Saturation (or press COMMAND/ CTRL-U).

3. Click the Colorize box in the lower right of the Hue/Saturation dialog box.

4. Move the Hue slider to achieve the color you want.

5. Move the Saturation slider to adjust the saturation of the image.

6. Click OK when finished.

? I have a hard time figuring out which color to add or subtract. Is there an easier way to decide?

Relax. Photoshop has a great Variations mode that allows you to compare several versions of the same image, each with a different color correction, and choose the one that looks best. Figure 10-1 shows the Variations dialog box. Follow these steps to use this tool:

1. Choose Image | Adjust | Variations to bring up the Variations dialog box. In the upper-left corner, you'll find thumbnail images of your original image paired with a preview, with the changes you've made applied.

2. Make sure the Midtones radio button is checked.

3. Immediately beneath the Original/Current Pick previews is another panel with the current pick surrounded by six different versions, each biased toward a different color: green, yellow, red, magenta, blue, and cyan. These show what your current pick would look like with that type of correction added. You can click on any of them to apply that correction to the current pick.

4. To the right of this ring is a panel with three sample images—the current pick in the center, with a lighter version above and a darker version below. If the lighter or darker versions look better to you, click on that preview to lighten or darken the current pick.

5. Click OK to apply your changes.

❓ It appears that the color shifts are more in the shadows and highlights than in the midtones. Can I fix these areas individually?

Yes. You'll often find that highlight and shadow areas can be a little off-color when the light source illuminating them is not pure. A person standing near a blue wall with the light coming from the opposite direction may have bluish shadows. Someone standing near an open window with daylight streaming in—but otherwise lit by reddish interior lighting—may have a weird blue/red mixed-color cast. Click in the Variations dialog box's Shadows radio button to adjust only the darker tones of an image. You can also choose the Highlights button to manipulate the lighter tones, or the Saturation control to adjust saturation.

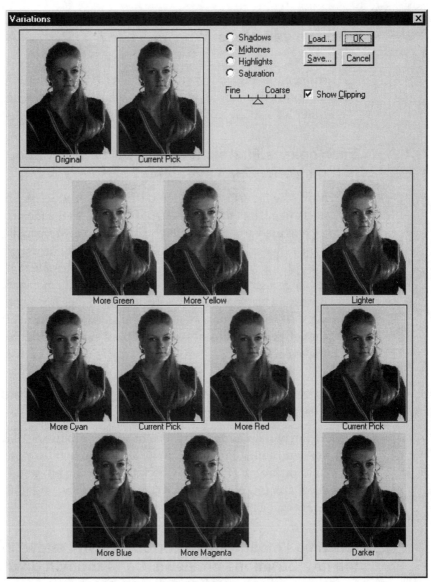

Figure 10-1. The Variations dialog box

? I don't see a lot of difference between some of the possible variations. What can I do?

Move the Fine/Coarse slider more to the right. Each variation will be stronger, giving you a better selection to choose from. Once you've determined which color you really want to add, you can move the slider back to the middle, then apply the color in small steps.

? Each color adjustment I make with the Variations feature is too strong. Can I avoid this?

Move the Fine/Coarse slider to the left to produce smaller increments of change. The Fine/Coarse scale determines the increment used for each of the variations displayed in the two lower panels. If you select a finer increment, the differences between the current pick and each of the options will be much smaller. A coarser increment will provide much grosser changes with each variation. You may need these to correct an original that is badly off-color. Since fine increments are difficult to detect onscreen, and coarse increments are often too drastic for tight control, I recommend keeping the pointer in the center of the scale.

? When using variations, sometimes I lose all detail in an area. What happened?

You may have added too much of a color, producing "clipping," which converts a highlight or shadow area to pure white or pure black (midtones aren't clipped). Check the Clipping box and Photoshop will show any colors that may be cut off in a contrasting hue so you'll know that clipping might take place.

? The area I most want to correct doesn't show up well in the tiny variations previews. Can I zoom in on that area as I work with the Variations dialog box?

Photoshop doesn't have this feature, but here's a workaround, shown in Figure 10-2:

1. Select the area that's important to you.

2. Choose Image | Adjust | Variations. The dialog box appears, showing only the selected area.

3. Make your color adjustments and click OK.

4. Use Select | Inverse (or press COMMAND/CTRL-SHIFT-I).

5. Choose Image | Adjust | Variations again. The color changes you last made will already be selected and shown in the preview.

6. Click OK. The color correction you made to the selection will be applied to the whole image.

? Can I apply the same set of changes to multiple images?

You may Load or Save the adjustments you've made in a session so they can be applied to the image at any later time. You can use this

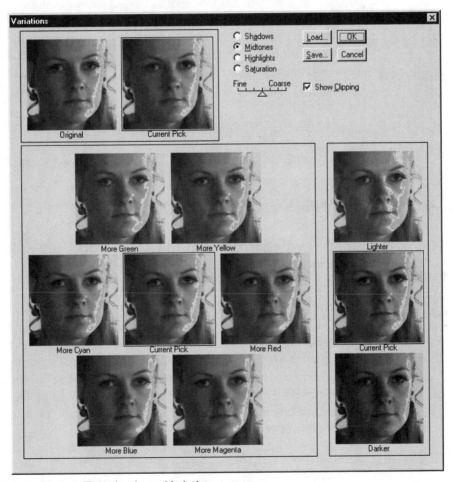

Figure 10-2.   Zooming in on Variations

option to create a file of settings that can be used with several similarly balanced images, thereby correcting all of them efficiently.

Selective Variations

In most cases, shadows, midtones, and highlights will need roughly the same amount of correction with the Variations dialog box. In others, though, the shadows or highlights may have picked up a color cast of their own (say, reflected from an object off-camera). Variations lets you correct these separately if you need to.

More often, though, you'll use the shadows-midtones-highlights option to improve the appearance of images that have too-dark shadows or washed-out highlights. Where any image editor's brightness/contrast control generally affects *all* the colors equally, this procedure lets you lighten shadows (bringing out more detail) or darken highlights (keeping them from becoming washed out) without affecting other portions of the image. The technique also lets you avoid nasty histograms and gamma curves.

CHANGING COLOR MODES

? When I switch from RGB to CMYK mode, my colors seem to change. Why is this?

If you switch back and forth between RGB and CMYK, your colors can, in fact, change. There are colors that can be represented by the RGB model that can't be duplicated in the CMYK model (and vice versa), so anytime you switch between the two, you run the risk of losing some colors. This phenomenon is especially pronounced when you change from one model to the other, then back to the original. Nor can all tones you see on your screen (RGB colors) be represented by printing inks (which use CMYK tones), so don't expect the printed version of your image to match exactly.

Photoshop uses a complex process to convert an RGB image to CMYK. It first changes the image to L*A*B mode, referring to information stored in your Monitor Setup preferences. Then, it uses information in the Printing Inks Setup and Separation Setup dialog boxes to create a color lookup table (CLUT) before converting the image to CMYK mode. Then, when the image is in CMYK mode, Photoshop converts the CMYK values back to RGB so that the image can be shown on your display.

Tip: *Use Photoshop's Preview mode (use Image | Preview, or press COMMAND/CTRL-Y), which lets you view CMYK color schemes without actually changing the file's content, so you can return to RGB with your colors intact. If you want to compare RGB and CMYK colors, open a second window on the same image using View | New View, then activate Image | Preview only for the second image.*

How can I tell which colors can't be represented by a particular color model?

Photoshop's Color Picker displays an exclamation point above the Current Color/Sample Color boxes when you've selected a hue that can't be printed. It offers a duller alternative color that does conform to the CMYK color model. You can also try working with the (slower) CMYK model as you edit an image. You can see the gamut alert in Figure 10-3. Photoshop also has a Gamut Warning mode you can activate with View | Gamut Warning or by pressing SHIFT-COMMAND/CTRL-Y. Any out-of-gamut pixels will be shown in a bright color, which you can select in the File | Preferences | Transparency & Gamut dialog box.

Some Photoshop functions can't be performed on a CMYK image. If I must create a CMYK file for output, how can I avoid switching back to RGB if I need to edit that image later on?

Save a copy in RGB mode, then switch to CMYK mode and save the duplicate. Edit the original RGB file if you need to later on.

When I switch from 24-bit color to 8-bit color, I get strange hues. What's going on?

If you change from either 24-bit models to Indexed Color (which boils all colors down to the 256 hues), you may get a good representation of your original or a horrid one. The results may be grainy, fuzzy,

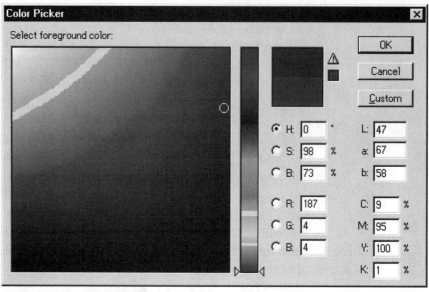

Figure 10-3.   Color Picker

perhaps with banding in the gradients, and not look anything like what you intended. Your carefully prepared desktop presentation can become a joke without your even knowing about it.

Prevent problems by converting images to 256 colors yourself, so you can preview them on your 24-bit display. After all, you might not *need* 24-bit color to represent a particular image.

Color Indexing

The 16.7 million colors possible with 24-bit color refers only to the palette of colors your image can draw from. No image will need anywhere near that number of colors. After all, a 640 × 480-pixel image has only 307,200 different pixels. If each of them were a different color, you'd need only 307,200 different colors—a far cry from 16.7 million! A 1024 × 768 image contains about 768,000 pixels, again many fewer than are available in a 16.7 million color palette.

Indexed color is based on the notion that many color images can be represented by far fewer than 16.7 million hues. Indeed, many can be displayed with 100 percent accuracy using only 256 different colors, producing a file size that is somewhat smaller—and one that can be viewed on PC systems having only 256-color video. Other images may have more colors than 256 but still look good when similar colors are combined and represented by one of the 256 in an indexed color palette.

The key is to create an *optimized* palette. What you don't want is an equal representation of all the colors in the spectrum. That might give you far too many blues, but not enough greens to represent a given scene. Think of a portrait of a man wearing a brown suit and a solid green tie. You may need only 10 to 20 different greens to encompass all the subtle shades of green in the tie. Another 50 or so browns might be required for the suit. Only a few blues, yellows, or other hues would be needed. The bulk of your tones might fall into the pinks or browns that make up flesh tones. By carefully selecting the most frequently used 256 tones in an image, you can often accurately represent a 24-bit file using 8-bit color.

Photoshop offers you a choice of methods for choosing the palette or CLUT.

? What's the best way to convert to 8-bit (256) color mode?

You'll use Image | Mode | Indexed Color to convert. Make sure you're starting with RGB color; Photoshop can't convert from CMYK color to Indexed Color and, while it can convert from Grayscale to Indexed Color, you won't notice any difference. Set the parameters for your CLUT/palette using one of the methods described next and click OK.

? My image actually contains few colors. Can I optimize how it's rendered?

In the Indexed Color dialog box, choose Exact from the Palette drop-down list. This choice will be available only if your image contains 256 or fewer colors. Photoshop will render the image in its exact colors.

？ I want my image to contain only the colors that can be represented by my operating system in 256-color mode. How can I do this?

Choose System or Uniform (the System choice changes to Uniform if you select a pixel depth of other than 8 bits/pixel) to create a CLUT that is evenly distributed among all the RGB colors. Separate System palettes are available for Macintosh and Windows machines. All colors in your image will be converted to one of the hues used by the operating system by default in its 256-color mode. You probably won't want to use this choice except for images with an even distribution of color.

？ My image contains a full range of colors. Do I have any hope of squeezing all of them into a 256-color palette?

Photoshop will make a valiant effort if you choose the Adaptive palette from the pull-down list in the Indexed Color dialog box. The software will examine all the colors in an image and create a palette that favors the most frequently used colors in the image.

？ How can I view the colors used in a palette?

Click on the Swatches palette to see the current colors used in the active CLUT. If you want to save the palette or load a new one, use Image | Mode | Color Table, shown in Figure 10-4. You'll find buttons for loading and saving palettes.

？ How can I use a palette I have saved?

In the Indexed Color dialog box, choose Custom from the Palette drop-down list. You can then load a previously saved CLUT. In this way, you can share color palettes between similar images, or apply the CLUT to a new image. The Previous choice applies the last custom CLUT you used in your session. (This option is available only if you've used the Custom command earlier.)

？ What is the Web palette I see in the Indexed Color dialog box?

Use that CLUT if you want to ensure that an image is browser-safe (i.e., that it contains the 216 colors common to browsers like Netscape

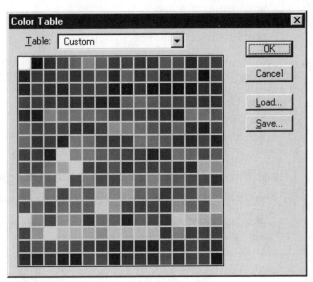

Figure 10-4.   The Color Table dialog box

and Microsoft Internet Explorer when used in 256-color mode). You'll find more on Internet color considerations in Chapter 14.

? What is the Color Depth entry in the dialog box used for?

If you are applying a Uniform or Adaptive palette to an image, you can choose either 8-bit color (256 hues), 7-bit (128 colors), 6-bit (64 colors), 5-bit (32 colors), 4-bit (16 colors) or 3-bit (8 colors). Use this to create a poster-like effect, or to specify color depths that you know will handle all the colors in your image. The Exact palette uses Other as a color depth, and other CLUTs all use 8-bit color.

? Even when I use an Adaptive palette, I get color bands in my image. Is there anything else I can do?

The dither parameter tells the software how to simulate colors that don't have a direct equivalent in the CLUT palette selected. Choose None and the software selects the closest color in the CLUT. Pattern can be used to create odd geometric arrangements of colors, but only if you chose the System palette option. You might like the special effects that result, but avoid this choice if you're looking for realistic color. Your best choice is usually Diffusion, which distributes the extra colors randomly and naturally. Note that dithering cannot be used with the Exact palette.

? Is it possible to edit the colors in a CLUT?

Yes. Use Image | Mode | Color Table. Select any color by double-clicking it. The Color Picker pops up and you can choose any color to substitute for the one selected.

? I need more blues in my 256-color image, which has a lot of sky and ocean. Is that easy to do?

Yes. You can create a custom CLUT that is top heavy with blues if you like. Here's how to do it:

1. With a 256-color image active, use Image | Mode | Color Table to view the color table.

2. Click and hold down the mouse in the first color of a range you'd like to change to blues.

3. Drag the mouse to encompass all the colors you'd like to replace with a blue range, then release the mouse button.

4. The Color Picker pops up with a label, "Select first color." Click in the color selection area to choose the initial color of the range.

5. Click OK. The Color Picker changes the label to "Select last color." Click in the color section area to choose the last color of the range.

6. Click OK. The Color Table dialog box appears again, with the boxes you selected containing a continuous span of colors between the first and last you chose.

7. Click Save to store the modified CLUT on disk.

8. Click OK to return to your image.

? I'd like to experiment with some outrageous color combinations. How can I get started?

Take a 256-color image, and substitute its CLUT with one of Photoshop's optional tables. Follow these steps:

1. Use Image | Mode | Color Table.

2. Choose either Spectrum or Black Body from the pull-down Table list. Spectrum is a set of 256 colors of the rainbow, spread evenly from magenta, through blue, cyan, green, yellow, orange, and red. The effect is a bit like solarization, and quite interesting. The Black Body CLUT includes only the colors you'd get from heating what scientists call a black-body radiator, which would start at black, glow a dull red, bright red, yellow, and eventually white. This is another interesting effect.

Tip: *Take an image colored with the Black Body CLUT, then use Image | Adjust | Invert (or press COMMAND/CTRL-I) to change the photo to a startling range of blues.*

When I change to Indexed Color mode, Photoshop insists on flattening my layers. Is there a way around this?

While Photoshop can change from some modes to others without flattening, it gives you no Flatten/Do Not Flatten option when going to Indexed Color. Solution? Save a copy with all your layers intact, then flatten and change to 256-color mode.

Digital Cameras and Scanners

Answer Topics!

Digital Cameras and Scanners @ a Glance

⇨ Digital cameras and scanners have a great deal in common. Both are equipped with a sensor that detects the amount of light reflected or transmitted by the subject or original artwork. One key difference between digital cameras and scanners is the way in which they capture images. Except for some high-end cameras that use a red/green/blue color wheel, still cameras grab the entire image in a frame in one instant, while scanners—scan.

⇨ *Scanning* is any technique for surveying a surface, often by sweeps of the scanning mechanism across the scanned area. A light source of some sort illuminates the artwork, which can be opaque or reflective artwork, such as a photograph or magazine article clipping, or translucent, such as a transparency. The amount of light reflected or transmitted by the artwork is detected by a sensor.

⇨ Scanners and digital cameras use charge-coupled devices, or *CCDs*, to capture images. A linear array like that found in flatbed scanners consists of a strip of tiny CCDs. The area arrays used in digital cameras are square wafers with rows and columns of CCD sensors.

⇨ Photoshop can manipulate color or black-and-white images created by scanners and digital cameras, just as it can any raster image. However, the means for importing such an image into Photoshop varies. Often, you'll need to use a special plug-in module to acquire the images. You can then edit them and save them in any format you choose.

This chapter deals primarily with the mechanics of image grabbing with digital cameras, scanners, and other options. Once the images are imported into Photoshop, the guidelines provided in other chapters on color correction, tonal adjustment, sharpening, and other qualities apply.

DIGITAL IMAGES

? How do I get images from my digital camera or scanner into Photoshop?

You'll have to use a special software module supplied by your camera manufacturer. Sometimes you'll receive two utilities. One is a stand-alone program that downloads and uploads photos, erases pictures already in your camera, arranges images into albums, and performs other tasks. A second module might be a plug-in for Photoshop that allows you to view thumbnails of the images in the camera and select which photos to download. You might even get a combination plug-in that handles both kinds of functions. Once you've installed the software, look for it in the File menu's Import or Acquire menu.

What is TWAIN?

TWAIN (reputedly standing for *Technology Without An Interesting Name*) is an interface for acquiring images captured by digital cameras, scanners, and video frame grabbers. TWAIN plug-ins are available for both Macs and Windows platforms. The modules are written by the vendor of the hardware and sit between the program, such as Photoshop, and the device. Photoshop can send standard commands to the TWAIN driver, which converts them into signals the hardware can respond to. A typical TWAIN driver is shown in Figure 11-1.

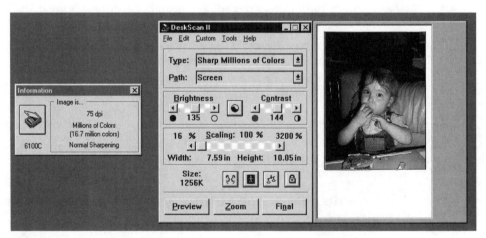

Figure 11-1.   A typical TWAIN driver

❓ I can't get TWAIN to work with my Windows computer. What's wrong?

If you're using Windows NT or Windows 95, you may be using an older TWAIN module intended for Windows 3.*x*. While some 16-bit drivers work under Windows 95, others do not, and Windows NT in particular requires newer 32-bit TWAIN sources. Vendors have been late in providing these special drivers for Windows NT. Check with the vendor of your scanner or digital camera for the latest modules. Once you have the module installed, follow these steps:

1. The first time you use a TWAIN driver, you'll need to use File | Import | Select TWAIN source (or Select TWAIN_32 Source) and choose the driver you want to use. That driver will remain as the default for future use of TWAIN.

2. Select File | Import and choose the TWAIN module.

3. A TWAIN driver dialog box will pop up. Make your selections for resolution or other functions, then click OK.

❓ Sometimes I can acquire images from my scanner or digital camera, and other times I cannot. What's wrong?

You've probably selected the wrong driver. If you have two devices that each use a separate TWAIN driver, you must remember to use the Select TWAIN Source command to switch to the appropriate driver.

DIGITAL CAMERAS

❓ When I import images from my digital camera into Photoshop, they don't look as sharp as they should. What's wrong?

If your camera has a resolution of 640×480 pixels, make sure you've set the camera for its "fine" resolution setting. In standard mode, it may actually produce images at only 320×240 pixels, which is good only for tiny snapshots. To see for yourself, take any sharp image and then use Photoshop's Image | Image Size command to change it to around 320 × 240 pixels. If it's a landscape (wide) image, type **320** into the Width field and leave the Height field alone. If it's a portrait (tall) image, type **240** into the Width field. Click OK and you'll see just how much resolution you can expect from a standard-resolution digital snapshot. Figure 11-2 shows an example.

❓ I have an upscale digital camera that has a resolution of 1024 × 768. Why do I still see pixels in my images?

In the digital camera world, 1024 × 768 isn't always the same. First of all, you shouldn't expect a camera priced under $1,000 to have three sets of sensors—red, green, and blue—for every pixel imaged. The only way to accomplish that kind of instantaneous exposure would be to use three separate CCD arrays, then split incoming light with a beam splitter so that red, green, and blue information is each directed to a different sensor. A system like that would be big, ugly, and expensive, and they call them production video cameras. Still cameras use another system.

Instead, CCD manufacturers coat individual pixels with red, green, and blue filters, arranged in alternating fashion, although a

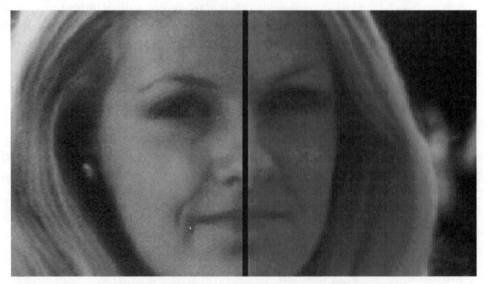

Figure 11-2.   An image at 640 × 480 pixels (left), and the same image at 320 × 240 pixels (right)

strict red, green, and blue pattern may not be used. One row of the array may be red-green-red-green-red-green, and so on, while the next row is green-blue-green-blue-green-blue. This excess of green-reading pixels is commonly used to compensate for a CCD's varying sensitivity to different colors of light.

Because a particular CCD pixel reads only one color of light, firmware in the camera interpolates using data from the nearest pixels of the other two colors to create the missing information. Interpolation produces images that are acceptable, even though not as good as if separate full-array sensors were used for each color. To make things even more complicated, some vendors use arrays of about 800×600 pixels, and use further interpolation to mimic higher resolutions. We've used some "megapixel" cameras that have many fewer than a million pixels.

❓ Can I get results equal to film?

Imaging scientists have determined that a full-frame field of view at a resolution roughly the same as a medium-speed film calls for a sensor with about 3000 (horizontal) $\times$ 2000 (vertical) pixels, a total of around six million individual samples. While there are cameras with true resolutions of 3060×2036 pixels or higher, they cost in the tens of thousands of dollars. These cameras give good results with prints up to 11×14 inches; however, to achieve the same resolution with a 640×480-pixel camera, you'd have to limit your output to wallet-sized 3×2-inch printlets.

❓ Whenever I try to crop a digital photo image in Photoshop, the pixels become obtrusive. Can I avoid this?

Yes, you can do a few things to minimize the pixelated effect. Try these tips:

⇨ Avoid cropping whenever possible. Move in close to your subject and try to frame the image exactly as you will want it when the picture has been imported to Photoshop.

⇨ When you crop an image, then print it in a larger size, you are, in effect, enlarging it without taking advantage of Photoshop's interpolation features. Enlarge the image size using bicubic interpolation, then crop to the size you need.

⇨ Sometimes, a slight amount of Gaussian blur can minimize the pixelated effect.

? Why does it take so long to download pictures from my digital camera to Photoshop?

You're probably transferring the pictures over a serial cable supplied with the camera. Here are some ways to increase the transfer speed:

⇨ Preview the thumbnail images in your camera, and download only the photos you really want.

⇨ Check your digital camera software and make sure you are using the highest serial transfer speed the software and your computer can support. You may have set the utility to use 19.2 Kbps when your computer is compatible with a setting as high as 115,200 Kbps.

⇨ Some digital cameras offer an optional parallel-port transfer mode for Windows PCs, sometimes using a special cradle to hold the camera. Parallel transfer can be up to eight times faster than serial downloads.

⇨ Your digital camera may use PC Card memory or one of the smaller memory cards that can fit into a PC Card adapter. If so, you may be able to use the PC Card slot in your laptop to transfer pictures directly without going through the serial cable. If you have a desktop PC, you can purchase a PC Card adapter for $100 or more.

? Can I change the resolution of my digital camera?

Digital cameras generally offer a fixed resolution corresponding to the number of pixels in the array, although consumer-oriented versions may give you a choice between low-resolution 640 × 480 and very low-resolution 320 × 240 pictures as a way to increase the capacity of the built-in storage.

Professional-level cameras start at roughly 1500 × 1000 pixels. That's about 1.5 million pixels, about three to five times as much resolution as low-end consumer-oriented cameras, which may have just 280,000-410,000 pixels.

SCANNERS

? **My scanner has a resolution of 300 × 600 samples per inch. How can this be possible?**

Since the same linear sensor is used to scan each line of an image, the vertical resolution is determined by the distance the array is moved between lines. That is, if the carriage is moved 1/400th inch between lines, the scanner has a vertical resolution of 400 dpi. Since the sensors in the linear array are smaller than .04 × .04 inches, it may be possible to move the carriage 1/800th inch or some smaller increment, providing higher vertical resolutions. That's why you'll see scanners with specifications listing 300 × 600 or 400 × 800 optical resolution.

? **Can I avoid interpolation?**

Interpolation can't always be avoided. However, you can choose to have an image interpolated or scaled in your scanner before the image is sent to Photoshop, or wait and resample it within Photoshop. The former may be faster, particularly if you're working with large images, while the latter can give you better control over this type of image manipulation. The best way to avoid interpolation is to work with an image that is closest in size, or larger, than the final output. If you hope to make an 8 × 10-inch print, a 5 × 7 or larger original will always look better than a 4 × 5-inch original at the same final size. An exception would be if the original artwork is grainy; an 8 × 10-inch print from a grainy negative won't have any more detail than a 4 × 5-inch print—it will just be grainier.

What's Interpolation?

In scanning, interpolation is the same as the resampling Photoshop does when you enlarge or reduce an image, or change its resolution. It is the process of creating estimated values for pixels based on known values acquired during a scan. A scanner may have to do some form of interpolation or scaling every time you request a scan at something other than the scanner's optical resolution and a 100 percent (1:1) scale.

Interpolation can be used to *reduce* the amount of information in a scan, or to *increase* it, converting a 600×600-dpi scanner's output to the equivalent of 300×300 dpi, or estimating the values of in-between pixels to simulate a resolution of 1200×1200 dpi.

Interpolating up or down is relatively simple if you happen to choose an exact fraction or multiple of a scanner's optical resolution. Converting a 600×600-dpi scan to 300×300 dpi can be accomplished by discarding every other pixel. Simulating a resolution of 1200×1200 dpi involves little more than duplicating each pixel. With any other resolution, the scanner ideally does not just discard or replicate pixels, but instead examines the available pixels and creates new ones based on the information found in the original samples.

❓ What's the difference between scaling and interpolating?

Scaling is just a way of selecting a resolution that will produce a particular size on a given output device. An image scanned at 150 dpi and printed on a 300-dpi printer will appear half its original size. An image scanned at 600 dpi and output to a 300-dpi printer will end up twice its original size. To insulate you, the user, from having to bother with calculations, scanners offer scaling options, usually as slider controls in the scanning software's dialog box.

So, if you had a piece of line art measuring 2×2 inches that was to be printed at twice its actual size—4×4 inches—on a 300-dpi laser printer, you could simply select a resolution of 300 dpi and a scale of 200 percent. A 600-dpi scanner will scan at 600 dpi. Request a scale of 400 percent and the same scanner will scan the image at 600 dpi and interpolate to the equivalent of 1200 dpi.

Scanners usually allow you to choose resolution settings in single-dpi increments and specify scales in single percentages, so you can choose 175 dpi or 133 percent if you need them. The algorithms used to carry out interpolation—either in your scanner's firmware or by your PC's software, can have a dramatic effect on the appearance of your final image. A 600-dpi scanner with a clumsy interpolation scheme can produce worse results than a 400-dpi scanner with more elegant interpolation routines. Scanners may use algorithms like binary rate multiplication, nearest neighbor interpolation, linear interpolation, or bicubic interpolation to optimize the guesses they make when creating new pixels or choosing which pixels to drop. Sloppy interpolation can give images with prominent diagonal lines obvious stairstepping, or "jaggies."

What's 30-bit color, and can Photoshop handle it?

In most cases, a scanner with 30-bit color (or 36-bit, or some higher figure) produces better results with contrasty originals, particularly color transparencies, than a typical 24-bit scanner. In both cases, the images are sent to Photoshop as 24-bit files. The main difference is that the 30- or 36-bit scanner has more colors to choose from in compiling a palette of 16.8 million colors for the 24-bit version.

High-Color Scanners

Until recently, desktop scanners always captured—at least on paper—eight bits of information per channel. That allowed 256 different grayscale tones for monochrome scans, or 256 different colors for each of the red, green, and blue channels—256 × 256 × 256, or 16.7 million colors overall. Eight bits per channel/24-bit color should provide you with plenty of colors, but in practice, color scanners always lose a little information because of the inherent noise in any analog electronics system, much like the way the sound on your car stereo suffers when you roll down the windows.

Noise affects a scan only from the time of capture until it is converted to digital format. Instead of eight bits and 256 colors per channel, you may end up with seven useful bits of information, and only 128 different colors per channel. When a system is capable of reproducing 256 different colors, but only 128 are available, it's likely that one of the available colors will have to be substituted for actual colors in an image. That can happen when scanning transparencies, which have a wider dynamic range— detail all areas from deep shadows to lightest highlights—and may easily contain 256 or more colors in a particular channel. Desktop scanner vendors offer models with CCDs capable of extended dynamic ranges that require 10, 12, or more bits per channel (30 or 36 bits overall) to capture. With 1024 colors per channel, there are a total of nearly 11 billion colors with 30-bit scanners, and 4096 hues and a total of 6.8 trillion colors with 36-bit scanners. You can see that these systems can afford to lose a little information to noise and still have plenty of data to interpolate down to an optimized palette of 16.7 million colors. Even grayscale scans can benefit from the extended dynamic range of such units.

? What resolution should I use for scanning?

As we noted in Chapter 4, unneeded resolution produces large file sizes and wasted time in printing, copying, or uploading those files. You will rarely need more resolution than your final output device, and with halftoned images, you usually won't see any difference in images scanned at more than 1.5 to 2.5 times the line screen applied to the photograph. Some scanner drivers have default resolution settings for various applications, which can be especially useful if you're scanning for a specialized application such as faxing, when any resolution above that usable by the fax machine is truly wasted.

? Can I calibrate my scanner for Photoshop?

Most scanners are furnished with some sort of calibration tool, usually a standardized target that you scan into Photoshop. So after scanning, print out the file on your color printer, and then rescan it. The scanner's calibration software then "knows" how to adjust colors so that what you print is closer to the colors of the known original target. Once the scanner software has been adjusted in this way, you can then use Photoshop's File I Color Settings I Monitor Setup dialog boxes to match your monitor to the original colors of the calibration target, so all three devices will match—at least as closely as they can.

? I have a black-and-white photo with colored stains. How can I fix it?

Scan it in full color, then use Photoshop's Image I Adjust I Color Balance to remove the color corresponding to the stain. Then convert to grayscale and edit. Figure 11-3 shows an image that has been rescued in this way.

? How do I scan color slides?

Photoshop is a perfect tool for working with scanned slide images. While there are dedicated slide scanners available for $750 to $2,000 and up, your scanner vendor may sell a special lid for your flatbed scanner that has a built-in light source or second set of scanning sensors. Hewlett-Packard offers an inexpensive ScanJet Slide Adapter that looks like a pyramid with mirrors inside. It reflects light from the scanner up, over, and down through transparencies. This device would work with any flatbed scanner from any vendor, if you can get one separately.

Figure 11-3.   Scan in color to remove a stain from a black-and-white photo.

? How do I scan an extra-wide image?

Place it the long way on your scanner, then use Photoshop's
Layer | Transform | Rotate feature to rotate it to the proper orientation.

? How do I scan images that are larger than my scanner's bed?

Scan the image in pieces, bring them into Photoshop, paste them into
a new document large enough to hold all the pieces, then use the
ARROW cursor keys to nudge the images around in their layers until
they line up. If you use the same settings and are careful not to skew
the images when scanning, quite good results can be achieved. You
may have to adjust lightness or contrast slightly in Photoshop before
flattening your images. Figure 11-4 shows an image that has been
stitched together.

Figure 11-4.   Extra-large images can be combined in Photoshop.

When scanning images from magazines, the printing on the other side shows through. Can Photoshop fix this problem?

You could tediously edit out the extraneous matter, but a simpler solution would be to place a piece of black paper behind the page being scanned. The lids of most scanners are white, which causes them to reflect any light that seeps through the page back to the sensor.

I need to size images I scan precisely. How can I do this?

Place a ruler face down on the scanning bed, and scan it along with your original. Then, in Photoshop, you can compare that ruler with Photoshop's own rulers to achieve the exact relationship of sizes you want.

OTHER METHODS FOR ACQUIRING IMAGES

I don't have a digital camera or scanner. How do I get images into Photoshop?

Actually, for the best image quality and flexibility, a conventional film camera coupled with automated scanning by your photofinisher onto Photo CDs is the best choice. For about $20 for 24 exposures, a photo lab can transfer pictures from your slides, negatives, or prints to high-resolution formats onto a CD-ROM that holds as many as 100 to 120 images. The entry fee is low: you can use any 35mm camera you already have, and just pay as you go to have images transferred. Those who own fancy SLRs (single-lens reflexes) with interchangeable lenses can capture more sophisticated images under more challenging conditions such as fast-moving sports events or poorly lit indoor scenes.

How do I import Photo CD images into Photoshop?

Use Photoshop's File | Open command and select Kodak Photo CD (PCD) format. The dialog box, shown here, allows you to choose from among any of the multiple resolutions included of each image.

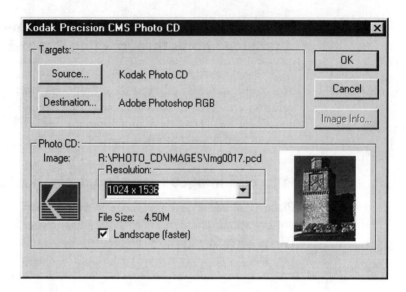

Available resolutions range from 128 × 192-pixel thumbnails to 256 × 384 previews to usable 512 × 768 and 1024 × 1536 images. An ultrahigh 2048 × 3072 version is also included, and will probably be sharper than anything you could produce with your own scanner. Kodak Pro Photo CDs have a sixth resolution of 4096 × 6144, which produces 72MB files you won't be eager to try and work with in Photoshop. Pro Photo CDs can also be scanned from original negatives and transparencies as large as 4 × 5 inches.

? I don't have that much memory. Can I work with those 72MB images in Photoshop?

Yes, but only a little at a time. Use Photoshop's File | Quick Edit option to select a portion of the image to edit. Save your work, then open a different section. You won't be able to apply a filter to the entire image this way, but can otherwise edit very large images.

? How long does it take to get Photo CDs?

Your local camera or retail store probably will need to send your film out to a lab offering Photo CD service. Mail order sources may take two to three weeks to turn around your order.

The wait may be worth it if you're not in a hurry. Photo CD images are sharp enough that you can crop tiny sections and still end up with razor-sharp graphics. If you don't need the whole image—perhaps you want to crop a head shot out of a group photo—the extra resolution of Photo CD can pay off.

? My Photo CD images open in the wrong orientation. What's wrong?

Photoshop opens all Photo CD images in landscape orientation, even if they are portrait-oriented images, if the landscape option is selected. Deselect it to enable Photoshop to open images in their native orientations.

? How do I save my images in Photo CD format?

You can't. Photo CDs are burned using a proprietary "image pac" format. You can load the images into image editors like Photoshop, but you'll have to save manipulated photos in one of the traditional formats, such as TIF, JPG, or GIF.

? Can I receive my digital images over the Internet?

Yes. The same photo labs that can transform your color negative or slide film to Photo CDs can now transfer images to Kodak Picture Disks, or post them for downloading remotely from the Kodak Picture Network. You'll find more information on both of these at *http://www.kodak.com*.

Picture Disks are floppy disks for Macintosh or Windows computers containing your digitized images. The disks lack the multiple resolution formats of Photo CDs, but they can be easily duplicated. Access to this service is as close as your mailbox.

Sign up for the Kodak Picture Network and you'll gain a password-protected account on a special Web site. Participating photofinishers can upload photos for your Web site that you can fetch online. There is also a workspace you can use to arrange your pictures for viewing and downloading by anyone you supply your username and password to. Your own photos may be uploaded to the workspace as well. Although aimed at consumers (reprints and photo postcards are also available), Web builders who need to retrieve images remotely will find these two services viable options.

Taking Action
with Macros

Answer Topics!

Taking Action with Macros @ a Glance

Macros are batches of commands that can be carried out with little or no user input, making it easy to automate repetitive tasks. As you might expect, macros are best used for a series of tasks that you do repeatedly, such as reducing a group of photos to a particular size or color depth, or applying a series of filters to several images. Conversely, macros are not very useful for tasks you intend to carry out just a few times.

⇨ Photoshop has limited support for external automation tools, such as AppleScript on the Macintosh or Object Linking and Embedding (OLE) commands from Microsoft Visual Basic (on Windows machines). In the latest versions of Photoshop, you'll find something better: the new Actions capability, which simplifies recording sets of commands for playback later. You may run a set of Actions on one file, or tell Photoshop to apply the macro's operations to all the files in a folder. The processed files can be saved under a new name in a different folder, if you wish.

⇨ Unfortunately, Actions works primarily with menu-oriented commands. You can apply filters, load and save files in different formats, resize images, change density or color balance, and perform many other useful tasks. You can't create repetitive paint strokes, make fancy selections, use the Paths palette, change between windows, or move objects. While you can leave "space" for the user to carry out nonrecordable actions, there are nearly as many things you can't do with Actions as those that you can.

BASIC ACTION SKILLS

❓ How do I record an action?

Recording actions is easy. The hardest part is thinking out a logical progression of steps to carry out. Once you've done that, do the following:

1. Open an appropriate file.

2. Click the New Action button in the Actions palette, or select New Action from the Actions palette's fly-out menu, shown in Figure 12-1.

3. When the New Action dialog box pops up, apply a name to the action and, if you wish, assign the action to a function key. You can always activate an action from the Actions palette, so all actions do not have to be associated with a function key.

4. You can check the Shift box if you want the SHIFT-(function key) to activate the action.

5. An action can also be assigned a color; you may want to group actions with similar or related functions under a similar color coding.

6. Click the Record button to begin recording your action. The Record button in the Actions palette turns red.

7. Use the commands as you want them recorded. You may select from menus or use keyboard shortcuts.

8. Enter the values you wish into any dialog boxes that pop up in response to your commands. Be sure to click OK when finished with a dialog box to record that command.

9. When finished recording a series of actions, click the Stop button in the Actions palette.

10. The action is ready for use and appears in the Actions palette for immediate use. If you want to store it on your hard disk for use in another session, select Save Actions from the Actions palette's fly-out menu. Photoshop will save the entire set of actions that are active in the Actions palette.

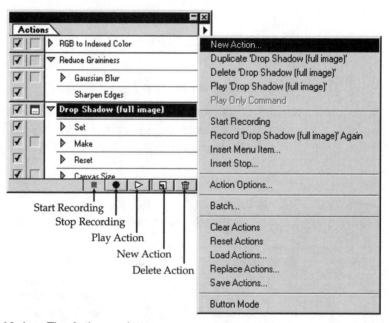

Figure 12-1.   The Actions palette

? **I can't use a tool in my action. What's up?**

You can't record any procedure you carry out with any tool from the toolbox. In some cases, you can use a recordable menu command to perform the same functions, such as fill a selection from Edit | Fill, which operates in the same way as the Paint Bucket. Of course, you must make the selection before running the macro, since making selections (except with the Select menu) is one of the things you can't do with actions.

? **Photoshop won't let me record an action that I know is valid. What's wrong?**

You probably don't have an open file. Photoshop won't let you carry out most commands unless a file is open, so you can't record those actions either. Open a file of the same type you'll be processing when you want to record an action.

? **I can't record certain commands, even though they're menu items I've recorded at other times. What's the problem here?**

Most likely, it's not the Actions feature that's blocking you but rather Photoshop itself, telling you that a particular command is inappropriate. If you want to apply certain color-correction commands to a file, Photoshop won't allow you to record the actions for those corrections if you're working on a grayscale file. It's an easy mistake to make, since it's common to record actions using a dummy or sample file instead of the real thing. Make sure the file you use to record an action is as close as possible to the files that will be used with that action.

? **Is there an easy way to play back only the first step in an action?**

Yes. Select the action, then hold down the COMMAND/CTRL key while clicking the Run button (the right-pointing triangle at the bottom of the Actions palette). You can also select "Play Only" from the Actions palette's fly-out menu. You can also select "Play Only xxx" from the fly-out menu.

GROUPS OF ACTIONS

❓ How can I make more actions visible on the Actions palette at one time?

In Default List View mode, the Actions palette shows a lot more information about an action than you might need to see. That's useful for editing actions, but slows you down when it comes time to apply them. Choose Button Mode from the Actions palette's fly-out menu. The actions will be shown on a set of buttons you can activate by clicking once.

❓ How do I apply a set of actions to every file in a folder?

Just follow these steps:

1. Make sure every file you want to process has been copied to the relevant folder. (Photoshop cannot root around through different levels of folders to find your files; they must all be in a single folder.)

2. If you'd like Photoshop to save the processed version in a different folder, create that folder now.

3. Select Batch from the Actions palette's fly-out menu. The Batch dialog box appears:

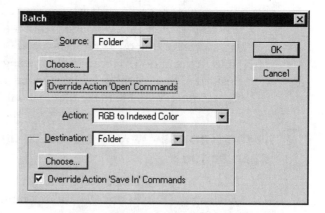

4. In the Source field, choose either Folder or Import. The former option tells Photoshop to use files that are already present on your computer; the latter allows you to acquire a series of images manually using the Import command (most likely using a scanner or digital camera), then automatically apply the rest of the action's commands to each file as it is imported.

5. If you've selected Folder, click the Choose button and find the source folder for the files you want processed.

6. In the Actions area, choose one of the macros you've already recorded from the drop-down list.

7. Select a destination from the Destination drop-down list. Your choices are

➪ **None** Photoshop leaves each file open.

➪ **Save and Close** Photoshop saves and closes the file in the same folder it was opened from.

➪ **Folder** You may choose a second folder to save the processed files in. When you do that, you'll retain both processed and unprocessed versions of the file (this is recommended). Click Choose and locate the destination folder.

Tip: *Any time you choose a folder, you should check the Override button if you want to ensure that files are stored in the destination folder you specify, and not one specified by the Save As command.*

I need some sets of actions for creating transparencies for presentations, and other sets for desktop publishing work. I don't want all my actions visible in the Actions palette at one time. Can I divide them up into sets?

Yes. You can save any set of actions using the Actions palette's fly-out menu (see Figure 12-1). The following commands are available:

➪ **Clear Actions** Deletes all actions. You might want to do this when beginning to create a new set.

➪ **Reset Actions** This restores the default actions Photoshop came with. You can replace your current actions with the default set, or append the default actions to the ones you already have loaded.

➪ **Load Actions** Appends a saved set of actions to the bottom of the list in the Actions palette.

➪ **Replace Actions** Removes the current actions, and replaces them with the set you specify.

➪ **Save Actions** Saves all the actions currently in the Actions palette under a name you specify.

WORKING WITH FILES

I managed to ruin my original file during an ill-fated attempt at recording an action. How can I avoid doing this again?

There is no way to keep Photoshop from executing the commands you are recording. Always use a copy of a file to record an original action, and another copy to test and debug your macro.

I want to apply several actions to all the files in a particular folder. Can I do that?

Yes. Photoshop can nest actions; that is, one action can call another action. Just create a new action that will hold all the macros you want to apply to the files. Use the Batch command for each action. Your finished macro will contain only the instructions to apply the other actions to a batch using the folders you specify.

I want to apply an action to all the files in several different folders. Can I automate this?

Yes. Just nest the same Actions command several times, each time to a different folder. Create a new action, but instead of calling several different actions, apply the same action to different folders.

Photoshop uses the same filename over and over when applying an action to every file in a folder. What's wrong?

When you recorded the action, you probably entered a filename into the Filename field in the Save As dialog box. Don't. Photoshop will then supply an appropriate filename. For example, if your batch of actions tells Photoshop to open every .TIF file in a particular folder, change it to Grayscale mode, then save it in a different folder as a .JPG file. Photoshop will retrieve the filename from each file in turn, make the mode switch, then store the changed file using the same root filename, but with the .JPG extension. You don't need to supply the filename.

Can I record a macro that converts a whole set of files from one format to another?

Yes. To simplify the task, just select File | Preferences | Saving Files and make sure the Append File Extension specification is set to Always. That will force Photoshop to use default file extensions (like .JPG or .PCX) whether you're using a Windows machine (which requires them) or a Macintosh (which considers them optional). Then, just follow these steps:

1. Move all the images in the source format to a separate folder. In this example, our source images will be .PCX files, and we'll convert them to JPEG format.

2. Create a second folder as the destination for your processed files.

3. Open one of the files from the source folder.

4. Click the New Action button at the bottom of the Actions palette. It looks like a page with the lower-left corner folded up.

5. When the New Action dialog box appears, apply a name, such as Convert to JPEG. Then click the Record button.

6. Choose File | Save As.

7. Choose JPEG from the drop-down Save As listing.

8. Click Save to store the file on the hard disk. Note that the old root filename will be used, but the file extension will be changed to .JPG.

9. Click the image's Close box to close it.

10. Click the Stop button to stop recording.

11. Now select the Convert to JPEG action and use the Batch choice from the fly-out menu, and select source and destination folders as described earlier in this chapter.

ADVANCED SKILLS

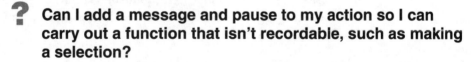 **Can I add a message and pause to my action so I can carry out a function that isn't recordable, such as making a selection?**

Yes. Select Insert Stop from the Actions palette's fly-out menu. The Record Stop dialog box will pop up:

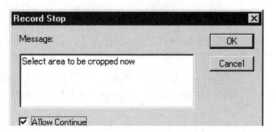

You can type in the message to be displayed, such as "Select area to be cropped now." Keep in mind:

⇨ If the Allow Continue box is checked, two buttons will appear in the Message dialog box: Continue and Stop. Clicking the Continue button tells Photoshop to go on with the rest of the macro. Clicking the Stop button stops the macro completely, but it can be restarted from that point by clicking the Play button (the right-pointing triangle) at the bottom of the Actions palette.

⇨ If the Allow Continue box is not checked, Photoshop will stop and allow you to perform the function. The only way the action will resume is when the Play button is clicked.

❓ I always want to apply a command to the second layer from the bottom. Can I do this?

The best way to do that is to record OPTION/ALT-SHIFT-[(left square bracket) as the first command, which selects the Background or bottom layer. Then record OPTION/ALT-SHIFT-] (right square bracket) twice to move up two layers.

❓ My action applies a command to the wrong layer of an image. How can I avoid that?

You may have recorded the action using an image with no layers at all, or a layered image with the bottom, Background layer selected. Since it's tricky to select a particular layer with an action, it's a good idea to count on performing a command on the Background layer. You can press OPTION/ALT-SHIFT-[(left square bracket) when you record the action. This selects the Background layer of both layered and nonlayered images.

❓ Can I create a macro that reduces the image size of a batch of images to a particular size?

Yes. You already know how to use the Batch command, so all you need to do is create an action that reduces the image to the desired size. Just follow these steps:

1. Click the New Action button at the bottom of the Actions palette. It looks like a page with the lower-left corner folded up.

2. When the New Action dialog box appears, call the macro Reduce to 640.

3. Click the Record button.

4. Choose Image | Image Size.

5. When the Image Size dialog box pops up, make sure Pixels is selected as the unit, and type in 640 as the width.

6. Click OK. The image will be resampled and resized to 640 pixels wide. If the image was already 640 pixels wide, nothing will happen. Smaller images will be enlarged to 640 pixels; larger ones will be reduced to that size. The height will be changed proportionately (e.g., an 800 × 600-pixel image will become 640 × 480 pixels).

7. Click the Stop button to stop recording the macro.

? I want to Hide or Show Rulers, Guides, and Grids all in one step. Can a macro do this?

Yes, this is a perfect application for an action. Just record the keystrokes for Show/Hide Rulers (COMMAND/CTRL-R), Show/Hide Guides (COMMAND/CTRL-; (semicolon)), or Show/Hide Grid (COMMAND/CTRL-" (quotation mark)). If you like, you can follow these three commands in your action with the Snap to Guides (SHIFT-COMMAND/CTRL-;) and Snap to Grids (SHIFT-COMMAND/CTRL-") commands (these choices are available only if the guides and grids are not hidden).

? I'd like to apply several filters to a group of images. Can I do this?

That's easy, too. Just start recording and apply any of the filters you like. You might want to apply the Dust & Scratches filter to reduce dust on an image, then soften it further with the Diffuse Glow filter.

? I can't seem to record rotation in an action. What's up?

Photoshop can't record transformations on a selection, unless you use Numeric Transform and type in the amount of rotation you want. The Numeric Transform feature can be also used to perform other changes that are otherwise unrecordable, such as scaling and skewing a selection. (Remember to make the selection before you run the action.)

REVISING YOUR ACTIONS

? I want to add one more command to an action. How can I do that?

Select the command before the one you want to insert, then choose Insert Menu Item from the Actions palette's fly-out menu. Choose the command you want to insert.

? Can I edit an action without re-recording it from scratch?

Yes. You may highlight any command in an action, then delete it, copy it, play the macro from that point, play only that step, or re-record only that step. Editing an action is an efficient way of fixing a "bug" in a macro or creating a new macro that differs only slightly from the old one.

? Can I change the values I've used for the dialog boxes in an action without re-recording the whole action from scratch?

Yes, select the action you want to modify and choose Record Action Again from the Actions palette's fly-out menu. Photoshop will run the action, pausing at each dialog box so you can enter new values, which will replace the old values.

? I want to change only the values for one of the dialog boxes, not all of them. Can I re-record just part of an action?

Certainly. Click the triangle next to the action that contains the command you want to modify. The triangle will point downward and show a list of all the commands in that action. Double-click the command you want to change. The dialog box will pop up. Enter the new value, and click OK.

? I'd like to create a modified version of an action without losing the original version. Can I do this?

Easily. Hold down the OPTION/ALT key, click on the action (or even a separate command) that you'd like to duplicate, and drag it to a new location on the Actions palette. Release the mouse button, and edit the duplicated action/command as required. You can also select Duplicate Action or Duplicate Command from the Actions palette fly-out menu, or drag the action/command to the New Action button at the bottom of the Actions palette.

Printing and Setup

Answer Topics!

PRINTING

? **When I print out my Photoshop images, an objectionable pattern of dots appears. What's gone wrong?**

Those are the halftone dots used by your printer to simulate continuous gray (or color) tones. You may have set the resolution of your printer too low in its dialog box, or perhaps your printer doesn't have a high enough resolution to reproduce images using small enough dots. Check the Printer Setup dialog box for your printer, and make sure it's not set in Draft mode, or another low-resolution mode such as 150 dpi. To get the best output from Photoshop, you'll need to use the highest resolution available—at least 300 dpi or higher.

Halftoning Images

Most desktop printers and printing presses can lay down nothing but solid ink or toner. To reproduce fine gradations of color or gray, the image is divided into dots or pixels with the proper mixture of black or colored ink/toner and white space, which the eye blends into the intermediate tone. For printing systems, this is done by varying the size of the dot itself. For example, for grayscale images, a very large black dot, which fills its allotted space, is seen as black. A so-called 50 percent dot, which covers half the area, will be seen as 50 percent gray as the human eye blurs the black space and the white space together. If you look at a newspaper halftone with a magnifier, you'll see that large and small black dots do make up the graytones you perceive in the printed picture.

On a printing press, the size of the dot can be varied continuously. On a desktop printer, individual dots corresponding to the resolution of the printer (e.g., 300 dpi, 600 dpi, 1200 dpi) are used to build up the varying dots you can produce on a press. The fewer pixels used to make up one of the superdots, the fewer the different tones available.

To understand this, consider a cell that measures two pixels on a side. You could leave that cell empty (white) or fill all four pixels. The cell could also contain one, two, or three dark pixels in between. That adds up to five different distinct tones, and four different gray levels, plus white. A cell 16 pixels on a side allows 256 variations in tone, but cuts the effective resolution of a 600 dpi printer to roughly 37.5 lines per inch. In practice, modern printers can achieve much more detail than this by using special hardware features that allow varying the size and placement of individual dots.

Color reproduction is much the same as grayscale printing, except that four different sets of dots are printed—cyan, magenta, yellow, and black—each color angled slightly to keep them from printing on top of each other.

? Can I create halftones within Photoshop?

Yes, you can—at least for grayscale images—although in most cases you won't need to. For example, any time you print to a PostScript printer, a continuous tone image will be output at a resolution appropriate to that device. However, if you're working with a non-PostScript printer or want to use special halftone effects for artistic purposes, you can do it. Just follow these steps:

1. Choose Image | Mode | Bitmap.

2. When the Bitmap dialog box appears, check the Halftone Screen button and click OK. The Halftone Screen dialog box will pop up:

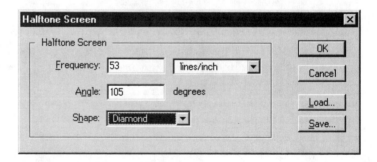

3. You can accept the default line frequency settings and angle, and choose from Round, Diamond, Ellipse, Line, Square, or Cross halftone dot shapes. Figure 13-1 shows how the image will look with each different setting.

4. Click OK to apply the screen.

? Once I create a halftone image, most of the layer options are grayed out. What's wrong?

Many Photoshop functions won't operate on a black/white bitmap. You'll find that only Transform and its rotational functions are active in the Layer menu. There's a good reason for that. When you resize or perform most other manipulations on halftoned images, the dots

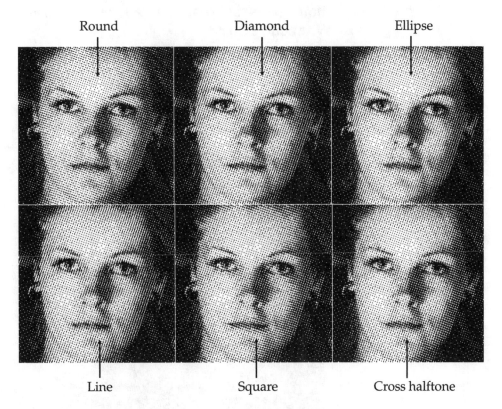

Round   Diamond   Ellipse

Line   Square   Cross halftone

Figure 13-1.   Examples of round, diamond, ellipse, line, square, and cross halftone dot shapes

become distorted and the image no longer looks good. Photoshop protects you from those problems by disabling potentially troublesome functions.

I want to skew a halftoned image for a special effect. Can I regain the layer functions Photoshop disables for a black/white bitmap image?

Yes, there's a workaround. You'll need to convert the image back to grayscale, using Image | Mode | Grayscale. When the Grayscale dialog box pops up, type in **1** for the Size Ratio field. You'll end up with a high-contrast, grayscale image of the black/white bitmap; you can perform any function possible on a grayscale image with the new version.

I'd like a halftone effect that uses a less regular-looking pattern. What can I do?

Convert the image to a black/white bitmap using Diffusion dither. You'll end up with an image like the one in Figure 13-2.

Figure 13-2.   Diffusion dither

I want to specify the halftone effect when I print an image, but don't want to convert it to a bitmap first. What can I do?

Photoshop's File | Page Setup menu has a Screen button, which produces a Halftone Screen dialog box that looks like this:

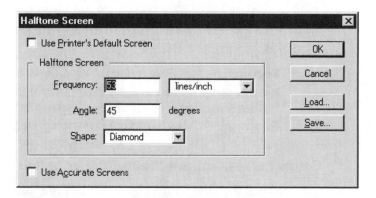

Normally, the Use Printer's Default Screen box is checked. Unmark this box, and you can select a line frequency, angle, and dot shape from the pull-down lists. If you're outputting to a high-res device equipped with PostScript Level 2, Level 3, or an Emerald controller, you can check the Use Accurate Screens option to ensure the optimum angles and screen rulings for high-resolution printing.

I scanned in an image that was already halftoned, and now I need to halftone it again. Terrible patterns result. Can I fix this?

You'll get an effect called moiré when you try to screen an image that has already been screened. Try blurring the image slightly to reduce the visibility of the screen. The Dust & Scratches filter often works. Some get better results with grayscale scans by capturing a full-color image, since the profusion of dots seems to blur together more easily.

? **I'd like to print some images and would like a border around each one. Can I add a border without editing the image in Photoshop to include one?**

Yes. Just choose File | Page Setup (or press SHIFT-COMMAND/CTRL-P) and click the Border button. You can choose a border up to .15 inches, 3.5mm, or 10 points wide in the Border dialog box that pops up.

? **I'm told I need to add registration marks to my hard copies. What are they?**

Registration marks are targets printed outside the image area of your file that can be used for aligning color separations, duotones, or other images that must be precisely lined up. Add them by checking the Registration Marks box in the Print Setup dialog box.

? **How can I compare the output from two different printers?**

When working with a grayscale file, print the file on each printer, checking off the Calibration Bars option in the Page Setup dialog box each time. The calibration bar printed below the image includes an 11-step grayscale, representing 0, 10, 20, 30, 40, 50, 60, 70, 80, 90, and 100 percent gray values. You can compare the bars from both prints to see how each printer reproduces that particular image.

If you're printing a CMYK image, a gradient tint bar is printed on the left side of each cyan, magenta, or yellow channel, and a progressive color bar is printed to the right.

? **How do I print out individual channels of a CMYK image?**

In the File | Print dialog box, check the Print Separations box. Individual pages for each of the color separations will be printed, plus a fourth for the black separation, which will have the 11-step grayscale below it rather than the tint and color bars at left and right.

? **I want to trim finished pages right at the edges of my image. How can I specify where the images are to be cut?**

Use File | Page Setup and check the Corner Crop Marks box. Lines will be printed outside the image area you can use as a guideline to trim the printed images.

? Even with crop marks, I manage to include some non-image area in my trimmed photos. Can I place the crop marks inside the image rather than right at its edge?

What you want is called a bleed, where the image goes right up to the edge of the trimmed piece. Use File | Page Setup, then check the Corner Crop Marks box and click the Bleed button. You can move the crop marks into the image by an increment you specify, up to about .125 inches.

? Can I print out a negative version of my image?

Yes, you can, without editing the image itself—and you might even have to do this when you're outputting a color separation that will be printed directly to film. Just use File | Page Setup, and check the Negative box.

? I want to label my images so I can identify them more easily. Does Photoshop let me include an identifying caption with my printouts?

Yes. One little-known feature of Photoshop is the ability to add information about an image using the File | File Info dialog box, shown in Figure 13.3. Add a caption, then check off the Caption box in the Page Setup dialog box; your caption will be printed below the image. Uncheck the box when you want a copy that doesn't include the caption. Under Windows, you can only add captions to Photoshop, TIFF and JPEG files; Mac owners can add this information to any format image.

? What other information can I add to the File Info about each image?

There are tons of fields in this dialog box. You can select six different sections from the drop-down list. They include the following:

⇨ **Caption**   A caption of up to 2,000 characters can be entered; a 32-character Caption Writer identification; a headline of up to 255 characters, and special instructions for that image up to an additional 255 characters.

⇨ **Keywords** You can type in a list of keywords that can be used to search your files for a particular match. Each keyword can be up to 31 characters long.

⇨ **Categories** This allows entering a three-character category code, additional subcategories, and a priority listing. Some organizations, such as the Associated Press, maintain a list of codes that can be used as categories. You're free to make up your own, if you like.

⇨ **Credits** You can edit up to 32 characters each for byline, byline title, credit, and source.

⇨ **Origin** In this section, you may enter information about where the image was made.

⇨ **Copyright & URL** In this dialog box, you may enter a copyright notice and an URL to a Web site with more information about the image, if applicable.

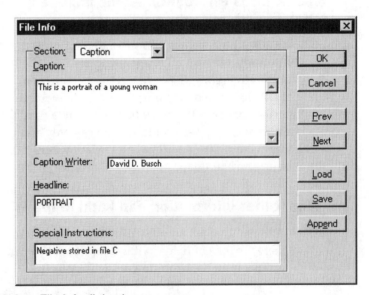

Figure 13-3.   File Info dialog box

CALIBRATING

? **My images look great on my screen, but when I take them to a colleague's computer or try to print them out, they look too dark. The hard copies look terrible, too. What's wrong?**

Your symptoms could be caused by several problems, all having their roots in the calibration of your monitor. First, many Photoshop users don't bother to calibrate their systems when they first install the program. They may be unfamiliar with the requirements of publishing because they've never had to reproduce their work, or they may have created only desktop presentations and other noncritical work exclusively. Second, monitors can change their brightness/darkness and color balance with age, a process called *drifting*, or someone may have used your computer and fiddled with the controls to make the image look better to them. A monitor's output can change simply by moving it from one location to another. You'll be happier with your results if you take the time now to calibrate your system. If you're using a Windows machine, calibration can standardize the way your images are displayed. On both Macintoshes and Windows workstations, calibration affects the relationships of color and density when images are printed out. If you do critical prepress work for offset printing, you'll want to use a hardware calibration tool, such as those from Radius or Daystar. Otherwise, you can do a fair job of calibrating your monitor by eye, using the File | Color Settings | Monitor Setup dialog box.

? **How do I calibrate my monitor?**

Make sure your monitor has been turned on for at least 30 minutes to allow it to stabilize. Then, use the File | Color Settings | Monitor Setup dialog box, shown in Figure 13-4. Note that the dialog box differs between Macintosh and Windows systems; the Windows box has an additional Calibrate button not available on the Mac—because the Mac already has systemwide monitor calibration. For both platforms, you need to provide the following information:

⇨ **Monitor** Here, if you're very, very lucky, you'll find the name of your monitor in the drop-down list and can select it. Photoshop

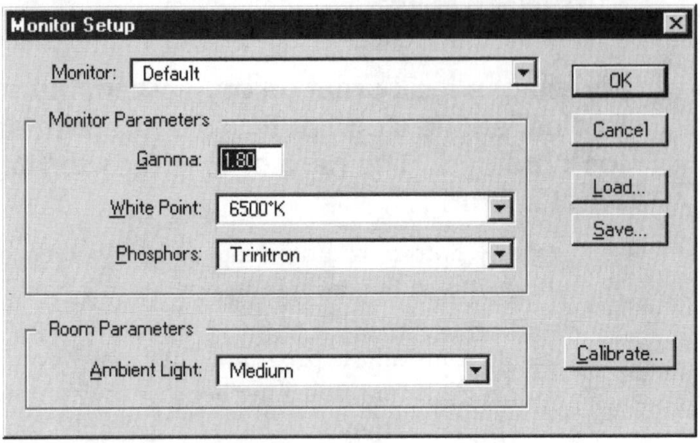

Figure 13-4.   The Monitor setup dialog box

Calibrating Your Monitor

Calibration is the process of adjusting a device to meet a known standard. If you're working only with RGB images, calibration doesn't have a great effect on how images are displayed (with one exception for Windows machines, discussed in the following paragraph). Photoshop takes the RGB values of your image, translates them into a signal your RGB monitor can display, and paints the image on your screen.

Under Windows only, however, you can adjust the gamma (lightness/darkness of the middle tones) for the display of RGB images. If you don't take this step, your images can appear to be too light or too dark on other Windows setups. The reason why Photoshop doesn't need to adjust gamma on the Macintosh is that Macs already have a systemwide gamma correction system that allows adjusting a monitor once for *all* the applications you run.

On both Macs and PCs, monitor calibration has the greatest impact on how images appear and are printed once they are converted to another color model, such as CMYK. When RGB images are transformed into CMYK, calibration ensures that they are displayed on your monitor as close as possible to the way they will be printed.

includes a list of a few popular monitors and can use some default settings for them if yours is listed. However, monitors vary quite a bit, so you're usually better off selecting Other.

⇨ **Gamma** If you have a Macintosh, fill in the system-level gamma setting you used when you set up your Macintosh's monitor. It will usually be 1.80 if your output will be printed. A higher gamma can be used if your destination is an RGB source, such as a desktop presentation on a video monitor. Windows users need to set up a gamma value for Photoshop, using the Calibrate button, which we'll look at shortly.

⇨ **White Point** This is the hue the monitor uses to display a neutral white. Set this to the color temperature of the light source that will be used to evaluate your printed output. Color viewing lights at print shops in the United States have standardized on 5,000K; elsewhere in the world, 6,500K is used.

⇨ **Phosphors** This setting specifies the colors used by a monitor to represent a fully saturated red, green, or blue. If you find your monitor on the drop-down list, select it. For critical applications, you can ask the manufacturer for xy chromacity values for your monitor, or use a hardware calibrator that actually measures these values. For most, the Trinitron choice will do a good enough job.

⇨ **Ambient Light** These apply changes that adjust Photoshop's output to your screen and printed material to compensate for the brightness of your room surroundings.

⇨ **Calibrate (Windows only)** Click this button to produce a dialog box that allows you to visually calibrate your monitor.

Then follow these steps:

1. Move the Gamma slider until the two sets of gray boxes match in tone.

2. Hold a piece of white paper next to your monitor.

3. Click the White Pt radio button, then drag the Red, Green, and Blue sliders until the white areas on the monitor (such as the gray step scale in the dialog box) match the paper stock.

4. Click the Balance button, and drag the sliders until the gray areas are neutral, without any color casts.

5. Click the Black Pt button, and drag the sliders until no color cast appears in the darker areas of the grayscale step strip.

6. After you've made all these changes, evaluate the gamma and color balance once more to make sure they are still calibrated properly.

7. Press OK when finished to return to the Monitor Setup dialog box.

 Tip: *Click the Load and Save buttons in the Calibrate and Monitor Setup dialog boxes to save your current calibration and setup values, or to retrieve an existing set for reuse.*

How can I calibrate my system for output?

This is a complex topic with no quick answers; entire books have been written on prepress topics. I'll provide just a brief introduction here. You'll want to know that Photoshop has three more calibration/setup tools you can use to adjust the system for output to CMYK printing systems, such as offset presses or your desktop color printer. You'll find the most critical application is usually offset printing, because the stakes are so high: even a short press run can cost thousands of dollars. The tools you use are

⇨ **Printing Inks Setup** This dialog box adjusts Photoshop so it represents on the screen the way your image will look when printed, as you can see here:

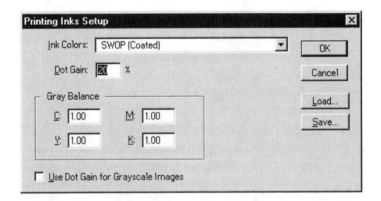

You'll probably want several versions of these settings, to represent each of the output paths you use. Specify the Ink Colors you desire. (In the U.S., SWOP, or Specifications for Web Offset Publications, prints on coated paper; other choices are available.)

You can also adjust for dot gain, which is the amount that halftone dots spread on the press due to absorption by the paper. Amount of dot gain is determined by measuring proofs with a densitometer; your print shop may be able to provide a value for you.

⇨ **Separation Setup** This controls the amount of ink placed on a page, plus the amount of black ink that will be used to replace equal amounts of the other ink colors. This saves ink costs and produces better output, because black ink is always snappier than the often brownish-blacks produced by "composite (cyan-magenta-yellow) blacks." There are two ways to generate blacks: Gray Component Replacement (GCR), which replaces equal amounts of cyan, magenta, and yellow with black in the overall image area; and Undercolor Removal (UCR), which replaces combinations of those colors only in neutral areas, allowing shadows to retain a bit more detail.

⇨ **Separation Tables** This dialog box allows you to build Printing Inks and Separation Setups tables using ICC Profiles (under Windows) or Apple Color Sync (Macintosh). Click the Build Tables button, then choose your printer from the drop-down list. You may need to contact your printer vendor to obtain a profile for your particular output device.

Photoshop on the Web

Answer Topics!

Photoshop on the Web @ a Glance

Graphics built the World Wide Web. Without images created by products like Photoshop, the Internet would probably have remained a text-based academic and scientific backwater. But there's more to creating good Web graphics than simply knowing how to use Photoshop. The Internet has some special requirements. Without understanding what those requirements are, the best Web pages are doomed to be more of a liability than an asset. Learning a few simple rules can help you create pages that sparkle with clean, lean, compelling images that rivet visitors' attention.

⇨ You should first learn how to create the smallest, easiest to download images you can. GIF files are great for images that have type or sharp edges, while JPEG files give smaller files and more colors at the cost of some sharpness.

⇨ Image maps are clickable graphics on a page that can send a visitor to another URL on the site, an anchor on the page, or to another site entirely. Photoshop can provide you with the coordinate information you need to set up separate image map files.

⇨ Transparent GIFs allow images to float on the page, while animated GIFs add the illusion of motion to your Web pages.

IMAGE SIZE AND QUALITY

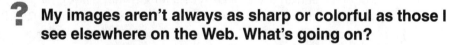 **My images aren't always as sharp or colorful as those I see elsewhere on the Web. What's going on?**

You may just be using the wrong image format—using GIF where JPEG would work better, or vice versa. Learn when each kind of image should be used and you can have better images in seconds:

⇨ GIF supports only 256 or fewer colors, but makes for excellent display on all Web browsers, regardless of the color capabilities of the visitor's monitor, and produces fairly small file sizes. Its lossless compression scheme retains all the sharpness of the original and tends to be best for images like charts and graphs that contain hard edges. In addition, GIFs can be made transparent to float on a background, interleaved so they can be progressively revealed as files download, and animated to add action to your Web page.

⇨ JPEG handles 16.8 million colors without breaking stride, so it's a good choice for reproducing full-color images. It offers even smaller file sizes than GIF, although the resulting images may not be as sharp. However, image editors let you trade off sharpness against file size to produce the best compromise. At present, not all browsers support progressive (interleaved) or transparent JPEG, so if you want to use those two features and remain as compatible with as many potential visitors as possible, you may want to stick with the GIF equivalents.

? **Other Web pages load fairly quickly even though they are studded with lots of graphics. My pages have only a few images, but still take too long to download. How can I speed things up?**

You may need to use Photoshop's Crop feature to select only the most important part of the image for your Web page, or the Image Resize feature to squeeze the entire image into smaller dimensions. Bigger is not better when it comes to Web graphics: even well-intentioned Web page designers sometimes don't take the simple steps needed to reduce the size of their images. One common mistake is to make images as large as possible to make them impressive looking on the visitor's browser.

Unfortunately, you have no control over the size of the browser window used to navigate your Web site. Many visitors will have screens with 640×480 pixel resolution, and part of that real estate is taken up by the browser's interface. Even those with 1024×768-pixel screens may have sized their browser window to a smaller size so they can view more than one application on the screen at once. So, the largest dimensions a single image can be may be 600×400 pixels on the wildly optimistic end of the scale, and should usually be much smaller than that. You'll get the best results with images that are no larger than 128×128 to 256×256 pixels, and even faster loading with buttons and thumbnails as small as 32×32 pixels. One of these tips might help you:

⇨ Click the Info palette's tab to make it visible. Then select the most important part of your image with the Rectangular Marquee tool. You'll be able to see the pixel dimensions of your selection in the lower-right corner of the Info palette. If the selected portion is a reasonable size, choose Image | Crop and reduce its size to the selection.

⇨ If you've selected only the portion of the image you can't live without and it's still too large, go ahead and crop it to eliminate the extraneous image information. Then use Image | Image Size and reduce the image to an even smaller size. For example, if you've cropped a large graphic to 480×320 pixels, you may be able to reduce it by half in each direction, to 240×160, cutting the dimensions by 75 percent in the process.

⇨ Don't be afraid to type in a specific pixel size for height or width, rather than selecting an "even" reduction increment. Photoshop does more than a good enough job of interpolation for Web graphics, which needn't have extra-high resolution in the first place. If you'd like an image 150 pixels wide, enter that value into the Image | Image Size dialog box, no matter how wide it is to start. You can always use Filter | Sharpen | Sharpen to improve the quality a bit.

? **I've made my images smaller, but they are still taking forever to load. Is there anything else I can do?**

Dimensions alone don't govern how large an image file will be. The number of colors in the image and the kind of compression used in saving the file can also make important contributions. A largish 256×256-pixel image with 16.7 million colors can amount to almost 200,000 bytes in raw form. Even under ideal conditions, it might take a visitor a minute or two to download an image that size. Even the most tolerant Web cruiser would probably have clicked the browser's Back button and moved on to a less time-consuming Web page at another site. After you've reduced the dimensions of your image to a reasonable size, make sure the file size is as small as possible?

To reduce file size after you've cut the dimensions to a reasonable level, follow one of these tips:

⇨ Use the minimum number of colors required to present your image. If your picture has just 64 colors, a GIF with only those colors will be smaller and load faster. You learned in Chapter 10 how to create files with the Exact palette.

⇨ If your image doesn't have text or lines that demand the bit of extra sharpness that GIF format affords, use JPEG instead. While GIF uses a lossless compression scheme that preserves all the information in an image, JPEG can discard redundant information and squeeze an image down 8 to 11 times, or even more.

❔ What's the ideal size for Web graphics?

The ideal size varies with the subject matter and its importance to your Web's message. Here are some simple rules of thumb you can use:

⇨ Try to keep each Web graphic no *larger* than 25–50K, especially if you plan to include a lot of them on a page. Things like rules and buttons can often be trimmed to 7K or smaller. Cropping or squeezing images with a bit more compression may be all you need.

⇨ Limit each page to a total of 200K or less in graphics.

⇨ Confine the heavy-duty images to certain pages, and provide your visitors with a warning before they enter them.

⇨ Include only enough graphics on your main page to entice visitors into your gallery of larger-scale images.

⇨ Small, thumbnail images can be placed on a page and used as a preview of a larger graphic image. You can place the full-size image on another page, or have it displayed when the visitor clicks on the thumbnail. That way, a visual clue is provided that helps the user decide whether to proceed with the full download.

❔ I tried using JPEG format to make my files smaller, but they didn't turn out as small as I expected. Have I done something wrong?

Photoshop allows you to choose the amount of compression to use when saving files. When you select the JPEG format and click the Save button in the Save As dialog box, the JPEG Options box pops up:

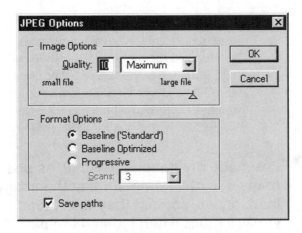

In the Image Options area of the dialog, you can use the slider to select quality values from 0 to 10; a value of 0 produces the maximum amount of compression, but the worst relative quality. A value of 10 generates the best image, but squeezes your file very little.

As an experiment, I took a very large 1400 × 1000-pixel 24-bit color file and saved it in the TIF format using the lossless LZW compression scheme Photoshop uses. The file in that form was about 3.3MB in size. Then, I saved it as a JPEG file using the maximum quality setting of 10. The file was squeezed down by almost 67 percent to 1.3MB. Finally, saving the file using the minimum quality/maximum compression setting of 0, I was able to produce an 82K file—more than 40 times smaller than the original. Yet, the image was still acceptable for Web use.

? What quality setting should I use in saving my JPEG files?

If the sharpness of your image is very important, try a setting of 7. Most noncritical images can be squeezed down further with a setting of 5 to 6. You can try settings of 4 or lower to see if the image is acceptable. For many kinds of images that don't contain important small details, the lower quality settings will be fine.

? How can I preview what my results will look like at each setting?

Unfortunately, Photoshop doesn't have a JPEG preview mode in its current release. Other image editors have such a feature, so expect to see it in the next version of Photoshop. The workaround is to save an image file several times, each time using a different quality setting. Then, load all the files into Photoshop and evaluate them in Zoom mode, and then at the size you'll be using for the finished image. Figure 14-1 shows a close-up of a sample image in compressed TIF format; JPEG format with a quality setting of 10 (on the left); and JPEG format with a quality setting of 0 (on the right).

?   I've made my images as small as possible, but visitors to my site still complain that the images take forever to load, or, worse, that they won't load at all. Everything worked great when I tested the pages on my computer. What's wrong?

Photoshop is probably not to blame here. No matter how picture-perfect its design, a page may hang if one or more of the images referenced in it inadvertently becomes unavailable to a visitor's browser. Instead of just skipping over the errant graphic, the browser may pause interminably waiting for it to download. What happens next? Your visitor hits the Back button and vanishes for greener and faster-loading pastures.

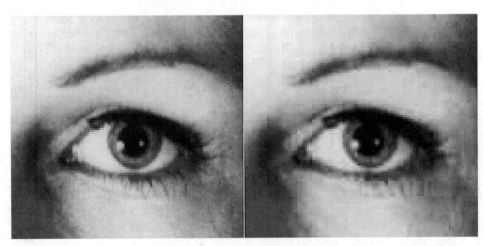

Figure 14-1.   JPEG qualities 10 (left) and 0 (right)

The reasons why an image goes AWOL aren't important. Perhaps there's an error in the <IMG SRC> tag in your HTML page, or you put the graphic in the wrong subdirectory. The problem can be as simple as a Web counter image on another server that happens to be running slow.

The best solution is to always, *always* include the height and width of a graphic image, using the <IMG SRC> tag's HEIGHT= and WIDTH= parameters. While most automated HTML authoring programs do this for you, it's an easy item to forget when you're editing a page, or hand coding from scratch. When the dimensions of the image are specified in the tag, the browser leaves space for it and moves on to download the rest of the page. If the image never shows up, your visitor sees a Placeholder icon, but can view the rest of the page.

WEB IMAGE COLOR

? Visitors complain of bizarre color shifts, funny speckles, and other strange effects that never show up when I view my Web pages. What's wrong?

If you're using Photoshop, you probably work with a 24-bit color display. Not everyone has a 24-bit display card like the one you used when preparing your Web graphics, or that you used when reviewing them once you've uploaded the graphics to your Web site. But guess what can happen when a visitor with an 8-bit, 256-color display visits your page and encounters those million-color JPEG images? Your visitor's system creates a palette of colors that *can* be displayed, and it's likely that many of the hues in your carefully crafted images will get tossed by the wayside. If you have more than one image on a page, even the "optimized" palette produced for the first one won't necessarily suit subsequent graphics. The result? Color shifts. Even 256-color images aren't immune to this process: there's no guarantee (or even likelihood) that all the graphics on a page happen to contain the same 256 colors. The solution has two parts: whenever possible, use the browser-safe palette of 216 Web colors built into Photoshop in the Indexed Color dialog box. If you must use a full 256-color palette, try to use the same palette for all the images on a page.

❓ How can I choose what palette to use?

You can only present 16.7 million color images using JPEG format; JPEG often gives the best overall set of colors, at the cost of some image quality. However, you can convert images that don't need more than 256 colors to 8-bit format. The trick is not just changing to 256 colors, but converting to the *right* 256 colors. What you don't want is an equal representation of all the colors in the spectrum. In an image of a human face, for example, an equal spread would give you far too many blues, but not enough pinks, reds, and browns to represent a living person. We looked at converting full-color images to 256-hue Indexed Color in Chapter 10.

As we noted then, Adobe Photoshop lets you fine-tune the palettes or *color lookup tables* (CLUTs) they work with. To be on the safe side, select a Web-oriented palette/CLUT if your software offers that choice. In that mode, the image editor will convert the image using a standardized palette of 216 specific colors most often used by Web browsers. However, if your image contains an atypical range of colors, a palette of the most frequently used colors in your particular image (a so-called *adaptive palette*) may be your best choice.

The second piece of the solution is to try to use the same palette for as many images as possible. Photoshop, for example, allows you to apply a previously defined CLUT to the next and subsequent images being converted. Even if a particular palette isn't the best one, at least the colors won't shift when several graphics are displayed together on a page.

❓ How do I use the Web palette option?

Just select Image | Mode | Indexed Color, and select Web from the drop-down palette list. Photoshop applies a 216-color palette of the hues common to Web browsers when viewing a page in 256-color mode. (The other 40 colors are reserved for the use of the system for its interface features such as menus, dialog boxes, scroll bars, etc.)

❓ Can I give visitors a preview of what an image will look like?

There are two ways to do this. You can save the image as an interlaced GIF file, using the File | Export | GIF89a Export command. Check the Interlaced box and the file will be saved as alternating sets of lines.

The browser will load one set first, producing a low-resolution image the visitor can view, then load the interlaced lines to produce the full-resolution image.

The second way is to save two versions of an image from Photoshop, a large, high-resolution version, and a smaller, lower-resolution version. Then, use the IMG SRC and LOWSRC commands in your HTML code. A browser will load the LOWSRC image first and display it while the full-resolution image is being loaded. This works for JPEG files, which Photoshop can save in Progressive format (similar to Interlaced), but not all browsers support JPEG files interlaced in this way.

? Visitors complain about not being able to navigate my pages. Have I done something wrong?

It's likely that you've concentrated too heavily on creating cool graphics with Photoshop and haven't considered that there are still thousands of Web cruisers using older text-based browsers that can't display graphics. Still more visitors to your site may have simply turned off automatic downloading of graphics because they're fed up with sites that are filled with large, slow-to-load images. These folks may not have a clue about what's really on your page, especially if you've put all the descriptive information to your links on clickable images or image maps that they can't see. (A discussion of image maps is next.)

There are two things you can do to head off letter bombs from those not equipped (or inclined) to appreciate your Photoshop graphics. First, if you use a clickable image or an image map as a link to another page or URL, make sure you also have a text-based link somewhere on the page. You can include it as a caption right under the graphic, or group all your text links at the bottom of the page.

Second, get into the habit of using the ALT= parameter with your <IMG SRC> tags, and make sure that the description is useful. If you create a button that reads, "Click Here for Page 2" or a picture of the Taj Mahal on your page, you should include "ALT=[Click Here for Page 2]" and "ALT=Photo of Taj Mahal." Your consideration will reward even graphics-capable visitors. Should your photo have no caption, the helpful label will pop up when the visitor's mouse cursor passes over the image.

IMAGE MAPS

 ### What are image maps? Can I create them with Photoshop?

Yes, Photoshop can be used to create image maps. These are graphics with embedded "hot spots" visitors click to activate a hyperlink, and can be the foundation of sleek, sinewy, and highly intuitive Web pages. Why rely on boring old buttons or text links, when you can incorporate multiple gateways to your site in an eye-catching graphic?

An image map is a graphic that has been divided into areas or regions a browser or Web server can recognize, using visible or invisible "borders" you define using a simple x-y coordinate system. An image map could use an actual map as a graphic—say, an outline of the United States, with each state or region corresponding to a hyperlink to your company's sales information for that state. Or, the boundaries within the image map can be more amorphous. A medical Web page might have an anatomical chart that links to other pages whenever a visitor clicks in the neighborhood of a particular structure.

 ### Are there any things I should be aware of when using image maps?

Like chocolate and fast sports cars, there's a downside to all the excitement. Clickable image maps are perhaps the most underused, least well understood, and most often badly applied graphic elements you're likely to find on a Web page. Even so, you can put these graphics to work for you effectively if you follow a few guidelines.

Reasonably sized image maps—under 50K or so—can make your site easier to navigate. A humongous graphic, whether used as a map or not, can convert a page into a nightmare that invites a Back button bailout even before the image completes its creep down a visitor's screen. Image maps can also be complex to create, since the information about the hot spots is not embedded in the Photoshop file itself but, rather, in a separate text file that stores the coordinates of the hot spots within the image.

What makes a good image map?

First of all, you want an alluring graphic that attracts visitors' attention. It should convey some information about the links nestled inside the image, and, most importantly, look enough like an image map to invite clicking. Visitors find nothing more frustrating than click-worthy images that contain no links, or hidden image maps that are stumbled upon by accident. An actual map, a dashboard full of buttons, a control panel, or similar graphics all make good image maps. Abstract shapes, unlabeled images, and large files that take a long time to download are poor choices for this technique. And don't forget to include text links for nonimage-capable browsers: if all your links are embedded in image maps, even a Netscape Navigator user who has shut off image display will be lost on your page.

? How do image maps work?

No mystical HTML incantations are needed to invoke this magic. The secret is in a simple ASCII file that contains little more than the coordinates of points defining any regions you want and the URL or link to be activated when a visitor clicks inside that area. A typical map file might look like this one:

```
<MAP NAME="usa">
<AREA SHAPE="rect" COORDS="245,355, 385,355"
HREF="colorado.htm">
<AREA SHAPE="polygon" COORDS="201,331,281,339,291,283,
359,334,294,357,198,358" HREF="ohio.htm">
</MAP>
```

This file creates an image map named "usa" and defines two areas within it—a rectangular region suitable for a regularly shaped area like the state of Colorado, and a six-sided polygon that hugs the borders of Ohio. Once the image map is deposited in the proper location (which can vary, depending on whether you're creating a client-side or server-side image map), an HTML reference in your Web page, such as the following, displays the graphic on your page and points toward the ASCII map file. The ALT tag is a courtesy for those viewing your page without graphics, as mentioned earlier in this chapter:

```
<IMG SRC="usa.gif" BORDER=0 ALT="USA Image Map"
USEMAP=#usa">
```

❓ What are client-side and server-side image maps?

Before the dust from the browser wars settled, the only practical way to accommodate the plethora of WWW client software out there was through server-side image maps, which monitor when you've clicked on a hot spot in a downloaded graphic and handle requests for the URLs and links specified.

You must include a CGI script on the server, have access to its cgi-bin directory, and adhere to either the CERN or NCSA conventions for defining an image map, depending on your server. (The syntax is similar, but not identical.) When a host is overloaded—and frequent access to maps can contribute to the overload—the response time can slow to a crawl.

Client-side image maps, in contrast, require nothing more than a map file on your site, appropriate HTML code to access the map, and that visitors have Netscape Navigator, Microsoft Internet Explorer, or another client-side, map-compatible browser. Client-side image maps can be tested and debugged locally, rather than on your server. As a bonus, as visitors pass their cursors over hot spots in your map, actual labels describing the link (rather than just coordinates, which is the case with server-side maps) appear. All the work is handled by the browser, which determines which URL is requested and passes the request on to the Web server.

❓ How do I create an image map with Photoshop?

If you've had any geometry, or worked with charts, creating a map file for your Photoshop image is simple. A region measuring 50×50 pixels, starting at the upper-left corner of the image, could be defined by a set of four numbers representing the x and y coordinates within the image: 0,0; 0,50; 50,50; and 50,0. That would set the four corners of the region at the 0,0 (upper left), 0,50 (upper right), 50,50 (lower right), and 50,0 (lower left) positions. In practice, a rectangle can be defined simply by specifying two opposite corners, such as 0,0 and 50,50.

If you want to use a region that's not a rectangle, just define all the corner points of a regular or irregular polygon, or the x and y coordinates of the center of a circle plus its radius in pixels. You can locate these points using the Info palette or equivalent in Photoshop, which displays the coordinates of the cursor within a graphic.

? What syntax do I use for the map file?

Because the syntax for CERN and NCSA image maps differ slightly, you'll want to check any good HTML handbook. But here are the basics: An AREA tag tells the browser that a new region is being defined. SHAPE is followed by an argument that specifies a rectangle, polygon, or circle, while COORDS provides the coordinates to be used for that area. An HREF tag directs the browser to the hyperlink accessed when this region is clicked. CERN and NCSA files look similar, except that the URL is placed last instead of first in a CERN map file, and NCSA uses shorter names, like rect instead of rectangle.

When you're finished, load the map file, map image, and HTML page onto your server. If you're using a server-side map, you'll need to reference the cgi directory in your hyperlinks:

```
<A HREF="/bin/cgi/mapprog/maps/usa.map">
<IMG SRC="usa.gif" ISMAP>
</A>
```

To be on the safe side, you can create an HTML page with a client-side image map that serves double duty as a server-side map, as well. Just create the client-side map on your page, then wrap a server-side map description around the URL reference, like this:

```
<A HREF="/bin/cgi/mapprog/maps/usa.map">
<IMG SRC="usa.gif" BORDER=0 ALT="USA Image Map" ISMAP
USEMAP=#usa">
</A>
```

That's all there is to it. Because the vast majority of Web cruisers today are using image-capable, client-side map-compatible browsers, expect to see this useful tool applied more often in the future. However, like blinking text, animated banners, and confusing frame layouts, image maps can be misused. Use some restraint and good taste, and maps can add interest and ease of use to your Web site.

TRANSPARENT GIFS

What Are transparent GIFs?

Transparent GIFs (and, someday, transparent JPG and PNG files when all browsers support them) make all the pixels surrounding the nonsquare object you want to highlight invisible, making triangles, other polygons, ellipses, and irregularly shaped objects valid fodder for your Web page graphics. You can create them using Photoshop's File | Export command.

Irregular Shapes Are a Snap

Whether it's a viewfinder on a camera, a picture frame on the wall, or an image on the Internet, humans try to squeeze all visuals into a square or rectangular format. While dropping every inline image into a box makes a browser's job easier, it complicates things for anyone who wants a round button, irregularly shaped rule, or even something as basic as fancy text to pop out of a page's background.

The secret is in the GIF89a format specification, which includes a provision for allowing a single color (and only one) to be designated as invisible, or transparent. When a program such as a browser displays such an image, it ignores that particular color anywhere it finds it and, instead, substitutes pixels representing the underlying background for the pixels of that color.

The background can be a background color, or, alternatively, a background image that is tiled, if necessary, to cover a page's window in the browser. So, while transparent GIFs are actually rectangular in shape (meaning that no text or other images can intrude on the area they cover), the actual GIF image merges smoothly into the background.

If you think transparent GIFs are nothing more than a tool for breaking out of the rectangular mold, think again. These graphics make great text and layout tools, too.

? How do I create a transparent GIF in Photoshop?

The easiest way is to create an empty, transparent layer in a document, and create the image there. When you select File | Export | GIF89a, the GIF89a Export Options dialog box appears, as you can see here, and the transparency of your layer is automatically selected to represent the transparent area of the GIF.

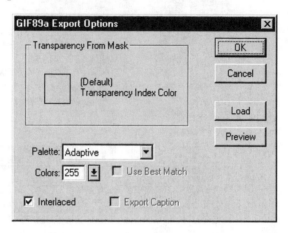

Because GIFs must be 256 colors or less, you'll have to choose from the Adaptive or System palettes and select the number of colors to be used. If you click the Preview button, Photoshop will show you the color lookup table (CLUT) that will be used. When you save the GIF and load it into a browser, the transparent portions will be ignored and your background color or image will show through.

? I have an existing image and don't want to work with a transparent layer. Can I specify which color should be made transparent?

Yes. While the GIF89a export filter converts a 24-bit color image to 256 hues, you can also perform this step ahead of time. Then, when you export the image as a transparent GIF, Photoshop asks you to select a transparency color, as you can see in Figure 14-2. Just use the Eyedropper to select the color that will be ignored by the Web browser.

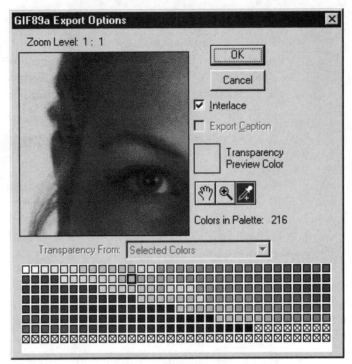

Figure 14-2.   Select a transparency color here

? **When I load my transparent GIF into a browser on the Web, the background shows through parts of the image that I don't want to be transparent. What happened?**

You selected a color for transparency that was within the image, as well as in the surrounding area. Go back to your original version of the image file (you did save a copy, didn't you?) and select some other color. You may want to change the surrounding color to some hue that isn't contained in the rest of your image.

? **I have a rather complex shape that I want to use for transparency, and it's made up of several different colors. Transparent GIFs can use only one color for transparency. What can I do?**

Select the area you want to be transparent using any of the selection tools. Then, save the selection. You might want to delete the area selected to see how your transparent GIF will look; the area will be ignored by the browser, so deleting it now does no harm. Then, reduce the image to Indexed Color and select the GIF89a Export option. In the Transparency From area, choose the name of your saved selection channel.

? I want to use special fonts on a page. Can transparent GIFs help me out here?

Yes indeed. Transparent GIFs let you use any font you like on a page, without resorting to Cascading Style Sheets or other HTML tricks. Create the text as an image using any font available to your image editor, add special effects, drop shadows, or other enhancements, and place it on the page as a transparent GIF.

? I want to create 3-D effects. Can transparent GIFs provide them?

In a manner of speaking, yes. See-through GIFs make it easy to create eye-catching 3-D effects. Holes, bumps, depressions, and other artifacts can seem to jump out of the page at you, given the right shading and transparent GIF display.

? Can I use transparent GIFs to help me place elements on a page?

Yes, while Cascading Style Sheets give you more flexibility over placement without forcing you to use large images, good old Photoshop can do the job, too. If you're dissatisfied with Left, Center, and Right orientation for your images, you can combine several images in any arrangement you like and define the area between them as transparent. Your dream layout can become a reality.

? Can I use transparent GIFs for image maps?

Transparent GIFs are a great way to display image maps, discussed earlier in this chapter. You can use them to create maps shaped like the objects they represent, whether it's a map of the United States or a clickable representation of a desktop computer.

? I need to use more than 256 colors in my transparent GIF. Can I do this?

Sorry, like all GIFs, the transparent variety supports a maximum of 256 colors, and if you want to use the palette of hues supported by most browsers, you may be stuck with 216 colors or fewer. You won't be able to create a good-quality transparent GIF of a full-color image.

? The edges of my transparent GIFs are rough. Can I fix this?

Only one color can be transparent, so smoothed, Anti-aliased edges are impossible. Your images need to have a hard edge, and everything outside that edge must be colored in the hue selected for transparency. When the Portable Network Graphics (PNG) format becomes established, this limitation, as well as the 256-color barrier will be vanquished. PNG supports both 8-bit transparency and full-color palettes.

? I really, really have to have smooth edges, and want to have a transparent component on my Web page. Is this possible?

Your best answer may be to fake a transparent GIF. Create your artwork on the same color background you'll be using on your Web page. Use all the smoothing and Anti-aliasing you like, and save it as a JPEG file. Then, when the image is loaded, it will appear to be floating transparently, as you can see in Figure 14-3.

Of course, this technique means you'll have to have a plain colored background instead of an image, but the shadows or other effects will look good. The easiest way to do this is to use a standard

Figure 14-3.   Floating transparent image

color like white or black as your Web page background. However, you can also use any of the background colors browsers have available. These are defined using three pairs of hexadecimal numbers representing the red, green, and blue amounts in the background. A yellow color might be defined by the string FFFF00 in your HTML line:

```
<BGCOLOR="FFFF00">
```

In your image editor, the same hue could be duplicated for your image background by dialing in the decimal equivalent of 255 Red, 255 Green, and 0 Blue. If you want to use another color, convert between decimal and hexadecimal and put it to work in both your browser and image editor.

 Tip: *Netscape Composer and other HTML editors can provide this information for you automatically. In Composer, choose Format | Color, and pass your cursor over a hue you want to use. A tag displaying both the decimal and hex values for that color appears.*

BUTTONS, BACKGROUNDS, AND OTHER ARTIFACTS

? Are buttons, backgrounds, rules, and other elements easy to create and use on a Web page?

Graphic backgrounds, buttons, rules, and techniques like drop shadows enhance Web pages by adding flavor without increasing the download time for your page significantly. A 10K background image or a 7K button or rule will transfer in a jiffy, even if your visitor has a 14.4K Internet connection, and then can be stored in their browser's cache for near-instant recall when reused on the same or subsequent pages in your site. They also add a unique stylistic flavor that makes your pages stand out from the rest. Best of all, none of these graphics are very difficult to create.

? How do I create background images in Photoshop?

Adding an interesting background to your page requires only a few words of HTML code (e.g. <BODY BACKGROUND="mygraphic.jpg">), and the image itself. The only tricky part is making sure the image is as small as possible and will tile seamlessly.

With that in mind, you can create a seamless background, like the one shown in Figure 14-4, from any image or texture. For this particular background, I created a blank image that was much larger than you'd actually want for a background—600 × 600 pixels. The extra large size was required because the filter I wanted to use as the background texture doesn't provide enough detail when applied to smaller images.

I selected blue as the foreground color, white as the background color, and activated Photoshop 4's Cloud filter to produce fluffy cumulus puffs reminiscent of the Windows 95 logo. You can use any texture offered by your image editor, or work with a photo or some other graphic. If you decide to have a nonrandom pattern as your background, center the object in the middle of the graphic.

As is, this graphic won't tile seamlessly. The edges show up, and with small background images, many, many duplicates will be tiled, producing a mosaic effect. Your image editor's Offset filter (with the Wrap Around option checked) rearranges the graphic so that the center is now displaced to the edges, where they can match with the edges of similar images when tiled. The secret is to use an offset that is *half* the width and height of the image (in this case, 300 pixels). Using your editor's Clone or Rubber Stamp tool, mask out the lines by

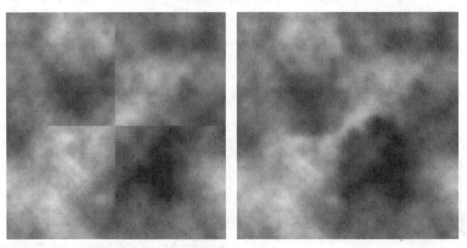

Figure 14-4.   Offset image for background

copying texture from elsewhere in the image over them. Try to stay away from the actual edges of the offset graphic—they should be left alone so they will tile invisibly.

The final step was to reduce the size of the background to 25 percent of its original dimensions (150 × 150 pixels) and save it in JPEG format.

? How can I create a button with a 3-D effect?

Follow these steps to get results like those shown here:

1. Create the button on a transparent layer.

2. Make a rectangular selection and fill it with a two-color gradient using a light and dark version of the same hue, which will enhance the 3-D effect.

3. Fill the selection with the gradient, starting at the upper-left corner with the light color, and continuing down to the lower-right corner with the dark color. Make sure the Preserve Transparency box is checked in the Layers palette so that the gradient tool will fill only the selection.

4. Next, reduce the size of your selection so it encompasses only the center of the button. With Photoshop, you can do this by using the Select | Modify | Contract menu item and then typing in a pixel value amounting to five or ten percent of the width of your button. You can also use Photoshop's Border command, which takes a selection and converts it into a band surrounding the object. Then, invert the selection so the center of the button is selected.

5. Fill the center of the button with the same gradient, but progressing from the lower right to upper left so the button will be darker in the upper corner and lighter in the lower corner. This produces the 3-D effect.

❓ How can I create a rule?

You can make a good rule out of any graphic or random artwork. Select one of Photoshop's brushstroke filters to add a painterly effect, then, squeeze the height of the rectangle and stretch it out lengthwise to produce a ruling line. Then apply the Burn/Darken tool (to the upper and lower edges) and the Dodge/Lighten brush to the center to create a more tubular effect.

 Tip: *When using graphics as rules, you should make them no wider than the smallest browser window your visitors are likely to use—400 pixels, or even smaller, is a good idea. Center the rule on your page so it will nestle in the middle at almost any window size.*

ANIMATED GIFS

❓ I've seen some graphics that move in an animated way on Web pages. Can I produce these animations in Photoshop?

You may have been looking at video files, Shockwave animations, Java applets, or Dynamic HTML, but it's more likely that what you saw were simple animated GIF files. These easy-to-create graphics can spin your logo, point visitors to your favorite link or ad banner, or simply add a little motion to flat pages. You can create the individual images in an animated GIF, but Photoshop itself can't produce fully animated GIF files. You'll need another tool, such as GIF Construction Set.

❓ How do I create the files for animated GIFs?

Produce the first frame in Photoshop, make a copy of the image, then add the variations to the copy that produce the animated effect. That might be as simple as moving the image slightly to one side. Photoshop owners can use the ARROW cursor keys to nudge a selection left, right, up, or down one pixel at a time, creating a simple animation.

Use Photoshop's layers to produce an animated GIF within one file. Then export the individual layers or copy them to an animation utility for assembly into a finished GIF. This approach is particularly good because you can turn layers on and off to preview your animation effects. In addition, using a single file simplifies using a single color palette for each frame of the animation. Create your first frame using a 256-color (or browser-safe 216-color) palette, and make all

Animating Your Web Site

Whether you're more familiar with flip books than Homer Simpson, you probably know how animation works: the eye is presented with a series of slightly different, progressive images, which the brain blends into smooth motion. While an average feature-length cartoon (before the age of computers) reportedly required a googol of separate hand-painted cels requiring 10,000 person-years of effort, one person can easily create GIFs with a few frames for fast, effective Web display.

Animated GIFs are GIF files that contain multiple images and the instructions that tell a Web browser how to display them. While you could theoretically embed a mini-movie inside an animated GIF, given the speed of Web transfers in most cases, you'll be doing your visitors a kindness if you stick to slim, trim animations. A two-image GIF can flash a message, attract attention to a link, or provide any simple kind of repetitive movement. With three or four images in your GIF, you can create a crawling marquee or produce the illusion of motion. An animation can display one time or cycle over and over. For the smoothest repeating effect, your animations should be created in *loops*, where the last image in the series flows right into the first one again.

To reduce download times, animated GIFs shouldn't cover much space on your Web page, either. A 36×36-pixel multilayered GIF will download four times faster than a 72×72-pixel version, which can make the difference between a tolerable 15-second wait and a painful one-minute delay. Nor should you overuse animations. In most cases you'll want just one, or possibly two, moving objects on your page. Any more than that and each animation will be competing with the others for your visitors' attention. You don't want to induce bouts of seasickness, either, with a roiling Web site. Keep 'em small, fast, and relevant, and everybody will be happy.

modifications on that version. If you start with a 24-bit color image, you may need to save the color table/palette and reuse it for each subsequent image. You'll need to use one of those techniques with

Photoshop, which doesn't allow you to convert a multilayer file to 256/216-colors without flattening or combining all the layers that make up your animation.

Create each frame on a transparent layer and you can build animated GIFs that dance around your background as if they were floating there. When you've created each frame, export them to GIF89a format using transparency. Use sequential names, like logo1.gif, logo2.gif, logo3.gif, and so forth.

? How do I convert all those GIF files into an animated GIF?

The final step is to use a GIF animation utility to compile the individual frames into a single, finished animated GIF you can place on your Web page using an ordinary IMG tag. There are dozens of shareware programs that automate this task, including GIF Construction Set for Windows, which you can find at *http://www.mindworkshop/alchemy/alchemy.html*, or GifBuilder for the Macintosh, found at *ftp:ftp.amug.org/pub/info-mac/gst/grf*.

15 Answers!

Tricks with Layers, Masks, and Adjustment Layers

Answer Topics

Layers, Masks, and Adjustment Layers @ a Glance

Additional tricks are available with layers, layer masks, transparency masks, and adjustment layers, which are all powerful features new in at least some aspects to Photoshop 4.0.

⇨ *Adjustment Layers* are special Photoshop layers that apply certain image manipulations (akin to filters) only to the layers of an image stacked below that "filter." In contrast to the same tasks performed directly on an image, Adjustment Layers can be turned on and off, modified with different parameters, or painted so the changes are applied only to a portion of the affected layers. Adjustment Layers offer a great way to experiment with effects, giving you the same freedom you'd have with the multiple Undo levels found in other programs (but which Photoshop sorely lacks). In some ways, Adjustment Layers are better than Undo: you can choose from among several different kinds of adjustments and modify only the ones you want, regardless of the order in which they were applied.

⇨ The Adjustment Layer feature allows you to create individual layers for adjusting Levels, Curves, Brightness/Contrast, Color Balance, Hue/Saturation, or Selective Color, as well as Invert, Threshold, and Posterize effects. You can create one or more Adjustment Layers, each dedicated to one of these manipulations, and arrange them in your Layers palette stack so only the effects you want are applied to the layers you want.

⇨ Each Adjustment Layer also has a *Layer Mask* that you can paint on to control the portion of the image that will be affected by the Adjustment Layer. Because the effects of an Adjustment Layer aren't permanently applied until the image is flattened, you can modify their settings at any time without affecting the underlying image. Yet, you can preview the exact effect you'll get, turn off the layer's changes entirely, or fade them in and out by manipulating the Adjustment Layer's Opacity setting.

ADJUSTMENT LAYERS

? **When I apply the Levels dialog box several times to the same image or layer, I find the multiple steps each cause my image to lose tones. Is there any way I can use Levels more than once without degrading the image?**

This is a perfect application for Photoshop's Adjustment Layers. Don't apply the same effect more than once: perform the manipulation on an Adjustment Layer so you can modify your changes at any time. To create an Adjustment Layer for your Levels command, just follow these steps:

1. Choose Layer | New | Adjustment Layer. The New Adjustment Layer dialog box appears:

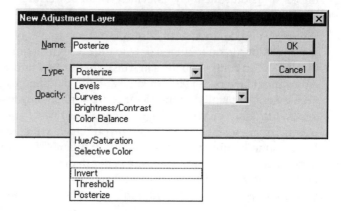

2. From the Type pull-down list, choose Levels.

3. Click OK.

4. The Levels dialog box appears immediately. You can make adjustments now, or click OK to return to your image. The new Levels layer appears in your Layers palette. A half-moon icon is shown in the far right column so you'll always be able to tell this is an Adjustment Layer, as you can see here:

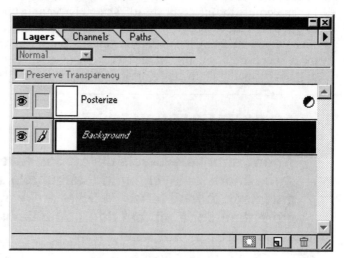

5. When you want to make Levels changes at any time, double-click the Adjustment Layer. The Levels dialog box appears, and you can make any modifications you like.

Tip: *To add an Adjustment Layer quickly, COMMAND/CTRL-click on the New Layer icon at the bottom of the Layers palette. The New Adjustment Layer dialog box will pop up, ready for your specifications.*

I want to produce different versions of an image, each with just one of the colors manipulated. How can I do this?

Create a Selective Color Adjustment Layer. The Selective Color dialog box, shown here, includes sliders for manipulating Cyan, Magenta, Yellow, or Black, or the complements of the color hues: Red, Green, and Blue.

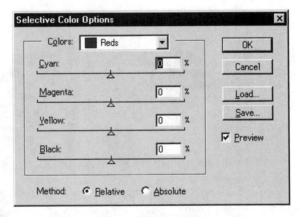

Make the adjustment you want, create a duplicate of the image, flatten it, and then save the changes. Then, return to the original and repeat for as many different variations as you like.

I want to apply these color changes only to the highlights of my image. Can I do that?

Certainly—just create a Color Balance Adjustment Layer and manipulate to your heart's content. As with all Adjustment Layer changes, make sure the Adjustment Layer and target layer(s) are visible when you flatten the image.

? I want to compare my original image to my new one, which includes changes made by an Adjustment Layer. How do I do that?

Just click the Eyeball icon next to the Adjustment Layer to turn it off. Its effects will be removed from the image, but you can flip back and forth between normal and adjusted views, as shown in Figure 15-1, by clicking the eyeball on and off.

? I want to see both adjusted and normal versions at once. Is that possible?

Yes. Create a duplicate image and turn the relevant Adjustment Layer in the copy on or off.

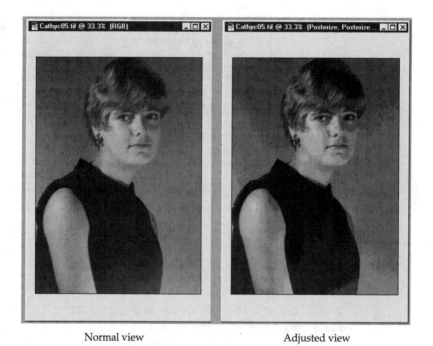

Normal view   Adjusted view

Figure 15-1.   Two different views of the same image

? **I have several photos that I'd like to manipulate using the same Adjustment Layer. Is there a quick way to duplicate these layers between images?**

Yes. You might want to use this feature to apply the exact same color correction to several images that were produced at the same time. Just drag the Adjustment Layer in the first image over to the Layers palette in the second image. The layer will be duplicated with all its settings intact.

? **Can I apply different adjustments to different layers?**

Yes. Photoshop allows you to create multiple Adjustment Layers and apply them to the layers you want. For example, you might want to invert one layer, and change the levels of all the layers. Just follow these steps:

1. Create the Adjustment Layers you want.
2. In the Layers palette, drag the Adjustment Layers so they are above the levels they are meant to manipulate.
3. Turn off the image layers and Adjustment Layers that you don't want affected by clicking their Eyeball icons, so they'll become invisible.
4. Make your adjustments.
5. Repeat with each set of layers and Adjustment Layers. Remember, affected image layers must be *below* the Adjustment Layers that will be applied to them.
6. When you're ready to flatten the image, merge Adjustment Layers with the image layers that they should be applied to by making only them visible, then using Layer | Merge Visible.
7. Turn other layers you want adjusted or protected on or off as appropriate, and merge them as well.
8. Once you've applied the adjustments to all the layers, turn on all of the ones you want included in the final image, and flatten.

❓ I'm satisfied with the results of two of my Adjustment Layers. Can I reduce the number of layers in my document by merging them?

No. You can only merge an Adjustment Layer with one or more image layers. You cannot merge Adjustment Layers with each other until you flatten the image and merge all of the layers together.

❓ Can I create more than one Adjustment Layer for a particular kind of adjustment?

Yes. If you want to apply, say, a different color balance to two different layers, you can create separate Color Balance Adjustment Layers for each one.

❓ When I create several Adjustment Layers for the same kind of manipulation, I get them mixed up. Is there an easy way to tell them apart?

You can apply a name to an Adjustment Layer the same as you can with any layer. Use Layer | Layer Options, or select Layer Options from the fly-out menu on the Layers palette, then type in a new name for your layer, as shown here:

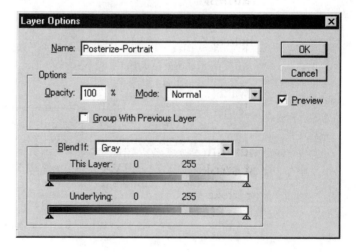

? I want to apply an adjustment to only part of a layer. I tried painting on an Adjustment Layer, but nothing happened. What did I do wrong?

To modify the coverage of an Adjustment Layer, you need to paint on the layer's Layer Mask *channel*, instead. Each time an Adjustment Layer is created, a layer mask is generated. To edit this mask, select the Adjustment Layer in the Layers palette, then click the Channels tab. Click the Eyeball icon to make the layer mask visible, if necessary. You can then paint on the mask using any painting tool. The selected, or active, portions of the Adjustment Layer will be shown in red, or whatever color you've specified. (Double-click the Layer Mask, and click the Color preview in the Layer Mask Display Options dialog box to change to another hue.)

? When I switch from Channels back to the Layers palette, the red mask color remains. How do I get rid of it?

You need to remember to turn the Eyeball icon off when leaving the Channels palette.

? I want to apply an adjustment to part of a layer, using a fixed mathematical increment, such as 25%. Can I do that?

The density of the "paint" you use on the layer mask determines the strength of the effect in the Adjustment Layer. Choose black as your foreground color, activate the brush or painting tool you want to use, then set the Opacity slider in the tool's Options dialog box to the level you want (e.g., 50% for a 50% application of the layer, 25% for a 25% application, etc.).

? I tried painting in the Adjustment Layer's layer mask, but no paint strokes appear. What's wrong?

Your strokes are being applied; you just can't see the strokes on the mask itself unless the Eyeball icon for the layer mask is visible in the Channels palette. Oddly enough, if you paint in the layer mask your strokes actually are applied, but you can't see the strokes until the mask is made visible. That's because only the mask itself can be painted on (the color layers are visible, but not active), so the mask is active by default.

? I need to apply an adjustment to an entire layer, but want to experiment with fading the amount of the change. Can I do this?

Yes. Simply select the Adjustment Layer in the Layers palette, then adjust the Opacity slider until you get the effect you want.

? When I'm using an Adjustment Layer, I run out of memory. What have I done wrong?

Adjustment Layers operate like any other editing function in Photoshop: the program creates a copy in memory for the Undo buffer, while keeping a duplicate of your edited layer in RAM as well. If you're running out of memory when you use Adjustment Layers, you'll probably be running out for other functions, too. You'll need twice as much memory available (either in silicon or hard disk form) to create an Adjustment Layer. Use File | Preferences | Plug-Ins & Scratch Disks to make sure you've allocated enough hard disk space. In many respects, however, Adjustment Layers are more efficient in use of your RAM and virtual memory, as you'll see in the next question.

? How do Adjustment Layers help save memory?

If Adjustment Layers weren't available, you might be tempted to make duplicate copies of layers you want to modify, and operate on those. The RAM and hard disk space required for each additional layer—particularly in a color image—can accumulate rapidly. Adjustment Layers, on the other hand, give you the ability to try out different effects on the original layer, without risk of actually modifying that layer until you're ready.

? When I save images and then reload them, the Adjustment Layers are lost. What's wrong?

You must use Photoshop's proprietary PSD format to save a file with its layers intact, including those with Adjustment Layers. You probably used Save a Copy, which lets you save an image with all its visible layers flattened, but with layer information lost. Use Save or Save As to keep the PSD format and your layers.

❓ My PSD images with layers are much larger than I expected. Is there any way to squeeze them down?

Yes. Use File | Preferences | Saving Files, and make sure the 2.5 Compatibility choice in the Options area is unchecked, as it is here:

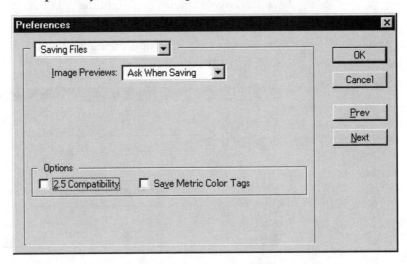

Unless you need to transfer images between Photoshop 4.0 and the (very) early Photoshop 2.5 version, this compatibility isn't necessary.

❓ I spent a lot of time making modifications of an image with Adjustment Layers, then noticed that I had previously worked on another copy of the same image. Can I combine my changes?

The capability to copy Adjustment Layers between images is one of the most valuable capabilities of this feature. Just drag the Adjustment Layer from one image to the other and position it in the Layers palette stack so it modifies the layers you want. You can even have two people working on an image independently, then combine their modifications to Adjustment Layers by copying the layers to a final image.

Tip: *Hold down the* SHIFT *key while dragging an Adjustment Layer from one image document to another to make sure they register exactly.*

? I want to save an Adjustment Layer to a separate file so I can use it with other images later on. Can I do this?

Yes. Follow these steps:

1. In the Layers palette, highlight the Adjustment Layer.

2. Choose Duplicate Layer from the Layers palette's fly-out menu or by selecting Layer | Duplicate Layer. The Duplicate Layer dialog box will appear:

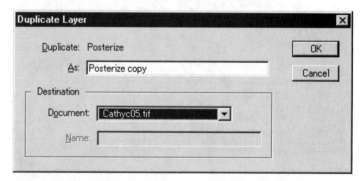

3. Select New from the drop-down Document list in the Destination area.

4. The Name field now becomes active. Type in a name for the document you want to store the Adjustment Layer in.

5. Click OK to save the copy of the Adjustment Layer.

Tip: *When copying Adjustment Layers between image documents, make sure that both documents have the same pixel dimensions so the layer will "fit" properly.*

? I want to create an image that is posterized in some areas and has a normal appearance in others. Can I do this?

Just use the Posterize Adjustment Layer, then activate the layer mask for that layer in the Channels palette and paint over the portion of the image you don't want posterized. You can achieve an effect like that in Figure 15-2.

❓ Can I apply filters to an Adjustment Layer?

Absolutely, although some filters, such as Lens Flare, may not be available. You can choose, for example, the Posterize Adjustment Layer, paint on the layer mask, and apply a texture filter to the area you've masked off for some great effects like the one shown in Figure 15-3.

MORE MASKS

❓ How can I create a halo-style vignette for an image?

An easy way to do this is through use of a transparency mask. Just follow these steps:

1. Create a new, transparent layer.

Figure 15-2.   Adjusting a posterized image

Figure 15-3.   Applying filters to an adjustment layer mask

2. Select an area corresponding to the shape of the vignette.

3. Use Select | Feather and specify a feathering radius of 40 pixels.

4. Use Select | Inverse to invert the selection.

5. Press D to make sure black and white are your default colors.

6. Use Edit | Fill to fill the selection. Make sure the Preserve Transparency box is unchecked.

7. Choose Select | Load Selection, and choose Layer Transparency from the Channel drop-down list.

8. Switch to the background layer of the image.

9. Press DELETE to delete the background image using the transparency mask.

10. Flatten the image. Your results should look like those in Figure 15-4.

? Can I edit a transparency mask?

You're better off using a layer mask, which also tracks the transparency of the pixels in an image, but which you can edit in the

Figure 15-4.   Final image haloed with transparency mask

Channels palette. (Layer masks were discussed in Chapter 6.) Create a
layer mask by highlighting the layer and choosing Layer | Add Layer
Mask. A second preview icon will appear in the layer in the Layers
palette, to the right of the original preview.

? Can I use a layer as a mask?

Yes. All you need to do is stack the layers so the one you want to use
to mask another layer is placed above it in the Layers palette. Select
the area you want to be revealed by the mask and delete it from the
masking layer. The area will become transparent and allow the
layer(s) underneath to show through.

? Is there a way to have a layer mask the one above it?

Yes, just group the layers together. Double-click the layer in the Layers
palette, then choose the Group with Previous Layer checkbox.

Glossary

Answers!

achromatic color   An unsaturated color, such as gray.

additive colors   The red, green, and blue (RGB) colors used to display images on monitor, and for Photoshop's primary image manipulation mode. All three colors added together produce white.

adjustment layer   A layer that can be used to modify the contrast, brightness, color, and other factors of the layers below it without changing the pixels themselves. Adjustment layers can be edited, turned on and off, and otherwise manipulated to provide flexible effects to the layers they are applied to.

airbrush   An artist's tool that sprays a fine mist of paint. Photoshop's version has user-configurable brushes that can apply a spray of a selected tone to an area.

Alpha channel   A grayscale layer of an image used to store selections. They may be copied from one image to another, saved with an image in formats like TIFF or PSD, recalled, and combined with other selections.

ambient lighting   A diffuse nondirectional lighting caused by light bouncing off the surroundings, use to fill in the dark areas not illuminated by one of the main light sources.

Anti-aliasing   A process which minimizes jaggy diagonal lines by using in-between tones to smooth the appearance of the line.

applications program interface (API)   A shared intermediate interface that allows a broad range of hardware and software products to communicate, such as the TWAIN interface used to connect Photoshop to scanners and digital cameras.

archive   To store files that are no longer active, usually on a removable disk or tape.

aspect ratio   The proportions of an image; e.g., an 8 × 10-inch photo has a 4:5 aspect ratio.

attribute   Characteristics of an object, including color, font, or line width.

background   The bottom layer of a Photoshop image.

backlighting   Lighting effect produced when the main light is located behind the subject.

baseline   An imaginary line on which type rests.

Bézier curve   An editable curved line like those produced by Photoshop's Paths tool.

bilevel   An image that stores only black-and-white information, with no gray tones; Photoshop calls such images bitmaps.

bitmap   A description of an image that represents each pixel as a number in a row-and-column format. In Photoshop parlance, each bit in the map can be represented by a 1 or a 0 (black or white), but in the rest of the world numbers as large as 32 can be used to describe the density, color, and transparency information in a pixel.

black   The color formed by the absence of reflected or transmitted light: e.g., the combination of 100 percent values of cyan, magenta, and yellow ink (in the subtractive color system), or 0 values of red, green, and blue light (in the additive color system).

black printer   A printing plate used to add black ink to a cyan-magenta-yellow image, emphasizing neutral tones and adding detail to shadows. A skeleton black printer adds black ink only to darker areas; a full-range black printer adds at least some black to all of an image.

bleed   A printed image that extends right up to the edge of a page, often accomplished by trimming a larger image down to a finished size.

blur   To reduce the contrast between pixels that form edges in an image, softening it.

brightness   The amount of light and dark shades in an image.

burn   To darken part of an image, using Burn mode of Photoshop's Toning tool.

cache   An area of memory used to store information so it can be accessed more quickly than data placed in slower RAM, on a hard disk, or other storage.

calibration   Adjusting a device such as a scanner, monitor, or printer so its output represents a known standard.

camera ready   Art work in a form usable for producing negatives or plates for printing.

cast   A tinge of color in an image, usually an undesired color.

channel   One of the layers that make up an image, such as the red, green, and blue channels of an RGB image, or the cyan, magenta, yellow, and black channels of a CMYK image. Alpha channels are additional layers used to represent masks or selections.

chrome   A color transparency such as Kodachrome, Ektachrome, or Fujichrome.

Clipboard   An area of memory used to store images and text so they can be interchanged between layers, windows, or applications. Photoshop has its own internal Clipboard, but can export and import to and from the Mac or PC's system clipboard.

clone   To copy pixels from one part of an image to another with Photoshop's Rubber Stamp tool.

color correction   To change the balance of colors in an image, most often to improve the accuracy of the rendition, or to compensate for deficiencies in the color separation and printing process.

color separation   The process of converting an image to its four separate color components—cyan, magenta, yellow, and black—for printing.

compression   Reducing the size of a file by encoding using smaller sets of numbers that don't include redundant information. Some kinds of compression, such as JPEG, can degrade images, while others, including GIF and PNG, preserve all the detail in the original.

constrain   To limit a tool in some way, such as forcing a brush to paint in a straight line, or forcing an object being rotated to a fixed increment.

continuous tone   Images that contain tones from the darkest to lightest, with an infinite range of variations in between.

contrast   The range of individual tones between the lightest and darkest shades in an image.

convolve   A process used by imaging filters that takes the values of surrounding pixels to calculate new values for sharpening, blurring, or creating another effect.

crop   To trim an image or page by adjusting the boundaries.

crop mark   A mark placed on a page showing where the page should be trimmed to produce its final size.

cursor   An icon that shows where the next action will be performed on the screen.

CYMK color model   A model that defines all possible colors in percentages of cyan, magenta, yellow, and black.

darken   The process of selectively changing pixel values to a darker value.

default   The value or parameter that is used for a tool, action, or function unless you specify otherwise using a dialog box or some other method.

defloat   To merge a floating selection with the underlying image.

defringe   To remove the outer edge pixels of a selection, often when merging a selection with an underlying image.

densitometer   An electronic device used to measure the density of an image.

desaturate   To reduce the purity or vividness of a color, as with Photoshop's Sponge tool. Desaturated colors appear washed out and diluted.

descender   The portion of a lowercase letter that extends below the *baseline*, such as the tail on the letter *y*.

diffusion   The random distribution of tones in an area of an image, often used to represent a larger number of tones.

displacement map   A Photoshop file used by the Displace filter to control the shifting of pixels in an image horizontally or vertically to produce a particular special effect.

dithering   A method of simulating tones that can't be represented at the current color depth by grouping the dots into clusters of varying size. The mind merges these clusters and the surrounding white background into different tones.

dodge   To block part of a photographic image as it is exposed, thus lightening its tones.

dot   A unit used to represent a portion of an image, especially on a printer.

dot gain   The tendency of a printing dot to grow from the original size when printed, as ink is absorbed and spread into the paper.

dots per inch (dpi)   The resolution of an image, expressed in the number of pixels or printer dots in an inch. Scanner resolution is also commonly expressed in dpi, but, technically, scanners use an optical technique that makes *samples per inch* a more accurate term.

driver   A software interface used to allow an applications program to communicate with a piece of hardware, such as a scanner.

duotone   A printed image, usually a monochrome halftone, that uses two different colors of ink to produce a longer range of tones than would be possible with a single ink density and set of printer cells alone.

emboss   A Photoshop technique that makes an image appear to be raised above the surface in a 3-D effect.

emulsion   The light-sensitive coating on a piece of film, paper, or printing plate.

emulsion side   The side of a piece of film that contains the image, usually with a matte, nonglossy finish.

encapsulated PostScript (EPS)   An image format for PostScript printers, which can include a bitmap description of an image file or an outline-oriented image of line graphics and text. Photoshop can import both bitmap and line-oriented EPS files, but can export only the bitmapped version.

export   To transfer text or images from a document to another format, using Photoshop's Save As or Export functions.

extrude   To create a 3-D effect by adding edges to an outline shape as if it were clay pushed through a mold.

Eyedropper   A Photoshop tool used to sample color from one part of an image so it can be used to paint or draw elsewhere.

feather   To fade the edges of a selection to produce a less obtrusive transition.

file format   A way in which a particular application stores information on a disk.

fill   To cover a selected area with a solid, transparent, or gradient tone or pattern.

filter   A Photoshop feature that changes the pixels in an image to produce blurring, sharpening, and other special effects.

font   Originally, a group of letters, numbers, and symbols in one size and typeface, but now often used to mean any typeface.

four-color printing   Another term for *process color*, in which cyan, magenta, yellow, and black inks are used to reproduce all the hues of the spectrum.

FPO   For Position Only. Artwork that is not good enough for reproduction, but can be used in a page layout to make it easier to visualize how the document will look.

frequency   The number of lines per inch in a halftone screen.

Gamma   A numerical way of representing the contrast of an image's midtones.

gamut   A range of color values that can be reproduced by a particular color model or device.

Gaussian blur   A method of diffusing an image using a bell-shaped curve instead of blurring all pixels in the selected area uniformly.

gray component removal   A process in which portions of an image that have a combination of cyan, magenta, and yellow are made purer by replacing equivalent amounts of all three with black.

gray map   A graph that shows the relationship between the original brightness values of an image and the output values after image processing.

gray scale   The range of different gray values an image can have.

guides   Grid lines that can used to help position objects in an image.

halftoning   A way of simulating the gray tones of an image by varying the size of the dots used to show the image.

handles   Small squares that appear in the corners and (frequently) the sides of a selection or object that can be used to resize, rotate, or otherwise manipulate the entire object or selection.

hexachrome   An image printed using black ink and five other colored inks.

highlight   The brightest values in a continuous tone image.

histogram   A bar-like graph that shows the distribution of tones in an image.

HSB color model   A model that defines all possible colors by specifying a particular hue and then adding or subtracting percentages of black or white.

hue   A pure color.

interpolation   A technique used to calculate the value of the new pixels required whenever you resize or change the resolution of an image, based on the values of surrounding pixels.

invert   In Photoshop, the process of changing an image to its negative, exchanging black for white, white for black, and each color for its complementary hue.

jaggies   The staircasing effect applied to edges of bitmapped objects that are not perfectly horizontal or vertical.

JPEG compression   A lossy method for reducing the size of an image by dividing it into blocks of varying sizes (depending on the amount of compression requested) and representing all the pixels in each block by a smaller number of values.

justified   Text that is aligned at both the right and left margins.

kern   To adjust the amount of space between two adjacent letters.

landscape   The orientation of a page in which the longest dimension is horizontal; also called *wide orientation*.

Lasso   A tool used to select irregularly shaped areas in a bitmapped image.

layers   Separation of a drawing or image into separate "transparent" overlays, which can be edited or manipulated separately, yet combined to provide a single drawing or image.

layer mask   A kind of grayscale mask applied only to one layer of a Photoshop image.

leading   The amount of vertical spacing between lines of text from baseline to baseline.

lens flare   The effect used by spreading light as if it were being reflected by the internal elements of an optical lens.

LHS color   A system of color based on the luminance, hue, and saturation of an image.

lighten   An image-editing function that is the equivalent to the photographic darkroom technique of dodging. Gray tones in a specific area of an image are gradually changed to lighter values.

line art   Usually, images that consist only of white pixels and one color.

line screen   The resolution or frequency of a halftone screen, expressed in lines per inch.

lines per inch (lpi)   The method used for measuring halftone resolution.

lithography   Offset printing.

luminance   The brightness or intensity of an image.

LZW compression   A method of compacting TIFF files using the Lempel-Zev Welch compression algorithm.

Magic Wand   A Photoshop tool used to select contiguous pixels that have the same color value, or that of a range you select.

Marquee   The Photoshop selection tool used to mark rectangular and elliptical areas.

mask   To protect part of an image so it won't be affected by other operations.

midtones   Parts of an image with tones of an intermediate value.

Moiré   An objectionable pattern caused by the interference of halftone screens, frequently generated by rescanning an image that has already been halftoned.

monochrome   Having a single color.

negative   A representation of an image in which the tones are reversed.

neutral color   In RGB mode, a color in which red, green, and blue are present in equal amounts, producing gray.

noise   Random pixels added to an image to increase apparent graininess.

opacity   The opposite of *transparency*: the degree to which a layer obscures the view of the layer beneath. *High opacity* means *low transparency*. Both terms are used in Photoshop.

palette   Tones available to produce an image, or a set of icons representing the available tools.

Photo CD   A special type of CD-ROM that can store high-quality photographic images in a special space-saving format that represents each image as a series of Image Pacs of increasing resolution, along with music and other data. Photoshop allows you to open any of the Image Pacs, but you cannot save in Photo CD format.

pixel   A picture element of a screen image.

plate   A thin, light-sensitive sheet, usually of metal or plastic, which is exposed and then processed to develop an image of the page, then placed on a printing press to transfer ink to paper.

plug-in   A separate module that integrates into Photoshop, usually a filter or import/export utility.

point   Approximately 1/72 of an inch outside the Macintosh world; exactly 1/72 of an inch within it.

Portable Network Graphics   A new RGB file format supported by Photoshop 4.0 and, eventually, Web browsers. It offers progressive, interleaved display and more sophisticated transparency capabilities than the GIF format, but is lossless.

portrait   The orientation of a page in which the longest dimension is vertical; also called *tall orientation.*

posterization   A Photoshop effect produced by reducing the number of tones in an image to a level at which the tones are shown as poster-like bands.

PostScript   A page description language developed by Adobe that allows any printing device to output a page at its highest resolution.

prepress   The stages of the reproduction process that precede printing, when halftones, color separations, and printing plates are created.

process colors   Cyan, magenta, yellow, and black, the basic ink colors used to produce all the other colors in four-color printing.

quadtone   An image printed using black ink and three other colored inks.

raster image   An image defined as a set of pixels or dots in row-and-column format.

rasterize   The process Photoshop uses to convert an outline-oriented image such as a PostScript file into pixels.

reflection copy   Original artwork that is viewed by light reflected from its surface rather than by light transmitted through it.

register   To align images, usually different versions of the same page or sheet. Color separation negatives must be precisely registered to one another to ensure that colors overlap in the proper places.

register marks   Small marks, also known as *registration marks*, which are placed on a page to make it possible to align different versions of the page precisely.

resampling   The process of changing the size or resolution of an image by replacing pixels with additional pixels or fewer pixels, calculated by examining the value of their neighbors.

resolution   The number of pixels, samples, or dots per inch in an image.

retouch   To edit an image, most often to remove flaws or to create a new effect.

RGB color model   A way of defining all possible colors as percentages of red, green, and blue.

right-reading image   An image, such as a film used to produce a printing plate, that reads correctly, left to right, when viewed as it will be placed down for exposure.

Rubber Stamp   A Photoshop tool that copies or clones part of an image to another area or image.

saturation   The purity of color; the amount by which a pure color is diluted with white or gray.

scale   To change the size of a piece of an image.

scanner   A device that converts an image of reflection art or a transparency to a bitmapped image.

screen   The halftone dots used to convert a continuous tone image to a black-and-white pattern for output on printers or printing presses.

screen angle   The alignment of rows of halftone dots, measured from the horizontal (which would be a 0° screen angle).

secondary color   A color produced by mixing two primary colors, such as yellow and cyan inks to create green, or red and green light to create magenta.

selection   An area of an image chosen for manipulation, usually surrounded by a moving series of dots called a *selection border,* or "marching ants."

separations   Film transparencies representing each of the primary colors (cyan, magenta, and yellow) plus black, used to produce individual printing plates.

serif   Short strokes at the ends of letters.

shade   A color with black added.

shadows   The darkest part of an image holding detail.

sharpening   Increasing the apparent sharpness of an image by boosting the contrast between adjacent pixels that form an edge.

smoothing   To blur the boundaries between edges of an image, often to reduce a rough or jagged appearance.

Smudge   A Photoshop tool that smears part of an image, mixing surrounding tones together.

snap   A Photoshop feature that causes lines or objects being drawn or moved to be attracted to a grid or guides.

spot   The dots that produce images on an imagesetter or other device.

spot color   Individual colors, often just one or two in addition to black, used on a page as an accent rather than to provide an accurate representation of a color image via a complete color separation.

subtractive colors   The primary colors of pigments: cyan, magenta, and yellow.

threshold   A predefined level used to determine whether a pixel will be represented as black or white.

thumbnail   A miniature copy of a page or image that provides a preview of the original.

TIFF   Tagged Image File Format. A standard graphics file format that can be used by Photoshop to store grayscale and color images, plus selection masks.

tint   A color with white added to it.

tolerance   The range of color or tonal values that will be selected, with a tool like the Magic Wand, or filled with paint, when using a tool like the Paint Bucket.

trim size   Final size of a printed publication.

tritone   An image printed usually with black ink (or another color) plus two other colored inks.

undercolor removal   A technique that reduces the amount of cyan, magenta, and yellow in black and neutral shadows by replacing them with an equivalent amount of black. *See also* gray component removal.

unsharp masking   The process for increasing the contrast between adjacent pixels in an image, increasing sharpness.

vector image   An image defined as a series of straight line vectors and curves, such as those produced with Photoshop's Pen tool.

wrong-reading image   An image that is backward relative to the original subject—that is, a *mirror image*.

x-height   The height of a lowercase letter, such as the letter x, excluding ascenders and descenders.

zoom   To enlarge part of an image so that it fills the screen, making it easier to work with that portion.

Index